THE COMING DEFEAT
OF COMMUNISM

Books by James Burnham

THE MANAGERIAL REVOLUTION

THE MACHIAVELLIANS

THE STRUGGLE FOR THE WORLD

THE COMING DEFEAT OF COMMUNISM

THE COMING DEFEAT

OF COMMUNISM

James Burnham

NEW YORK

THE JOHN DAY COMPANY, INC.

5ʋ

COPYRIGHT, 1949, 1950, BY JAMES BURNHAM

This book is published by The John Day Company, 62 West 45th Street, New York 19, N.Y., and on the same day in Canada by Longmans, Green & Company, Toronto.

MANUFACTURED IN THE UNITED STATES OF AMERICA
BY THE CORNWALL PRESS, INC., CORNWALL, N. Y.

Who says A, must say B.

CONTENTS

Part One. REVIEW

Part Two. ANALYSIS

Part Three. PLAN

Part Four. ORGANIZATION

THE COMING DEFEAT
OF COMMUNISM

REVIEW

CHAPTER I

The Catastrophic Point of View

WE HAVE GROWN rather weary at having been told so often in recent years that we have reached a "turning point," a "crossroads," or a "crisis." The rhetoric of catastrophe weakens with the general semantic palsy of our time. Boredom is in any case the most insistent response to senility, and boredom becomes further soured by derision when, as so often, the "crisis" is that of the sardine-canning industry, or the "crossroads" an episode in the career of the local Parent-Teachers' Association.

The middle-mind of common sense reasserts itself. It is enough to remember the umbrella when it looks like rain, and to pay the insurance premiums regularly. The rhetoric of catastrophe is converted into a mannerism, apt for an after-dinner speech or the catharsis of a guilt-obsessed nuclear physicist. The soiled omens of disaster are washed by theo-Freudian best sellers. Businessmen settle down to making money, bankers demand economy in government, farmers call for higher parity prices, politicians conjure votes, labor leaders thunder against the Taft-Hartley Act, diplomats test their stamina on procedure, and everyone denounces taxes and the high cost of living.

If it is true, as a thousand books and ten thousand editorials have informed us, that catastrophe does indeed threaten us, that "the fate of mankind" is now at stake, that civilization is at the edge of destruction, what are we to make of the behavior of the leaders of the West—those men of the Western nations, that is to say, who are powerful or rich? Their acts, on that hypothesis, seem to lag most haltingly behind the reality; they hardly succeed, as Marxists would put it, in uniting theory and practice. Though atom bombs grow more powerful and more numerous, though laboratories master the techniques of biological warfare and supersonic flight, these men do not noticeably alter the course of their accustomed rounds.

There is less attention paid to the fall of China than to the bizarre shooting of a baseball player. France, darkened by the premonitory shadow of Soviet conquest, appoints a Communist party member head of her Atomic Commission. The torture of bishops and cardinals fails to cancel an afternoon of golf; a revolution in Indonesia or Costa Rica is not permitted to interfere with a long weekend. Elderly ghosts from another age, weighted with the somehow forgotten record of failure and cowardice and stupidity—of unemployment and appeasement and squandered victory, of 1932 and Munich and Yalta—are still propped into position at the wheels of State. Though Europe is bleeding from a severed central artery, the Union of Europe remains a debating subject for congresses of polite liberals. Delegates to IRO's and ECCA's and UN's and ILO's and UNESCO's meet at Beirut and Lake Success and London and Mexico City and Paris and Geneva in an aura of stenotypists, experts, and translators—never have so many talked so much about so little. Graft, corruption, barratry, deals, bolster once more the sense of the normal.

Methods, traditions, slogans, and ideas are carried over from a pre-crisis past. Citizens who believe that agents of an implacable enemy should be labeled, and ousted from sensitive posts of government, are accused from on high of "hysteria." Observers who take seriously the communists' professed aim of world conquest are dismissed as "fanatics." Analysts who doubt the wisdom of remaining passive until general possession of nuclear weapons guarantees total devastation are denounced as "fascists" and "warmongers."

Professors, writing in the tranquil air of untouched college towns, produce, as is their métier, an ideological defense of business-as-usual. The sense of catastrophe, they find, is a subjective aberration. Neurotic individuals, out of adjustment with their environment, imagine that the world is going to pieces, though in fact it is only their own mental and emotional processes that are dislocated. If we look back through history, we discover that every age thought itself to be in a crisis, at a turning point. There have always been wars and depressions and famines and revolutions. Mankind has always lived through them. The introduction of firearms was, historically speaking, as critical as the invention of nuclear weapons. We shall get along all right if we regain perspective, and keep our heads.

There is here posed an issue that is fundamental not simply in theory but in pervasive consequences for social, political, and individual actions. The issue is this: is ours in truth, in a special sense not generally applicable, an age of crisis, a catastrophic age? Or are we merely suffering the usual human lot, and viewing our normal predicaments with the habitual human tendency to egocentric distortion? This issue is fundamental because, if our age is no different in kind from others, then there is no need for particular urgency or drastic solutions. The methods and ideas of the past have no doubt failed to produce a world of unmixed happiness and peace. But they have managed to get us by; and they could be relied upon to do so once more. If, however, we live in a period not of ordinary troubles but of crisis and catastrophe, then it is reasonable to suppose that the old ways are not enough, that we must, if we are not to be engulfed, cut sharply from the past, and turn to ideas and methods sufficiently new and drastic to meet the drastic novelty of the crisis.

2

An examination of the records of the past will indeed show us that in many centuries there have been men who believed themselves to be living in an age of crisis, of transition, revolution, or even catastrophe. This would seem, then, to be evidence to calm us about our own troubles.

It is, however, by no means the case that a widespread sense of crisis has been usual. To discover, in any given generation, one or two individuals crying general havoc is of little significance. We are entitled to explain their feelings of disaster by individual psychology, and to investigate their merely personal circumstances as the presumed cause of their expressions. Moreover, the bare judgment that "we are in an age of transition" is any empty tautology: the idea of "transition" is implicit in the idea of "time"; the present is, by meaning alone, the moment of transition from past to future; and it is therefore self-evidently the case that every age is an age of transition.

The sense of crisis is almost altogether absent from classical writings. "Time" and "history" were not orienting concepts in the Hellenic world-view, and there was therefore little substance out of which to form the derived category of "historical crisis." Socrates, Plato, and to a lesser extent Aristotle were reformers, disapproving of much that was around them, and aware of grave social problems. Nevertheless, they never thought or felt in terms of "social catastrophe," in spite of the fact that there might seem to have been some objective occasion for them to have done so. During the lifetime of Socrates and Plato, the foundations of their own Athens and the Greek city-state polity of which it was the leading element, were, as it turned out, irrevocably shattered.

You can search long in English writing of the 18th century before finding more than sporadic, atypical expression of a sense of crisis. To imagine Spengler surrounded by Dryden, Addison, Steele, and Dr. Johnson is an essay in fantasy. Duns Scotus, Alexander of Hales, Albertus Magnus, Thomas Aquinas, the troubadours and chroniclers and singers of their time, Bertran de Borns, Arnaut Daniel, Chrétien de Troyes, Guido Guinicelli, and the rest, are not concerned with social catastrophe. The problem of the Victorian novel or the French 17th century theater is not that of major revolution, and the possible end of organized society.

It is true that, from the 16th century on, there have been extreme evangelical sects of Protestant Christianity that have preached disaster and catastrophe. Their doctrines have, however, been of a special character, derived from a literal apocalyptic version of religious dogma, deliberately unrelated to historical fact, and plainly separated from the mainstream of post-Renaissance opinion. In Western civilization, the dominating historical idea from the 18th to the 20th centuries, and to some extent even from the 16th, has been that of indefinite Progress, the extreme contrary of the idea of catastrophe.

Individual exceptions may be granted in some abundance without altering the conclusion from the record, that the sense of crisis and catastrophe has not at all been typical of human thought and feeling. A general sense of crisis is comparatively rare, and confined, it would seem, to a very few historical periods. One of these, perhaps the most notable, is that of the 3rd and 4th centuries A.D., especially among the Christian writers of that time. There we do find, not atypically and by exception, but so generally as to be a style of syntax as well as of content, the conviction of crisis.

The world itself now bears witness to its approaching end by the evidence of its failing powers. There is not so much rain in winter for fertilizing the seeds, nor in summer is there so much warmth for ripening them. The springtime is no longer so mild, nor the autumn so rich in fruit. Less marble is quarried from the exhausted mountains, and the dwindling supplies of gold and silver show that the mines are worked out and the impoverished veins of metal diminish from day to day. The peasant is failing and disappearing from the fields, the sailor at sea, the soldier in the camp, uprightness in the forum, justice in the court, concord in friendships, skill in the arts, discipline in morals. Can anything that is old preserve the same powers that it had in the prime and vigor of its youth? It is inevitable that whatever is tending downwards to decay and approaches its end must decrease in strength, like the setting sun and the waning moon, and the dying tree and the failing stream. This is the sentence passed on the world; this is God's law: that all that has risen should fall and that all that has grown should wax old, and that strong things should become weak and great things should become small, and that when they have been weakened and diminished they should come to an end.*

A second such period, if we discount the admixture of secular optimism and judge by the writings of the more extreme religious revolutionists, is the first half of the 16th century.

The world did not end, as some of the writers of the 4th and the 16th centuries predicted, nor was mankind destroyed in a new equivalent of the Flood, nor was the Last Judgment pronounced. Nevertheless, the catastrophic writers of those two periods cannot be dismissed as maladjusted neurotics, fanatics, or victims of hysteria. Considered historically, they were correct in their intuitions, and it was their normal contemporaries who were in error. Though the world and society in an abstract and physical sense were not to be destroyed, the given historical world and society were exactly in the process of destruction; that process was, moreover, subsequently completed; and history's Last Judgment, thrusting them to the left and downward, was rendered.

Once again, in our day, the sense of crisis has spread from individual utterance to wide and thereby social consciousness. It will not be felt if our reading and listening are confined to the stories of the *Saturday Evening Post* and *Good Housekeeping,* the selections of the big book clubs, or the speeches at Rotarian and Optimist Club luncheons. It is, however, present everywhere in the words of our great poets, in their shattered grammar no less than in their metaphors of destruction. The poetic symbols of 1920 have proved much more literal than the contemporary prose of the spokesmen for "normalcy"—

* St. Cyprian, quoted in *A Monument to Saint Augustine* (New York: The Dial Press, 1930).

> What is the city over the mountains
> Cracks and reforms and bursts in the violet air
> Falling towers
> Jerusalem Athens Alexandria
> Vienna London

It thrusts between the broken or distorted forms of Picasso, and the antiharmonics of Schoenberg. It is bodied in the fables of Joyce and Faulkner and Gide and Mann, and shows quite openly in Malraux and Silone and Koestler. It gives relevance to the neo-Lutheran theologies and the existentialist philosophies. And it undergoes ideological transformation in the books of Spengler and Toynbee as well as the pamphlets of Rosenberg and Lenin.

3

In a measure that has been reached only twice before in Western history, we are being told that we live in an age of crisis, that we face the possibility of catastrophe. But the question whether men today have the sense of crisis, believe themselves to be in the midst of crisis, is after all secondary. The more central question is not of belief but of fact. Whatever most men believe, is it in fact true that our age is in crisis? Is the catastrophic point of view, as we might call it, justified?

Two world wars within a generation, with the destruction of from 50 to 100 million human lives and several trillion dollars' worth of human products, would seem, alone, to be enough evidence for a positive answer. These wars, however, are only an item in a long list. Six million Jews slaughtered in death factories must be added; 15, 20, 30 million persons thrown into slave camps; millions of peasants killed because they loved their land; crowds of tens of millions, refugees and displaced persons and exiles, wandering across Eurasia in swarms that make the barbarian hordes of the 3rd and 4th centuries seem as minor as neighborhood gangs. An economic depression that shakes the structure of the entire world, wild inflations that wipe out the money and savings of a dozen nations, trials and purges that liquidate hundreds of thousands of men of every variety, are not phenomena of normality. The great wave of revolution that broke in 1917 has waxed and ebbed, but has never since then subsided. It pounds at every shore, from the islands of East Asia to the borders of the Panama Canal.

From the watchtowers of Westchester, Lake Forest, the Peninsula, Grosse Pointe, and the Main Line, from those social islands where crises are confined, as a rule, to the bedroom and the country club, it is difficult to sight catastrophe. Yet Hiroshima had also its well-kept gardens. The lawns and trees of Zehlendorf were not proof against bombs and fire and rape. Destruction at Coventry was not selective in its victims, and there were bankers and industrialists in the large houses around Cologne. The *dachas,* near Stalingrad, of plant managers and politicians disintegrated along with the workers' tenements.

The crisis of our time is not a vague foreboding. It is presented to the senses, most palpable. It is there to be seen from the streets of Darmstadt, along which not a single building is whole. It can be noted from the porch of St. Paul's, where the blocks of empty cellars, from which weeds and even trees now grow, comment on the future of London's City. Its terms are given by the jammed freight cars that roll toward Siberia from the Baltic, carrying three nations to dissolution, or by the tribunals at Budapest and Prague and Bucharest. It can be touched at Leningrad, in the center of Rotterdam or Beauvais, or in the narrow, shell-crumbled alleys of the small hill towns of Italy. It is acutely visible to one who, standing at the edge of Berlin's Soviet Sector, looks back over the acres of wasteland, surrounded by the ruined walls of the great embassies, that are the heart of the once imperial city.

The visible crisis is of necessity past. But these material symbols of what has lately been show also to the inner eye what may well come. Not all the towers, or governments, have yet fallen; the forced wanderings of the peoples hardly seem to have come to an end. The most sanguine observer cannot find in our world the sufficient premises of stability.

Arthur Koestler is fond of translating his own catastrophic vision into an argument of this sort: You believe that we have a good chance to prevent a third world war? But it is true, is it not, that there have always been wars in the past, and that in the past of our own century there have been the greatest and most devastating of all wars. Unless, therefore, fundamental causal factors have changed, we must expect the same pattern in the future that has held in the past. If you are right in expecting peace in our age, then the burden of proof is on you. Can you show us that, in truth, the various causes that have operated toward war in the past have now been eliminated? Or will you not find that the chief among them are present among us in a degree more exaggerated, perhaps, than ever before?

There are many phases to our crisis. It appears, for example, as a moral and religious crisis, as a crisis in the arts, and as a crisis in the economic structure; and each of these furnishes the groundwork for a correlated possibility of catastrophe. In this book, however, my chief concern is with only two phases of the crisis, and with the first only in its bearing upon the second. There is what might be called the physical crisis, the content of which is the existence of the nuclear, biological, and similar weapons of mass destruction. This physical crisis presents the possibility of catastrophe as the annihilation of civilized society, and perhaps of mankind. There is, finally, the political crisis. This is constituted through the fact that there now exist in the world only two major power centers, and the further fact that these two power centers are incompatible with each other. The possibility of catastrophe, as given by the political crisis, is the conquest of a monopoly of world power by communism.*

*I have stated the general terms of the world political crisis in *The Struggle for the World* (New York: The John Day Company, 1947). This present book is a concrete extension of the analysis of the earlier.

4

The totalitarian political movements of our century, particularly the communist, have accepted a catastrophic point of view. In 1916, totalitarianism, limited at that date to a few thousand outlaw associates and followers of Lenin, was so negligible a force as to be altogether unknown even to the politically literate public. Today, 34 years later, it dominates about a quarter of the world, and closely threatens the rest. The contribution of the catastrophic point of view to this rise, which is quite without precedent, has been much more than minor. It has been so because the catastrophic point of view, as a perspective on our age, has been correct.

From the perspective of normality, those who hold the catastrophic point of view seem comic or fanatic, and usually both. This has been the invariant estimate of democratic public opinion on all the totalitarian leaders. The estimate is popularly and profoundly expressed in the cartoon and movie stereotypes of "reds" and "fascists." But informed as well as vulgar opinion rated Lenin and Trotsky as scholastic cranks, Mussolini as a clown (I remember what fun my learned French teacher at school in 1922 used to poke at Mussolini), Hitler as a comic-neurotic (as Chaplin fixed him), Stalin as a dull pedant, Franco as a light-opera colonel. In 1930 and '31, London and Washington and Paris judged the political and business leaders of the Weimar Republic to be responsible, serious, and able; and Hitler, a mountebank. Democratic commentators are always explaining how the totalitarians interfere with "their own best interests" ("Hitler's greatest mistake was to persecute the Jews"; "The Kremlin would have done so much better if it had adopted a conciliatory policy after 1945". . .). They can never understand how the totalitarians can believe in "such ridiculous theories" as nazism and Marxism-Leninism-Stalinism. Even toward the 1949 trial of the eleven U.S. communist leaders, the normal response is to classify the defendants as "nuts."

Neuroticism, insanity, and the comic are, however, largely a matter of context. Behavior and ideas that would have proved insanity under Queen Anne may have a very different meaning in the 20th century. Putting money each week in the savings bank is not sensible behavior during an unrestrained inflation; bringing suit for libel is not a mark of sanity in a revolution. What is historical madness depends upon what historical reality is. Mussolini and Hitler and Lenin and Stalin and Franco are no doubt still to be judged in some respects mad. But what then of the Baldwins and Chamberlains and Blums and Daladiers and Stresemanns and Eberts and Hoovers and Roosevelts and Azañas, many of whose actions can be explained only by the hypothesis that they imagined themselves to be living in another century than their own?

The totalitarians believe that we live in what Lenin defined as "an era of wars and revolutions," in an age of crisis. They count on crises, and make these the fulcrum of their policies. Lenin was sure that there would be a world war, and his energies were directed toward seizing power in the breakdown which he was sure would come during the course of the war. Hitler was sure that the German peace treaty not only could not be enforced but would shatter in spectacular fragments, and he planned to take power over the ruins of Versailles. Who, outside of the Kremlin, had heard in 1939, or even 1942, of Hoxha and his dozen or two adherents? But Hoxha knew that his time—a time of war and civil confusion and breakdown—would come, and in 1945 he duly took power in Albania. Stalin counted on fierce rivalries among "imperialist powers," and he was ready to exploit these by signing with Hitler or fighting him, by making agreements with the West and by breaking them.

The democratic leaders have regarded the crises as abnormal exceptions to the flow of history, as errors that can be avoided by doing each day its daily short-term task. They have therefore failed either to utilize the crises or even to prepare for them. They find themselves in the paradoxical position of having suffered the greatest social defeats from the two wars in which they have won the greatest military victories of all time. Munich and Yalta might have been model diplomacy in the 17th or 18th centuries, but we are dealing now not with kings and emperors and czars, but with totalitarian mass revolutionists. The day of the Congress of Vienna and the Holy Alliance is over.

Given time, we hear the argument, we can gradually work our way out of the mess. The League of Nations—or the United Nations, the Marshall Plan—or the Dawes Plan, the gold standard—or Keynesian deficits, the Kellogg Pact—or conferences of foreign ministers, will step by step build up confidence and solve the problems and bring us peace and prosperity. But we are not given time, and there is now loose in the world a mighty force dedicated to the proposition that we shall not have peace and prosperity.

We are, historically, in an *extreme situation*. It requires a novel and extreme solution. Our problem is to avoid the threatened catastrophe by meeting the urgency of the crisis that is its forerunner. The analysis that I undertake in this book, and the plan of action that I propose, are predicated upon what I have been calling "the catastrophic point of view." The analysis and the plan depart from our accepted ways of thinking and acting in international affairs. If I am wrong in my assumed point of view, if the crisis is an illusion and the catastrophe an anxiety complex, then there can be no justification for either the analysis or the plan. But I do not believe that I am wrong.

CHAPTER II

The Inadequacy of U. S. Foreign Policy

AT SOME POINT during the spring of 1949, it became customary in the United States to say that "we are winning the cold war." In editorials, speeches, and articles, U.S. foreign policy was judged and found not wanting. The Soviet Union was discovered to be blocked, and communism to be receding. "The tension had lessened"; internal affairs began to take precedence again over foreign in the business of Congress and the plans of politicians.

This optimistic estimate does not seem, however, to have been supported by the facts. We should not regard a businessman as particularly successful if, instead of going bankrupt as feared, he had finished two or three millions in the red. Nor would we label a man healthy if, instead of dying, he had only lost a half-dozen limbs and organs.

Let us, in order to disentangle our judgment from day-by-day moods, compare the world position of the United States in 1939 to its position ten years later. In 1939, what was taken to be the principal concentration of enemy power was confined to a limited area of central Europe. Within this area was a population of less than 100 million. The enemy technological level was high, and his military machine formidable. He lacked, however, both the possession of, and direct access to, many of the most essential raw materials. His power was extended outside of his boundaries by the manipulation of fifth columns within other nations; but, since these were cemented only by a narrowly chauvinist and racial ideology which could have no wide appeal, their strength was negligible.

The enemy power concentration in 1939 was, in fact or potentially, counterbalanced by several other autonomous power centers of some magnitude: the Soviet Union; Great Britain with her Empire and Dominions; France; Japan (as well, of course, as the United States, from the point of view of which the outline is being drawn).

In 1949, the enemy power concentration is based upon a vast territory which includes the most favorable strategic position of the world, the heartland of Eurasia. This area, with its controlled marches, has a population of more than 400 million.* Though technologically backward, the enemy's military machine is also formidable, and he has at his disposal nearly all essential or important raw materials. His fifth columns, not handicapped by overt chauvinism or racialism, have penetrated deep into the tissue of all political organisms outside of his direct control, and are in their own right massive fighting forces.

Moreover, except for the United States itself, there no longer exist any other counterbalancing power centers of any magnitude. Germany (the previous enemy concentration) and Japan have been broken; France dissolved; and Great Britain, with her Empire shorn and her economy in desperation, though by no means finished is no longer capable of independent action.

To pose the comparison as between 1939 and 1949 may, however, seem inappropriate. In 1939, the enemy was Germany and nazism. Foreign policy with respect to Germany and nazism was successful, since these were defeated and eliminated as a major power threat, even though certain inconveniences linger on. That chapter was closed in 1945, so that probing before that date becomes an academic appraisal of no practical importance for the present and future.

This objection, it may be remarked, is not well taken. The historical life of a nation, until it finally dies by conquest or absorption, is continuous. The division of its life into stages or periods is merely for our analytic convenience. Throughout its life, the nation is in an

---

* Malenkov, in his address at the 1949 celebration of the aniversary of the Bolshevik revolution, had already added China to the Soviet family: "With the victory of the Chinese people the countries of Popular Democracies in Europe, together with the Soviet Socialist State, number about 800 million people."

always shifting power equilibrium with other nations, both severally and in their totality. The power relation is now more, now less favorable to the nation that we are considering: which it is to be is not decided by the names of the other nations that happen for a time to be most conspicuous, but by the facts of power. For Sparta to defeat Athens does not necessarily improve the power position of Sparta if thereby she has aided the rise of first Thebes and then Macedon. Holland could not long rejoice over the elimination of the Spanish Navy when she saw it replaced by the ships of England. Britain's defeat of Napoleon made possible also the rise of Prussia.

Nevertheless, let us begin again with 1945. Since 1945, the Soviet Union has proceeded steadily with the reduction to its domination of the nations of Eastern Europe. In spite of the fact that in 1942 and 1943 it had been thrust back hundreds and in many directions thousands of miles inside its own frontiers, and was close to total defeat, the Soviet Union has stretched an ever tightening hand over Lithuania, Latvia, Estonia, Poland, East Germany, Czechoslovakia, Hungary, Bulgaria, Rumania, Albania. By careful diplomacy and infiltration, it has gained a foothold in the Near East; and, by exploiting the social difficulties in Egypt, the Belgian Congo, and South Africa, it has for the first time made a crossing of the land bridge into Africa. It has developed task forces in nearly every Latin American nation, and has carried through major actions in Colombia and Costa Rica—immediately north and south, that is, of the Panama Canal.

In France and in Italy, the two major countries of Western Europe, mass communist parties, surrounded and covered by millions of voters, give the Soviet Union a veto power over economic recovery and political decision, and induce a permanent paralysis of military potential. Through minor but skillfully planned actions in Greece, Turkey, and Berlin, the Kremlin, at a minimum cost to itself, continues to drain vast sums and energies from the United States.

On the ideological front, there has occurred a cumulative growth of despair and the feeling of betrayal among the peoples of Eastern

Europe. The morale of these peoples depends upon the conviction that their present subjection to the Soviet empire is temporary, and that the perspective of the West includes their liberation. No important actions of the West have furthered or even sustained this conviction. The Atlantic Union, as this has been publicly presented, runs directly counter to it; the make-up of the Union, and its announced defensive purpose, seem to imply acceptance of the present division of Europe. So also do the commercial agreements that have been negotiated between Western nations and the communist satellite governments. Meanwhile, at the United Nations and in every international conference, the Soviet representatives maintain the ideological initiative. This is plain even in their supposed "retreats." The first proposals always come from the Soviet spokesmen, who always set the direction of the proceedings. The spokesmen of the West, even though their showing is often better than in the days of Teheran or Yalta, are always "reacting" to the Soviet moves.

In drawing up the balance of these years, the purges and liquidations that have been going on continuously within the Soviet empire must not be omitted. In these purges, millions of persons have been executed, imprisoned, or sent to slower death in the slave labor camps. These millions include especially those who have been, or might have been, oriented toward the West: that is, it is our allies and potential allies who have been purged. Their ranks are the equivalent of more divisions than the Atlantic Pact is going to produce.

By far the greatest triumphs of communist policy during these years since 1945 have, however, been in Asia. Manchuria and northern Korea have been brought within the Soviet empire; a considerable part of China proper has been overrun; and on the southern flank, in the big islands and in Burma and Malaysia, turmoil has been successfully maintained. The probing into southern Korea and Japan has begun.

From the standpoint of the Kremlin, it would be hard to overstate the importance of the Asian victories. From the beginning of the

Russian Communist party, "the Chinese question" has played a central role. Only a few years after the 1917 Revolution, even before the Bolsheviks had fully consolidated power at home, their direct intervention into China began. Tens of thousands of Chinese revolutionists have been trained, often for many years, at Soviet institutes; and thousands of non-Chinese, for work in China. In the dispute between Stalin and Trotsky, the Chinese question was one of the fundamental points at issue. Stalin's writings show that the Chinese and general Asian problem has been one of his own principal preoccupations. He is himself in large measure responsible for the policies that have been followed, and that are now so close to definite success.

During these same years, since 1945, the Soviet Union has suffered only one major and unambiguous setback: the defection of Tito. This setback, however, is not yet final; and it was not gained by our policy.

In the spring of 1949, the publicists hailed "the great victory of Berlin." But of what did the victory of Berlin consist, and what is its content? From June, 1948, until the spring of 1949, we "held at Berlin." During those same months, the communists conquered China. How do these two weigh against each other?

In judging the success or failure of recent U.S. foreign policy, we must be careful not to distort our readings. It is true that the results, however melancholy, are not as bad as they could have been. If we had continued the 1943–46 line of conciliation and virtual capitulation to every Soviet demand—if we had adopted the line of Henry Wallace—then the balance would have been still more heavily weighted. Without the turn to a tougher line, without the Truman Doctrine and the Marshall Plan and the airlift, the communists would by now have Iran, Greece, and perhaps Turkey, and they would quite possibly be in control of France, Italy, and Germany. Moreover, it would be utopian to suppose that any policy, confronted by the problems of a world crisis, could have had or could have quick and easy success.

We must, however, dispel illusion. Though U.S. policy has so far avoided the worst possible, and has cut some threatened losses, it has as yet produced no clearcut and positive gains. The supposed or real gains are at best negative or potential; none that is concrete and positive has yet been realized. The Soviet Union has given up nothing, nothing whatsoever, and has added much. Nor is it true that 1948–49 marked a "righting of the balance"; 1948–49, let it be repeated, marked the conquest of China. The commented-on relaxation of tension, and the overtures toward greater East-West trade, far from indicating a positive gain for the West, are simply a new device manipulated by the communists in an effort to get the West to do some of their work for them.

World politics is, at present and until the issue is settled, the field of struggle between the United States, as representative of Western civilization, on the one hand, and communism, with its primary base in the Soviet Union, on the other. Every other development in world politics has historical significance only in relation to this determining struggle. A positive gain for U.S. foreign policy means, therefore, an alteration of the world power balance in its favor as against the Soviet Union. Such an alteration can take place in a variety of ways. An internal strengthening of the United States, in morale or organization or arms, without a corresponding strengthening of the Soviet empire, is one possibility, to which an internal weakening of the Soviet empire without a corresponding weakening of the United States is equivalent. The winning of new territories, peoples, and resources for the anti-communist (that is, the United States) bloc is another, as is the increase and hardening of anti-communist sentiment within any nation, including the nations of the Soviet empire. A loss by the Soviet empire of territory, peoples, or resources is a gain for the United States.

The weakening or elimination of the communist fifth column within nations outside of the present Soviet empire is a gain, and could be a very considerable gain, for United States policy. For example, the economic, political, and military recovery of Western Europe—which has been adopted as an objective of U.S. policy—is in fact a positive gain for the United States only to the extent that the Western European nations are firmly anti-communist in their orientation. This is frequently overlooked, though it is certainly obvious if stated in reverse: the recovery of Western Europe, if it had a firm pro-communist, pro-Soviet orientation, would undoubtedly be a loss for U.S. policy; and in such a case it would be far better for Europe to be weak than strong. It follows that the United States might well have much more to gain, in the near future, from the smashing of the French Communist party—which now prevents the French nation from having a firm and unified anti-communist orientation—than from the arming of a few French divisions.

If we estimate the results of our foreign policy by such an objective test in terms of the power balance, it is usually rather easy to show whether a given move has led to success or failure. Such testing will, I believe, confirm the impression that during the past few years since 1945 we have had no major positive gain except the gift of Tito's defection, and that we have suffered a number of major positive losses. Our action in Greece, or the Berlin airlift, cannot be counted as positive gains, because they did not alter the power balance in our favor except perhaps to a minor extent through a positive influence on anti-communist morale. They prevented, or checked, positive and major losses, and have therefore been politically justified; but no more.

Moreover, it does not seem likely that U.S. foreign policy, if it continues along its present course, will in the future produce major positive gains. Where are they likely to come from? Where, even, are they being deliberately sought? History is not so obliging as to distribute its favors to bashful suitors.

If we did not live in an age of crisis, if what I have called the catastrophic point of view were a neurotic phantom, then there would be no occasion for special concern. We could even permit ourselves a certain complacency. After all, we have as a nation learned a good deal since 1945. In those days we were gladly donating to the Soviet Union great batteries of power—in Germany, the Balkans, in Manchuria and Korea. Today we at any rate hold back and grumble. In time, we could be expected to complete our lessons by the gradual pressure of historical circumstance. In time, yes; but there is not much time. There is an outside and strict time limit to our course of schooling: the date when the enemy will possess in quantity the weapons of mass destruction, and the means of employing them.

2

The directing principles of U.S. foreign policy are not static. From 1942 until 1946, the U.S. based its relations toward the Soviet Union on conciliation, military solidarity, and the attempt at friendship. These relations were unilateral. At no time did the Soviet Union have any notion of conciliation or friendship toward the United States, and its military solidarity was at most no more than partial. In 1946, as was publicly indicated at that time by the then Secretary of State, Byrnes, a change took place. Military solidarity was no longer in question. The attempt at close friendship cooled, and conciliatory moves alternated with what came to be called "toughness." During the following year the tough line was broadened by the Truman Doctrine and the call for the Marshall Plan. In 1948 the general implications of the new stage were made explicit in the famous article, reputed to have been written by George Kennan of the State Department, which was published in *Foreign Affairs*. According to this intelligent and carefully reasoned presentation, the guiding principle of our foreign policy should be summed up as "the containment of communism."

Nevertheless, in spite of these changes, which have been very considerable and even very rapid for a large and complex democracy to have made within so relatively short a time, the foreign policy has continued to be unsuccessful. At the very least, even if the unfavorable estimate is not accepted, the policy has not been successful enough in the light of what has to be done. It is advisable, therefore, to try to analyze why it has failed, what its principal defects are. If this analysis can be agreed on, we shall then know better what revisions ought to be made.

The principal defects in U.S. foreign policy are, I believe, the following four:

(1) The policy is not sufficiently unified. From this it follows that a move in one direction tends to have its results canceled by another move in a counterdirection. This has been true at every stage of the policy as it has developed since 1945. For example, we rush in money, goods, and even military help to "contain communism" in Europe at the same time that we decrease or withdraw efforts to contain communism in China. We condemn communism in Czechoslovakia by denouncing the persecution of the Church, and at the same time accept overtures to ourselves and our allies for increased trade with Czechoslovakia of a kind that is certain to aid the communist rule of that country. We help Tito against Stalin by making economic deals with Tito, and at the same time solidarize ourselves with Stalin against Tito by signing a joint agreement on Carinthia. We spend hundreds of millions against the communists in Greece, and at the same time, by withdrawing economic aid, hinder the Dutch in their efforts to control communists in the East Indies. We denounce De Gaulle as a fascist because he wants to suppress the communists; and at the same time denounce the Third Force French government as hopeless because it fails to suppress the communists in Indo-China.

On the same day, one government leader will give a speech proclaiming that the communists are irreconcilable and will never abandon their aim of world revolution, while another will insist that the Kremlin is "sincere" in wanting to decrease tension, increase trade, and come to some agreement. In laying down the perspectives for the Marshall Plan, we list as one of its goals the revival of trade between East and West Europe; and immediately thereafter we draw up lists of prohibited exports from West to East. We expose communist propaganda as lies and moral poison, and at the same time permit UNESCO, the international propaganda organization financed largely by our money, to be infiltrated, exploited, and to a large extent controlled by fellow travelers and Communist party members. We enter into an Atlantic Pact that can have no content unless it is directed against the Soviet Union, and insist to the world that it has no relation to the Soviet Union. We protest the economic draining of other nations by the Soviet Union, and at the same time agree, in discussing an Austrian treaty, on how the Soviet Union shall be permitted to pillage the Austrian economy.

In a democratic nation, where there is no monolithic government structure, and where differing social pressures and differing points of view are not merely likely but desirable, we cannot expect and should not hope for the kind of unity that is part of the essence of totalitarianism. Still, it does not seem extravagant to think that we might, without succumbing to internal totalitarianism, have a little more unity in action than has prevailed during these recent years. It seems not unreasonable to believe that the heads of the various departments of the government should at any rate carry out roughly the same policy, and that their subordinates should be required, at least, not to sabotage policy in action, however much they may disapprove and rightly try, by persuasion, to change the direction of policy.

This disunity is not merely stultifying by its direct effect on our own policies and their implementation. It is equally injurious through its effect on the confidence of other peoples in us. The rest of the world is bewildered and disoriented by what it observes, and cannot help observing, of the practical conflicts in U.S. policies. The dramatic conduct of the Berlin airlift seems to call for a spirit of firm resistance to communism, and much of the rest of the world responds. Just as its spirit rises to the contest, it learns of secret friendly negotiations between U.S. and Soviet representatives; and the President of the United States expresses his reliance on the Kremlin's sincerity. It reads a brave speech that seems to promise the liberation of the nations behind the iron curtain; and the next day it learns that Gromyko and Baruch and American industrialists are talking about big trade on the present political basis. It hears of a great welcome in New York and Washington to Soviet deserters and refugees; and in the DP camps, the International Refugee Organization, financed by U.S. funds, propagandizes other refugees and deserters to return to what they know will be death or enslavement in their homelands. The observed contradictions in policy, which are at first experience a puzzle, tend to lead toward cynicism and despair.

(2) The policy is too narrow. Unlike communist policy, U.S. policy is not yet based on the clear realization that the present struggle for the world proceeds simultaneously and integrally along political, economic, ideological, sociological, and military lines. What happens in each of these fields affects what happens in every other. It is difficult, for example, to solidify political relations with Britain if economic measures harmful to Britain are undertaken. Communist lies spread in Europe about the United States cannot be combatted unless the truth about the United States is made widely available in Europe. The Chinese are not encouraged to resist communist rule if American business insists on aiding the Chinese communists by trade.

The United States is accused by communist propaganda of being "militaristic." In the sense meant by the communists, this is almost ludicrously untrue. However, in another and very important sense, U.S. policy might well be considered too militaristic. There is a tendency for Americans to reason, not altogether consciously, somewhat as follows. After all, we have at our disposal nuclear and other weapons of mass destruction. These can be relied upon. However many mistakes we make, whatever deficiencies and omissions there may be in our day-to-day actions, and even if we sustain a good many setbacks, all can quickly be made right when the showdown comes by dropping a few hundred bombs at the right spots. U.S.

"militarism," that is to say, does not mean a militarization of our society—which, though doubtless increased as compared with our previous history, remains at a lesser degree than that of almost all other nations. We do run the danger, however, of being narrowly militaristic in our historical attitude, in this seldom expressed but widely held belief that arms alone, that force can if necessary solve all our problems. This belief is not only dangerous but false. Though great historical problems cannot be solved without force, force alone solves nothing.

I shall return in other connections to the need of broadening the front of our operations in the struggle for the world. The defect of narrowness is understood by many within the government and the armed services, and during recent years steps have been taken to overcome it. The Marshall Plan, the Voice of America, and the intervention of both the A. F. of L. and the C.I.O. in the international trade-union movement are recognitions of the importance of, respectively, the economic, the ideological, and the sociological phases of the struggle.

(3) The policy is defensive. So far as U.S. foreign relations since 1947 have been integrated into a single policy rather than a loose collection of conflicting policies, this has been done through the conception of "the containment of communism." The containment of communism is unquestionably something to be desired. "Containment," however, cannot be the end objective of a policy. More generally, a defensive policy—and containment is a variant of the defensive—can never win.

It is curious how persistent are the errors on this point, in spite of the ever repeated lessons of history and experience. It is especially curious that military leaders, trained in military history, could even for a moment have been led to accept the doctrine of containment. Moreover, what is proved by military history about the limitations of the defensive holds equally for all realms of human activity. It is just as sure that the defensive will not, in the long run, save a fortune or a business as that it will not win a war.

The defensive has, of course, its appropriate use, both as tactic and as strategy. In a battle by which an army implements an offensive strategy, there will always be individual units which, for a time or even for the entire battle, remain on the defensive. Not only the tactic but the strategy of an entire army or group of armies may be correctly defensive, as in the case of Eisenhower's armies at the end of 1944. Even a nation, or a coalition of nations, may be, and be correctly, on the defensive, as England necessarily was in 1940, after the fall of France. (The Anglo-French coalition had, in fact, been on the defensive from the beginning of the war; and this is an indication of why the Allied nations could never have won the war unless the United States had joined them. They could never have passed successfully to the strategic offensive without United States support. This Churchill knew, and he consequently, and correctly, made the task of drawing the United States into the war his primary objective during the first two years.)

All this is true of the defensive. Nevertheless, the defensive never wins, except for rare and uncontrollable accidents where the opponent is already in a state of internal collapse to begin with, and in reality licked before he starts. In the case of dynamic social forces, whether nations or classes or competitive business organizations or even rival garden clubs or families, victory and even, in the long run, survival come only by carrying through an attack, only by passing to the offensive. The defensive, properly understood, can never be more than a partial and temporary expedient. Certain elements can be placed on the defensive in order to support indirectly an offensive by the remainder. A general defensive can, and often must, be used in order to gain time, to complete preparations, to hold out until support comes, to consolidate an internal position; but the preparation must always be *for* something, the time gained must be so that something can be *done* in the future; and what the preparation is for, what is to be done, is either the offensive or meaningless.

Every businessman knows that under competitive conditions a soap company, for instance, cannot rest content with the products and methods it already has, and the markets it has already won. Sooner or later its competitors would be underselling it, would have devised new products and procedures, and would be grabbing its markets. The certain end would be bankruptcy. It is no different in political, social, and military affairs.

A perpetual defensive is impossible in general, and it is particularly fantastic in relation to the struggle against world communism. The containment line is almost immeasurably vast. It is not limited to the tens of thousands of miles of the Soviet Empire's border, which is itself far too great to encompass. By the methods of propaganda, subversion, and infiltration, the communist front is carried into and through every nation of the world on both sides of the border. The "front" itself is not merely geographic, but ideological, sociological, and political as well. How could a front of such magnitude be held? A concentration of forces for containment on one sector necessarily opens up another sector—as China so plainly proves. The enemy behind this world front, moreover, is not passive but in the highest degree dynamic and aggressive, ready at any moment to thrust with any of a most varied arsenal of material, political and psychological weapons toward every symptom of weakness, every unguarded opening. To suppose that such an opponent can be countered indefinitely by a policy of containment is to concede him victory.

(4) The policy has no objective. Perhaps it would be more accurate to say that U.S. foreign policy, as understood by those who devise it and carry it out, has a number of objectives which are mutually inconsistent. This lack of an objective, or of a consistent set of objectives, is the decisive defect.

If anyone believes that there is a clearcut objective, let him then declare what it is. No unequivocal answer has yet been authoritatively given, nor is it implicit in the actions that have been taken.

Eternal containment of communism cannot be an objective; it is both empty and impossible. Containment can make sense only as a temporary device for the sake of some genuine objective to be gained later on.

Is the objective an agreement, a deal, with communism? If so, what kind of deal? A deal that leaves communist power intact where it is now established, and communist fifth columns free to extend that power wherever they find or make an opportunity? If so, what business do we have denouncing internal measures taken within the Soviet Union itself and within the satellite nations? What concern is it of ours that Hungary or Czechoslovakia tortures or kills priests who, by their standards, are enemies of the state? Why do we impose embargoes on exports, and order FBI agents to guard ships sailing in from behind the Iron Curtain? What objection have we to Mao Tse-tung or to the Political Bureau of the American Communist party? If we want an agreement, we should listen to Henry Wallace or Professor Schuman or Harlow Shapley. They can tell us the kind of agreement we can get, and how to get it. But if not a genuine agreement, then what do we want? It illuminates nothing to seek refuge in vague abstractions about "peace" and "international law" and "friendship" and "cooperation." We must be concrete: what kind of peace, on what basis? whose law, enforced by whom? what terms of friendship? cooperation toward what ends?

This lack of clearcut objective, which vitiates so many even of those policy moves which in themselves are intelligent and promising, is not by chance. Obscurity here reflects a profound hesitation. We have not been willing to face the fact that there is only one possible objective of U.S. foreign policy: the destruction of communist power.

3

I wish to illustrate these defects, in particular the last two, by several examples. In order not to prejudice the evidence, I shall select policy moves which have been among the wisest and most successful. It would hardly need discussion to prove that the policy followed toward China has been defective.

(1) The Berlin airlift. The dazzling technical and human achievement of the Berlin airlift makes the attempt to strike an objective political balance of its motivation and results seem irrelevant, and ungracious. The courage and skill of the pilots, the loyalty and work of the ground crews, the organizational achievement of the Air Force staff, the fearlessness and endurance of the Western Berlin population, cannot be overcommended. Political analysis, however, cannot rest satisfied with a distribution of rhetorical ribbons. What, we must ask, did the airlift accomplish politically? What was it even supposed to accomplish?

In the spring of 1948, as the communists gradually choked off access to Berlin, the United States leadership was challenged by the developing situation to a decision. The practical situation was novel, without exact historical precedent. The United States, together with its allies, was manning an isolated enclave deep within enemy territory, without local resources or secure communications. In law and in fact the status of the enclave was equivocal in the extreme.

Two intelligible decisions were possible. One was to regard the position as untenable, and to withdraw. This would have meant a defeat, which could have been explained and perhaps justified, but which could not have been hidden or exempted from a long series of weakening consequences. The other was to deny the enemy the right to blockade, to refuse to recognize the barriers, and to send armed convoys through with supplies. It is widely believed that General Clay, then military governor for the United States, was in favor of this second decision.

To send armed convoys through would have risked an armed clash; and an armed clash before the gates of Berlin would have risked, however remotely, the outbreak of general war. This risk cannot be denied. However, well-grounded opinion in the spring of

1948 and almost universal *ex post facto* opinion rate this risk as negligible. Everything in Soviet behavior indicates that the armed convoys would have got through without armed opposition.

The minute risk was linked to the chance for enormous gain. The direct smashing of the Berlin blockade would have been a rolling defeat for the Soviet Union which would have had cumulative repercussion throughout the world, and above all in Eastern Europe. It would have proved in action that the communists are beatable. I have talked to many persons in Germany who believe that the Soviet position in their German zone would have been so undermined that they would have had to withdraw their forces from Germany. That is perhaps too optimistic. But there can be little doubt that the communist defeat would have roused all the satellite peoples to new hope and new determination: it would have been the first reversal since 1944 of the ascendant communist trend in Eastern Europe, the first and so much needed proof that the Iron Curtain has not been drawn to stay.

The United States made neither of the two possible decisions. Instead, without a previous plan and without knowing what could or should be done or for how long, the airlift was improvised. But the airlift was not a decision; or, if a decision, it was a decision not to decide. It was a means for temporizing, for putting off decisions. After it turned out to be a great technical success, and had excited the admiration of the world, it could of course be advertised as a brilliant victory. But a victory means the achievement of a goal. And what was the goal?

In the spring of 1949, as usual on Soviet initiative, a Foreign Ministers' Conference was held, and the Soviet blockade partially and irritatingly lifted. What was the net political gain from the triumph of the airlift? Were the communists anywhere driven back? Were the communications to Berlin any more fully secured and guaranteed? Was the Soviet veto that operates at every level of international contact abolished? Was it a great gain that once more the foreign ministers waste time and money in futile conferences from which no concrete profits have ever been drawn except by the Kremlin? And let us remember that the year of the airlift was also the year of the communist conquest of China.

I do not mean to suggest that the airlift—the decision, that is, not to decide—was necessarily incorrect in the practical sense. It is often advisable and necessary to temporize. The United States may not have been ready to take even the slight risk of a positive decision on Berlin. But we should, then, know what we are doing and have done. We should realize that a delay, a temporizing, a failure to decide, is what it is, is not a goal in itself, and can be justified only if through it we become better placed to make a decision after the temporizing is over. My failure to decide today is justified if I shall be able to decide tomorrow with a better chance of success. If, however, I make indecision itself the basis of all my behavior, I become the passive tool of circumstance.

(2) *The intervention in Greece.* From 1947 on, as part of what has become known as the Truman Doctrine, the United States has carried out in Greece an intervention of massive scope in relation to the size and population of the country. Hundreds of millions of dollars' worth of food, supplies, machinery, and weapons have been shipped in. Personnel from the United States has aided in the supervision of economic reconstruction, has considerably influenced internal Greek politics and government measures, and has been in close liaison with the Greek armed forces.

If it had not been for this intervention, it is almost certain that the communists would have taken control of Greece. The Soviet Empire would thereby have been extended well into the Eastern Mediterranean. Tito's defection would have become much more difficult, perhaps impossible. The Near East would have been directly threatened, and the road to Africa smoothed. The intervention has blocked these disastrous results; and thus, as we have seen, is rightly considered a success, though it is only a negative success. The United States has gained nothing by the Greek intervention, but has merely avoided an important loss. The relative cost of the negative success has been high: as against the vast resources poured out by the United States, the communists have committed a few thousand auxiliary troops, conscripts, and dupes, small amounts of arms, and a core of trained leaders.

It is apparent that the Greek intervention, both in conception and in execution, is purely defensive. This is what proves its inadequacy, when it is placed within the context of the world struggle. "The Greek problem" has not been solved, and cannot be under the present policy. Moreover, the concentration of defensive efforts in Greece leaves holes more open elsewhere, as has been demonstrated.

To solve the Greek problem would mean secure borders and internal political stability. The latter is impossible without at least a functioning Greek economy. Greece, during and since the war, has been ravaged materially and socially by the Italians, the Nazis, and by a series of revolutions and uprisings. Greece is a small country, poor in natural resources. In modern times, her economy has been kept precariously going by shipping, and by an export trade in which the principal item has been tobacco marketed in Central Europe, especially in Germany. Most of her shipping was destroyed in the war. Since the war, many of her capitalists have disloyally operated ships with no benefit to Greece by transferring their corporate selves or their registries to foreign nations. The German tobacco market has been nonexistent. The Greek borders cannot be secure while at their edge is the dynamic force of world communism. The communist-led partisans cannot be finally wiped out while they have safe refuge and safe sources of new supplies of men and materiel behind the borders. If the Kremlin so decides, it can on its own initiative suspend the Greek civil war, just as it can suspend the Berlin blockade. But security does not result, because the civil war—or the blockade—can at any moment, on a new initiative of the Kremlin's, be resumed.

Once again the conclusion is inescapable. Under present U.S. policy, the Greek intervention, like any other foreign policy moves, can at best have only negative success, and cannot result, except by accident or luck, in positive gains.

Since this present chapter is primarily critical, I do not intend here to anticipate the different policy which it is the business of the latter half of this book to present, and by which positive gains, in Greece and in general, would become possible. However, it is perhaps advisable to note very briefly what must be kept in mind in the case of Greece.

Greece's military and political problem cannot be solved within Greece itself, but only in the Balkans beyond Greece. That is, there can be no secure defense at Greece's borders from the Balkan communist forces; and therefore these forces must be got rid of. Tito's break with the Cominform, the unrest in Albania, and Bulgaria's violations of the peace treaty present the chance of doing so at perhaps less cost than that of two years of Greek intervention.

Greece's economic problem can be solved only if the European economic problem is solved. This consideration, however, leads to a third U.S. policy move, with a summary discussion of which I wish to conclude this chapter.

(3) *The Marshall Plan.* There were a number of motives that led the United States to adopt and put into effect the Marshall Plan. From the point of view of the general public, there is little doubt that a directly humanitarian motive was prominent. The European peoples had been our allies in a great war. They had suffered far more than we, and in part from our own bombs and shells. We ought, then, to aid their reconstruction.

There were also economic aims. Just as a penniless tramp is not a good customer for a storekeeper, so an impoverished Europe would be useless for trade. Moreover, not a few American businessmen saw that through the Marshall Plan credits they would have a European market for export products that could not otherwise be sold. Unquestionably, some sections of American business saw the Marshall Plan as a device that could be used to increase American economic supremacy, though there was the difficulty that through the Plan the United States would also be strengthening potential trade rivals.

The political motive, however, was derived from the containment policy. Europe, in its shattered postwar condition, was an easy mark for communism. The economic reconstruction of Europe would permit European political stability; and the two together would give Europe a better chance to resist communism both internally and externally. From a political standpoint, thus, the Marshall Plan was exclusively defensive in conception. As always, the defensive move is inadequate, even to fulfill the defensive purpose.

With the help of the Marshall Plan, the West European economy has somewhat improved. The communist movements within the West European nations are somewhat weaker, though still very powerful. Nevertheless, the European economic position remains fundamentally unsound, and, granted a continuation of the present policy, it will be so at the conclusion of the Marshall Plan and of any number of post-Marshall Plans. It is not difficult to understand why this must be.

The economy of continental Europe has always functioned through an interchange between the East and the West, with the East exchanging food and minerals and other raw materials for the machines, finished goods, and capital of the West. Moreover, the Continent as a whole has had to trade with the rest of the world. In addition, the development of production methods at the present time has become incompatible with the political division of Europe into small, rigidly independent states.

European economic recovery, therefore, is possible only if the European Iron Curtain is lifted, if some measure of European unification is brought about, and if the whole world is opened up to relatively free economic interchange. One further condition should be added: West European economic and political reconstruction is impossible so long as there are mass communist movements within the major West European nations, since these movements can and will block the reconstruction.

To achieve these conditions of European recovery is an offensive task. Many measures of the Marshall Plan might contribute to the fulfillment of that task if they were linked to a positive, offensive general policy conception. But they have not been; the Plan has been restricted by the defensive framework of containment. Therefore, once again, the Marshall Plan can have no more than a negative success; it cannot produce positive gains. Consequently, when the Plan's termination is reached, the power balance will not have significantly altered. The same problems will be present as those that originally called forth the Plan. If the same reasoning is used, a second—and a third and a fourth—Plan will have to be successively launched.

The problem is to escape from this treadmill.

CHAPTER III

The End of Traditional Diplomacy

SINCE 1943 THERE has been a long series of high-level conferences in which the Soviet Union and the United States have been the principal participants. These have taken place among the heads of state or foreign ministers at Teheran, Yalta, Potsdam, London, New York, and Paris, and they are still taking place. The meetings of the United Nations, both of the Security Council and of the Assembly, are a running addition to the series which, at lower levels, has been almost continuous in one or another field of international activity from refugees to trade regulation to freedom of the press.

The labors of the diplomats in the conference delivery rooms never fail to give birth to public words—memoranda, "understandings," and even treaties like those for Italy, Hungary, Bulgaria, and Rumania. If we consider these documentary offspring singly and at face value, they do not seem at all bad from the point of view of the United States. They are always polite and often friendly. Agreement, at least up to a point, is always reached. There seems, from the documents, to have been a meeting of minds, a give and take, with points conceded and points won on both sides. Democracy, freedom, law, and justice are invariably upheld.

Nevertheless, the historical accompaniment of this succession of documents has been the steady advance of communist power, and the loss of one after another anti-communist position. It somehow works out that when a conference document assigns an asset to the communists—territory or port rights or reparations or administrative control or economic privileges, then that asset is always taken over, usually with back interest. But when the documents allot an asset to non-communists—free elections or political rights (in Berlin, say, or Dairen) or powers of intervention under peace treaties (in the Balkans, for example) or respect for a church or non-communist political parties—then somehow the asset evaporates during the months succeeding the proclamation of the document, and even turns into a liability.

Something seems to have gone wrong with these conferences and their verbal issue.

The historical function of diplomatic conferences and the agreements or treaties which such conferences produce is very generally misunderstood. In spite of the contrary conviction of most diplomats who attend them, and who need the conviction in order to sustain their own sense of self-importance, diplomatic conferences seldom have much independent causal force in history. Important historical problems are settled by wars, and by the semi- or non-military clash of economic, political, social, and ideological forces. The conferences reflect and articulate the real power equilibrium that has been reached by other means.

The documents must be understood primarily as records and symptoms: records of the situation, the power equilibrium, at the time of, or rather just prior to, their formulation; symptoms which indicate, often very indirectly, shifts in the relevant power relations.

A nation is not defeated in a war because it signs an unfavorable treaty. Obviously enough—but not obvious enough, it would seem, to be kept in mind as a principle of analysis—it signs the unfavorable treaty because it has been defeated. Britain did not go to war in 1914 because she had signed a treaty with France; Britain signed the treaty with France because Britain knew that her interests required her to go to war when Germany made the attempt to smash the European and world power balance. Poland was not submitted to the Kremlin either by the terms of Yalta or by the violation of those terms. The ambiguous words of Yalta were merely reflecting the halfway stage of the actual communist conquest of Poland, which was begun long before Yalta and finished thereafter. Germany was not divided into four impossible zones at Potsdam. The Potsdam provisions simply recorded the impossible political relations among the four nominal allies.

We are periodically told that there ought to be "another meeting" —of Stalin and Truman, the heads of the Big Four states or their foreign ministers, of experts or United Nations delegates—in order to "come to an agreement" or to "settle things." But there is really very little that a meeting or a conference can do about agreeing and settling. If basic disagreement exists on the plane of fact, of the real relations of forces, then the conference can only, in the semantically obscure way that conferences have, express that disagreement (express it, perhaps, by coming to an apparent positive agreement on secondary and irrelevant points). If real relations are confused and unsettled, then the meeting will only be symptomatic of that condition by the confusions of its own proceedings. A conference can come to a productive agreement only when the real basis of agreement exists independently of, and prior to, the conference itself.

It does not follow that international conferences are of no use whatever. Merely to record and formalize the facts of political and economic relations is itself a useful function. Then, though their causal influence on history is slight, it is not quite zero. So far as the conferees operate within a common frame of interest, even if that common frame is very spare, their deliberations can show positive results. A peace treaty will always favor the victor, but the shrewdness or objectivity of statesmen may make it less rather than more injurious to the defeated and to the common civilization to which both parties may belong. A conference between a great imperialist nation and an African tribe is a formal joke, because there is no political ground common to the two. The whole proceeding is a mere ritual of power. But if Britain and the United States wish to agree about the exploitation of the oil resources of the Middle East, a conference on the subject is more than a gesture. A conference could accomplish nothing if there were not already the wish for agreement in general; but granted the general wish, there is still to be settled the exact terms and methods and relative advantages.

We may state the rule in another way. International conferences can be productive to the extent that the conferees are seeking the same things. This statement may seem to be paradoxical. It is usually assumed that conferences are held precisely because the various parties are not seeking the same thing, and want a means to compromise and settle disagreements. But the paradox holds. The conferences most certain of success are those called, after complete agreement has been reached beforehand, for the purpose of formalizing what has already happened.

All Communist party congresses, or congresses arranged by Communists, are examples at hand. Short of this, conferences are productive when areas of dispute are secondary to agreed-on aims. After Yorktown, England and the united colonies were agreed that they wished to bring the revolutionary war to an end, that the united colonies were to become an independent nation, and that the two sides wished to regularize their mutual political relations. The conferences in Paris could therefore result in a productive treaty in spite of the many lesser disagreements. The chief parties to the Congress of Vienna, with Napoleon defeated and the dynamic of the French Revolution for the time being confined, knew what kind of Europe they wanted. Their discussions, arguments, and final agreements were therefore productive and significant.

But if I want war and you want peace, what is there for us to confer about? The speeches made prior to battle in primitive times by orator-champions were not international conferences. A social purpose was served by the speeches, but the purpose was not to come to an agreement.

The diplomats of the nations of modern Western civilization have usually entered international conferences with the assumption that, whatever the disputes that divided them, there existed a fundamental basis of agreement; that, with respect to at least certain aims, they were seeking the same thing. Each knew that he was expected to press the particular interests of his own nation as skillfully as he could; but he was aware that these interests were limited on the one hand by his nation's power and on the other by the common framework. If a war had been fought to redress the broken balance of European power, each did as well as he could for his own; but all were agreed that a reasonably viable European structure was the objective. If England and the United States were in dispute over a boundary line, each argued for the most favorable parallel, but both assumed that the line was going to be drawn somewhere, and without war. No one aimed at the literal destruction of peoples. Each might want a favoring arrangement on extradition or tariffs or exchange or radio bands or marine law, but all wanted some arrangement.

The Western representatives have carried this same assumption into the conferences with the Soviet Union. They are not so naïve as some of their critics imagine them to be. They understand, and have understood from the beginning, that there are multitudinous conflicts between the interests of the Soviet Union and those of the Western powers. They have not expected the task of resolving those conflicts to be short or easy. They have also, however, assumed that they and the Soviet representatives share at least some basis of final agreement, however narrow, and seek also at least some of the same things, however few. The Kremlin, they have known, wants as much as it can possibly get—but not, they have thought, everything. The Kremlin is at least agreed that peace, however hard to assure, is desirable. It strives for the most one-sided possible agreement in its favor; but at least it aims at some agreement, on some terms. And therefore the conferences, however dreary, are necessary and justified.

In their assumptions, the leaders of the Western nations have been deceived.

2

Communism, more than any other political movement in history, imposes on itself what communists call a "union of theory and practice." By this is meant that communists always have a theoretical justification for, and explanation of, their concrete political actions. The justification and explanation are found in the systematic body of communist doctrine which they refer to as "Marxism-Leninism-Stalinism," the up-to-date version of the philosophy of "dialectical materialism." The communists display a considerable flexibility in their tactics, which are adapted to the changing contingencies of the moment; but this flexibility in tactics accompanies and is limited by a rigid adherence to fixed principles and unyielding strategic conceptions.

The communist objectives with respect to meetings in which non-communists also participate were defined in the early years of this century by Lenin. They were stated explicitly and unequivocally in resolutions adopted by the second and third congresses of the Communist International. Though, subsequent to these romantic early years, communism has become less open and indiscreet in its public declarations, there has been no change in either doctrine or practice. These meetings or conferences, organized by or with the consent of non-communists, are, like congresses or parliaments in non-communist nations, "agencies of the class enemy." The communist representatives to them are not negotiators, but "agents of the Communist party within the camp of the enemy." A resolution of the Second Congress of the International threatens with immediate expulsion any communist representative who, forgetting that he was only an instrument of the party, might undertake bona fide negotiation with the non-communists.

The communist aims in the conferences (meetings, parliaments, Leagues of Nations, United Nations, whatever the form that the counterrevolutionary organizations might take) are the following:

(1) To use the conference as a "forum" from which to speak to

"the masses," and to influence world public opinion in the direction of world communist policy. It is this aim that explains the long and florid orations of Molotov or Vishinsky or Gromyko or Manuilsky that seem so irrelevant or even ridiculous to the non-communist delegates. The communists rate very high the uses of the type of forum which the conferences (or the United Nations) provide. They know that when they speak in their own name from their own platform many ears are closed in advance against them. Therefore they must seek means for addressing the masses which are not themselves plainly identifiable as communist, means which can give the whole proceeding a non-communist, more "objective" label.

(2) By these appeals to the masses, to weaken and to undermine the non-communist representatives and their governments in relation to their respective citizens. Thus, through their agitation in the conferences of recent years, they seek to persuade especially the citizens of the United States (the main enemy) that the U.S. government is "reactionary," "imperialist," and "warmongering."

(3) To use every opportunity offered by the inside position at the conferences to divide and embitter relations among the non-communist delegates and governments. Along this line they have seized every chance to widen potential rifts (over Palestine or Germany or trade or the East Indies or whatever the issue may be) between Britain and the United States especially, or between either of these and China, France, Holland, the Arab nations, and Latin America.

(4) To block or shunt aside, again from the advantageous inside position, attempts by the non-communist governments, particularly by the United States, to develop and pursue an independent anti-communist policy.

(5) To use the conferences as a cover, a screen, a diversion, under the protection of which world communism can proceed with a minimum of hindrance in the carrying out of its own communist policy: namely, the preparation for the open stage of the third world war and the triumph of the world communist empire. Thus a conference

on Trieste can cover a coup in Czechoslovakia; or a long, futile meeting on Berlin and Germany can divert attention from China.

It is not excluded that at a particular conference the communists may actually want, for reasons of immediate expediency, agreement on some definite point, usually secondary. They will, if this is consistent with the tactics of the moment. And, after wearing out the other representatives with weeks of apparently pointless discussion that seems to be getting repetitiously nowhere, they usually succeed in gaining their point as a minor clause or subparagraph in the final memorandum.

In general, however, communists do not go to these international conferences—whether of foreign ministers or their deputies, or of heads of state or of United Nations—in order to get agreements. They go precisely in order to block agreements that might inconvenience their plans, and to implement those five aims which I have just summarized. The communists and the non-communists at the conferences are not, thus, in any respect "seeking the same thing." There is no common ground, however restricted, between them.

The result is that, so long as we enter them with the point of view of traditional diplomacy, international conferences with the communists can never serve our interests. Conferences with non-communist nations can be, and are, fruitful for us because there is at least a sufficient area of agreement, because at least to some degree we are mutually seeking the same thing. But conferences with the communists, if they are approached with the same presuppositions that we apply to conferences with non-communists, are never to our advantage. This conclusion, which can be, as I have done, deduced theoretically from communist doctrine, is not abstract. The record from 1944 shows that, when judged by the objective terms of the world power balance, we have lost from every conference that has ever been held with the communists, and they have invariably gained. No matter what seemed to have gone on at the conference— Yalta or Potsdam or London or Teheran or New York or Paris, no matter what memoranda or contracts were signed and published at the conclusion, the aftermath never shows a net gain for us, and always shows at least some gain—ranging from a factory or a ship to entire nations—for the enemy.

These uniformly negative results cannot be explained by accident or by the personal ineptness of our representatives. There is no reason to suppose that our representatives are, on the average, any less intelligent or loyal or learned than the communists. The cause of our failures lies in part in the inadequacy of our general foreign policy, and partly in our lack of understanding of the meaning of these conferences with the communists.

Let us put the truth more sharply. For the communists, the international conferences are not mechanisms whereby to secure deals, bargains, adjustments, agreements, or steps toward peace. For the communists, these conferences are battlegrounds; and the performances of the communist delegates are acts of war. Against an enemy who does not fight back, they inevitably win all the victories.

They will continue to do so, until we revise our assumptions, and realize that our problem is not to debate issues but to defeat an opponent.

CHAPTER IV

What Can Be Expected of Europe?

THE HISTORIC DRIFT of the inhabitants of the United States has been to the West, thereby continuing the direction which originally brought them to America. From the Eastern Seaboard, they crossed the Alleghenies and infiltrated the Mississippi basin. They drove through the Rockies and around by the sea to the Pacific Coast. Not stopping, they moved on over the Pacific. A century ago, with their warships as key, they opened the sealed doors of Japan. They demanded free entry into China, and in their first great imperial ventures, they took command of the islands of Hawaii and the Philippines. With earlier rivals humbled or weakened, the Pacific is now a lake under their dominion.

In spite of this historic drift, however, the United States has always sensed that its destiny is more irrevocably linked with Europe than with Asia. The United States has realized in its own way that its civilization is a projection of Western, Christian civilization, the source of which lies in Europe, not in China or India or central Africa. It has felt, rightly, that the modern age has been the time of the world leadership of Western civilization, and that all the vast spaces and swarming peoples of the non-Western cultures have not counterbalanced the science, technology, and will to power of the West.

In this century, the United States has fought two great wars in order to control the outcome of contests begun within Europe. Though the second of these wars was fought simultaneously in Europe and Asia, the United States leadership judged, correctly, that the decision would come in Europe, and therefore made the

44

European battle its primary concern. Following this war, the United States, under a variety of formulas, has thrown into Europe aid and energies in unprecedented billions.

There are those who argue that this primary orientation on Europe, even if once justified, has become an error. The fate of the world, they say, now rests in Asia, especially in China and India. Europe is finished. Resources poured into Europe are wasted to no purpose, above all if by vainly sustaining Europe we divert means that might save Asia.

This criticism is well made in its insistence that we must prevent China and India from being swallowed and digested by the enemy. But in its comparative estimate of Europe and Asia, it confuses, I believe, the long run with the short crisis. Two or three generations from now, in our grandchildren's time or in their children's the new age of Asia may come. The survival of the United States (if it still exists) may then be decided in China or India. For the next decade, however, which is the period of the present crisis, the period within which the United States may be obliterated before it has to face the full challenge of Asia, Europe remains the more decisive area. Not only do China and India lack the science, industry, and technology for the determining conduct of modern war; they lack also the trained workers and technicians and administrators, and the social and political cohesion without which their potential power cannot be channeled. These lacks cannot be quickly remedied even by the communist sorcery.

If, on the other hand, all Europe were assimilated by the communist empire, even a weakened and shattered Europe; if Europe's trained population and her stores of knowledge, her machines and formulas and historic experience, were joined to the present communist resources, then the scales would be heavily weighted.

We rightly, then, think first of Europe. We must, however, think carefully, about the Europe that is, not Europe as it has been or might be.

2

Travelers in Western Europe during the spring or summer of 1949, if they had also been there during 1946 or 1947, could quickly note many symptoms of improvement. In England in 1949, food was still very poor, and life rather drab in appearance; but there was no unemployment, the shop windows were full, the bomb rubble cleaned away, and the movies crowded. Figures could prove to you that production was greater than prewar, and many types of exports at their highest levels in history.

On most of the Continent, the restaurants were at their most delicious, the wines triumphant, and the goods in the shops, which even a year before had been poor in quality and scarce, were admirable and abundant. In France, the thousands of bombed railroad bridges and culverts had been rebuilt, the tracks of the marshaling yards relaid. During one entire twenty-four-hour period in April, the proud *cheminots* brought every train in France into every station exactly on time. No one in France was unemployed. If the hotels still did not supply soap, they had been redecorated, and well stocked with wine and food and servants. The racetrack at Longchamps was still the most beautiful in the world; the valley of the Loire was rich with the stores of two good harvests and the promise of another. In Italy, there were fine new docks in Naples, and a fine new row of hotels along the Bay to replace those that the bombs and shells had destroyed. In Milan and Parma and Florence and Bologna, masons and carpenters were busy on railroad stations and police headquarters and apartments. In the Low Countries, as in England, thousands of new small houses were finished or in process, and factories were busy. The Louvre and the Uffizzi were never more splendid, with pictures cleaned after their war hiding, and walls repainted for the first time in decades.

In western Germany, a year's change had been the most dramatic of all. Though the buildings were still shattered, and much of the rubble still remained within the shells, factories were working, trains and cars were running, fairs were being held, and it was possible to buy more things and food—almost any thing, almost any food. In June, 1948, the magic wand of the currency reform had conjured out of empty cellars and attics and warehouses the needles and cloth and shoes and bicycles and sugar and meat and pots and pans that had disappeared from the face of the German earth. The next real trouble in Germany will start, they said, if the occupation authorities reduce the German standard of living to that of England.

Even politically, though there was not much that was impressive, there seemed to be a favorable contrast to 1947. In Britain, the government was firm and the opposition loyal. On the Continent, the governments were not so firm, but they were managing to hang on without too much disturbance. The communists, who looked almost ready to take over several countries in 1947, were still there. After the Italian elections, however, and the failure of the French general strikes, it no longer seemed likely that they could, unaided, take power from within.

To the casual traveler, the European surface could give such impressions in the spring and summer of 1949. But it would not have taken him long to discover, if he chose, that this surface was not a mirror but a distortion of what lay beneath. Lend-Lease, UNRRA, and the Marshall Plan, together with the episodic upturn that was bound to follow the war and occupation, had served to obscure and warp, but not to alter, the European realities.

Inflation had wiped out Germany's money, and had carried other currencies down to a tenth or a thirtieth of their prewar values. The governmental budgets of France and Italy were wholly dependent on deficit financing. Britain was balancing its budget and paying for its too rapid nationalizations and social service extensions by taxes that meant not only a grim austerity but a rise in costs that was pricing her out of world markets. Everywhere the dollar crisis was strangling free world trade. If there were no unemployed in France, there were many in Italy, which was nevertheless increasing its population at a rate of half a million a year. There were goods in the shops, but there was not enough money in the pockets of the masses to buy them—the workers needed every franc or lira or Deutsches-mark to get food and a minimum of clothing. The factories, ma-chines, and mines were old and inefficient. In France and Italy, the huge capital plant represented by the homes of the people was worn out and literally crumbling; in Germany millions of persons lived in odd corners left half intact by the bombs. Eleven million refugees from Silesia, East Prussia, and the Sudetenland pressed on the west German economy, which was bare of capital and deprived of the greater part of its European and world markets. Throughout Eu-rope, huge and sterile bureaucracies sucked at shrinking resources.

For centuries, Britain has maintained her economic position through her relation to her great Empire; through her merchant ships, which carried half the sea trade of the world; through her position as the world's money and insurance center; by acting as the principal entrepôt for trade with the Continent; and by enor-mous foreign capital investments. Now all that has ended. Italy too had and has lost an empire; and France's empire since the war has cost the billions of francs that have gone into the attempts to suppress revolt and dissension.

The European economy has for centuries been organized in terms of an interchange between Western and Eastern Europe—the grains and minerals of the East for the finished goods and capital of the West. And now the Iron Curtain cuts that interchange to an un-workable trickle. Europe has acted as banker and workshop for the world; but now the advancing armies of communism progressively reduce the area of the world accessible to Europe, while tariffs and exchange controls paralyze the markets in the remainder.

Modern technology and modern industrial methods, with the mass production and reduced costs which modern economy must have and which they alone can bring, require great and ready internal markets. The European countries, laced tight within their national boundaries, and burdened with all the expenses and delays of multiplied bureaucracies, taxes, currencies, laws, tariffs, stamps, controls, and regulations, cannot provide such markets.

The European economic realities force an inescapable conclusion. Granted the present basic structure and conditions, the Marshall Plan will not succeed in its avowed objectives. When the Plan comes to an end, in 1952, European recovery will not have been secured, the dollar deficit will not have been overcome. More generally: granted the present conditions, Europe will never recover. It will not until the basic structure and conditions are themselves changed.

3

The political realities beneath the relative quiet of the European political surface in the spring and summer of 1949 were only a shade less dark than the economic. Some of the smaller nations (notably Switzerland, Holland, Norway, and Sweden) were political going concerns. And Britain, in spite of the immensity of its difficulties, was a going concern. The British government was a genuine government, a sovereign. The opposition, except for the communist traitors, was loyal: loyal to the nation and the government, however sharply critical of the party that was leading the government. The law in Britain was law, and the courts gave justice under the law. Taxes were levied, and paid. There was no black market, or almost none; and official graft was so slight that the results of the Lynskey Tribunal were more ludicrous than shocking. In accepting the restrictions which they knew to be necessary to their country's survival, the citizens, though they grumbled, were responsible and disciplined, in their homes as well as in public. It was clear that Britain was not ready to quit. Her economic desperation might force her into temporary measures that helped the enemy—as did some phases of her trade pacts with Poland and with the Soviet Union itself, as well as her Chinese policy—but in the showdown of the world struggle there could be little doubt that Britain would stand firm, that she would never freely yield.

But in France and Germany and Italy, the chief and determining countries of the Continent, all was still in doubt. The citizens were contemptuous of their governments, cynical, disillusioned, and often corrupt. Black market manipulations in gasoline and foreign exchange, privilege and favoritism and graft were open and accepted scandals. Taxes were a matter of deals with officials, not of law and regulation. With two or three exceptions, newspapers were the paid propaganda sheets of individuals and cliques who subsidized their deficits. Fascism, nazism, occupation, and the two terrible wars in which even the victors had been defeated had left the unhealed scars of moral deterioration.

There was evident in these three nations a partial dissolution of the community. The inhabitants were functioning as semi-autonomous individuals, groups, and factions, not as members of single national communities. Peasants, bankers, merchants, financiers, industrialists, trade union officials, bureaucrats, soldiers, police, political parties, each subgroup was out to do the best it could for itself, with little concern for the effect on others or on the interests of the nation as a whole.

Under such circumstances, the governments were not genuine governments, not truly sovereign (in Germany, of course, with the occupation and the East-West division, there could not in any case have been a genuine government). They were interim, liaison committees in which the various divisive real interests intersected and, by a process of endless manipulation, were compromised just enough to keep things going.

The mark of sovereignty is the ability to decide. These governments were incapable of decision. In France, they could not decide to tax the peasants, who were prosperous; and in southern Italy, they could not decide to distribute land to the peasants, who were poor. They could not decide to discharge useless bureaucrats, or to force efficiency on high-cost nationalized industries. They could not discipline middlemen who were fattening on outrageous profits, or put an end to the raids of speculators in international exchange.

They could not decide what kind of army they wanted, or how to get it. They could not suppress the communists, or live without them. They could not cut social services, or find means to pay for them. Though they knew that Europe must be united, they could take no actual step toward unity. Above all, they could not decide whether to commit themselves finally in the world struggle against the advancing communist empire.

The ministers of these governments were chosen by the central committees of various of the many parties into which the formal political life of the countries was divided. Most of the parties and their central committees, however, had lost all living contact with the respective peoples. With the help of systems of proportional voting, which prevented any direct check by local constituencies, the central committees were self-perpetuating, and were able to select all candidates and functionaries. The party leaders were old in years and older still in political age; the parties themselves were the ghosts of a past era. Military defeat after Italy's fascism and Germany's nazism, liberation after France's occupation, found those three countries with no political structure or leadership corresponding to the real movements within the masses. A makeshift political scheme was imposed, partly on the insistence of Britain and the United States (reasoning as parliamentary doctrinaires). The old parties were dragged up from the dustheaps, given an address, and printed on ballots. Old leaders, who had shown courage in concentration camp or exile but now represented only a shattered past, or had lived aside in a university classroom, or who had simply kept drearily alive with a record of error and cowardice and even betrayal, were eased into the party offices and the parliaments.

Why should we expect these men, with their parties, to be able to lead Europe? Are we to rely on Daladier, the apostle of Munich? on Reynaud, the veteran of boudoirs and banks? on the friends of Badoglio and Ciano? on Blum, who made the communists a force in France by welcoming them into the united front? on Queuille or Schuman, who survived by a studied policy of remaining obscure? on the chauvinists of the Ruhr and Bavaria who use the German Christian Democratic Union? on Heine and Oilenhauer, who chiefly remember, from their German Social Democratic past, the means of assuring majorities in party conventions?

In France, the unsovereign government has taken the name of "Third Force"; and the term Third Force has been generally applied to the type of government which is now prevalent on the Continent. It is one of the oddest of ironies that the idea of the Third Force has found much favor with the literate public and also with the government of the United States.

The real meaning of the "Third Force" is to be discovered in its origin: a speech delivered by Juan Perón of Argentina, early in 1947. The Third Force idea, Perón said, was the expression of Argentina's determination not to take sides in the world struggle between the Soviet Union and the United States. This continues to be the basic meaning in Europe, in spite of the local variations, and the ideological decoration given by popular intellectuals.

In France, the two serious organized political forces, both of which do have genuine roots in the masses, are the communists and the Gaullists. Together they command the adherence of a majority. Neither, of course, was represented in the government of 1949—which is one most obvious indication of why the government is not a genuine government, why it can decide nothing. The French governments since 1947 have, in relation to the internal political situation, been able to exist only by balancing the two real internal forces—Gaullism and communism—against each other; and this has been possible only because the issue between these two forces has not been settled. This internal balancing is only the local expression of the more general international performance. The Third Force, in political fundamentals, is the attempt to balance internationally between "Soviet dictatorship" and "American imperialism" (as they are called by the ideologists of the Third Force); the attempt to avoid taking sides, definitively and irrevocably, with either one or the other; the attempt to be neutral in the world struggle.

That this is the meaning of the Third Force is openly stated, in Europe, by the leaders and publicists of this hermaphroditic political tendency. (For publicity in the United States and England, the point is put more palatably: "to avoid dictatorship whether of the left or of the right.") Beneš of Czechoslovakia, who was always the personal and political friend of the present Third Force leaders in Western Europe, was a model Third Force statesman. Today, the spokesmen of the Third Force in France, Italy, and western Germany seem more inclined to Washington than to the Kremlin. That is because today the pressure on them from Washington is heavier than that from Moscow; and the nature of the Third Force is to yield to the heavier pressure. But in Prague, the weight was from the East, not the West, as tomorrow it might be in Berlin or Frankfort or Paris.

The Third Force cannot suppress, or even materially weaken, the internal communist movement, because the communists are necessary to the existence of the Third Force—you cannot balance unless there is something to balance on. If the communists were removed, the Third Force as a political tendency would automatically and simultaneously disappear. The Third Force cannot in external policy take an unyielding stand against Soviet communism, because the world meaning of the Third Force is the attempt to avoid the consequences of the world struggle between the Soviet Union and the United States.

I have said that it is oddly ironic that the European Third Force has been favored by many in the United States, and by many within the United States government. It is ironic because the Third Force is in reality a sticky obstacle to the development and prosecution of an adequate U.S. policy. The favoring attitude, however, is also natural. The United States has not yet fully made its own decision, and therefore feels a lingering sympathy toward the Third Force for the very reason that the Third Force is the distilled essence of political indecision.

4

The question confronting Europe is, simply: "Will Europe survive?" Perhaps, today, the question is, more exactly: "Does Europe wish to survive?" If it does not wish to, it certainly will not.

It may seem absurd to ask this second question; yet, just as in the case of individuals, so in that of social organisms, there can come a point where the will to survive vanishes. In that disappearance, perhaps, as much as in external attack, lies the explanation of the collapse of Sparta or Egypt or Rome. It may be that modern Europe has undergone too much, that the perpetual struggle no longer seems worth while. Centuries of wars and sufferings and tyrannies and revolutions have culminated in the unparalleled ravages of this century. And what is there, or may there be, ahead? Another war, still more terrible, atomic and biological. Europe again the battleground, again the scene of occupation, and no less threatened by liberation than by defeat. Why not, then, quit now, live for the present, and adjust passively to whatever future comes?

There is evidence of the weakening of the will to survival in the loss of the sense of community, to which I have referred, in the demoralization and separatism and cynicism. There is further evidence in the mood that a stranger feels in the books and conversation and art, in the popular café philosophies, like Sartre's form of existentialism, and in the attitudes of profound indifference (*je m'en fichisme*). When the communists staged their great Paris "Congress of the Partisans of Peace" in April, 1949, no anti-communist Frenchman even cared enough to picket or to denounce; no one had been sufficiently indignant to tear down any of the thousands of posters on which Picasso's sinister dove was advertising the Congress.

At a Florence street café, one spring evening in 1949, I saw the insolent leader of a small gang of neo-fascist schoolboy hoodlums punch and kick a little headwaiter (because, apparently, he was an Algerian—a "foreigner"). The Italian crowd (in Florence, which had a communist mayor), and the other waiters, and the café's professional bouncers (the police not even appearing) went no further in their concern than a half hour of loud and elaborate mass talking, after which the hoodlums retired singing, in good order. A row of twenty Swiss businessmen, in town for some sort of conference, were so strict in their neutrality that they did not even stand up to see what was going on.

In Marburg, the first lifting of the Occupation ban on student clubs was at once followed by a revival of the student dueling that for so many generations has put the scars on German cheeks. A general of the Air Force Staff Headquarters at Wiesbaden told me how proud the west Germans were of the Berliners, and how grateful for the airlift. Absorbed by his technical task, he had doubtless not heard the west German complaints over the penny stamp "for Berlin" which they had to put on their letters, or the west German saying, "If the Americans want their war, let them fight it."

It is easy to be deceived in one's judgment of mood and feeling. In the case of Europe, however, there are more objective tests of the wish for survival.

We have already observed that Europe cannot survive unless the following four conditions are realized:

(1) Eastern Europe must be brought back into active relation with Western Europe. But this cannot be done so long as Eastern Europe is under communist domination.

(2) Europe as a whole must get at least some measure of economic and political unification.

(3) The communist movements within the Western European nations must be reduced to impotence, since, so long as they are powerful, they are able to, and they will, sabotage European recovery.

(4) Europe must find outlets for its population, energies, products, and capital in less developed sections of the world.

Europe's will to survival can, therefore, be measured by the extent to which it wills these conditions, and takes steps, or at least attempts to take steps, toward their realization. The fact is that the governments and official leaders of the major Continental nations are doing almost nothing of importance with respect to any of the four. Far from promoting any policies that aim to push the Iron Curtain eastward, they draw trembling back from all concrete proposals that might have that effect. They permit their internal communists to have complete freedom, and take no steps against them even when the communist leaders openly announce their treason—as they have done in their declaration that party members will not under any circumstances obey orders to fight against the Red Army. The principal moves toward European unification made by the major nations are eloquent speeches by ancient politicians at polite conferences, while in practice the nationalistic restrictions are continued and in some cases increased. The tendency is withdrawal from rather than expansion in the rest of the world. Individual Europeans who write, for example, that Europe must begin the major development of Africa are laughed at as dreamers.

Under these circumstances, it is hard not to wonder what is to be expected from the proposed European rearmament program. In order to resist, the first requisite is not arms but the will to fight and if necessary to die—the will that is the first derivative and the primary demonstration of the general will to survive. If Europe does not wish to fight, what good will arms be? Those men in whom the will to survive has been strong have usually managed to find arms, or to take them.

Under the present French government, the post of the head of the Atomic Commission, the most sensitive and perhaps the most vital of all posts bearing on modern war, is held by a member of the French Communist party, Frédéric Joliot-Curie. Under his administration, the Atomic Commission is laced with agents of the MVD. It was Joliot-Curie who was chairman of the communists' Congress of the Partisans of Peace. At that congress, one of the principal speakers was Yves Farge, the sole French observer at the Bikini atomic tests. How close a military liaison do the U.S. Joint

Chiefs of Staff want with a government which considers such arrangements fitting? What return should be expected from the arms with which it might be supplied?

Indeed, granted the present European circumstances, the North Atlantic Pact is itself a doubtful device. It, too, is an expression of the containment policy. It does not say to the communists, "Go back," but only, and not very loudly, "Come no further (in Europe)." It adds not an ounce of real weight in the power balance between the Soviet Union and the United States. It can, moreover, become a kind of psychological and diplomatic Maginot Line, under the illusory protection of which the need for more dynamic action may seem less urgent.

5

To the question which this chapter asks—"What is to be expected from Europe?"—the answer must be: from Continental Europe, under its present circumstances, very little, and perhaps less than nothing. However, the present governments and governmental parties are not identical with Europe, and the present circumstances are not necessarily eternal.

The communists stand actively for the death of Europe—its death, that is to say, as a historical, cultural, and moral entity, since the victory of communism would entail the destruction of the set of values and historical traditions which give Europe its meaning.

The attitude of many of the European political parties and leaders, and of some at least of the West European governments, is equivalent to a passive acceptance of the death of Europe, since they are not willing to initiate those steps upon which European survival depends.

There remain in Europe, at the same time, many millions of persons in whom the will to European survival is not faded, however its expression may have been frustrated by the artificial, unreal political structure that has been straddled over Europe during these recent years. Some of these persons are organized, or beginning to organize, though often in curious ways. Others are isolated, sometimes bitter individuals. Some are resting, as if by a collective understanding, on the sidelines, until they have some assurance that action —and sacrifice—shall be to some purpose. The anarchist workers of Belleville, the silent peasants, the engineers and foremen blocked by an outworn economic organization know, better than Paul Reynaud or the ideologues of the Third Force, the catastrophic nature of the European crisis. But they are not willing to respond with action to the men and parties and the ideas that have spent the 20th century in proving their incompetence.

It is toward these millions that American eyes ought to be turned, and on them that American policy ought to be oriented. The fact of the European situation is simply this. Europe, under the blows of the 20th century, has been battered into a condition in which it cannot itself take the initiative toward its own revival. This was in effect recognized by the proposal and acceptance of the Marshall Plan. In this condition, the voice from the East counsels suicide, the acceptance of death. The problem for the United States, therefore, is to counter that negation with a clear summons to renewed struggle, and a clear assurance that the struggle will be worth making. This summons and assurance must be communicated not merely to ministers and bureaucrats, after the manner of traditional diplomacy, but to those men, not now prominent on the official surface of European events, in whom the will to European survival is still firm.

The United States must itself, in other words, announce, implement, and be prepared to enforce the program of European revival. The main lines of this program we have already noted: the shattering of the Iron Curtain; the unification of Europe; the smashing of communism; and the opening up of the entire world to a new period of economic, social, and political advance. A European correspondent of mine summed up the problem in a sentence of a letter which he wrote as the rumors of a lifting of the Berlin blockade first began to spread: "What the European masses need is not another conference of Big Four foreign ministers, but a demonstration that the United States will have a firm and consistent policy against the Soviets." This is an adequate summation because the Soviet policy is in general and in each detail a guarantee of the death of Europe. The Soviet policy is to maintain and advance the Iron Curtain; to block by every means any moves toward European unification (on any other than a communist basis); to increase the power of communism within every nation; and to prevent non-communist access to ever widening sections of the world. A program for European revival, consequently, can only be, in every respect, an anti-Soviet, anti-communist program.

In Part Three of this book I shall discuss some of the specific measures by which the United States can carry out a dynamic European program. I wish here merely to state the general answer to the question, "What is to be expected of Europe?" The United States can expect of Europe that which the quality of United States leadership calls for. If the United States appeases, yields to the Soviet Union and communism, then to the degree of the appeasement, the United States will contribute to the further deterioration and the final annihilation and death of Europe. If the United States, under the illusions of a purely defensive policy of containment, drifts with those forces in Europe that have neither intelligence nor will left for anything more than drift, then the United States may perhaps prolong but will not avert the agony. If the United States accepts the responsibility, assumes the initiative, and offers the leadership, then—and only then—Europe will respond creatively. The Europe that today seems to be like an aged parent who clutters up the house, drains his child's substance, and querulously runs up doctors' bills, will again prove a wise counselor, and a brave partner in the building of a new world order.

Part Two
ANALYSIS

CHAPTER V

The Nature of Modern War

IT IS GENERALLY agreed that the principal 19th century advance in the theory of warfare was made by Von Clausewitz. Clausewitz' conception was summarily stated in his famous principle: "War is nothing but the continuation of politics by other means." (Von Treitschke condenses the content even more tersely: "War is only the violent form of politics.")

This principle, on its negative side, abandons the definition of war as an "exceptional event," an "accident," a "punishment." So long as wars are looked upon as historical accidents or exceptions, there cannot indeed be any scientific theory of war, because the business of science is to explain apparent exceptions by showing their lawful relation to other phenomena. There is, however, a powerful human tendency to cling to the view that wars are exceptions to "the normal course of historical development." It is then felt to be easier to avoid moral responsibility for the occurrence of wars and for what goes on during them. We wish to believe that wars somehow happen in spite of our conduct and intentions, that our killing and destroying in wars does not count morally, and that we are to be judged and may judge ourselves solely by our "achievements" of "peacetime."

Clausewitz' principle cuts cruelly through this understandable moral sentimentality. In effect he is saying that the struggle for social power—the struggle of different classes, groups, cults, and nations for the maintenance or relative increase of their power, prestige, and privilege—is historically continuous. This struggle is conducted part of the time by the means of peace: economic means, political and diplomatic manipulations. And part of the time this struggle—the same struggle, for the same ends—is fought by the means of war. Wars, therefore, are not accidents in history, but integral and even normal parts of the process of history. Periods of war and periods of peace mutually complement each other. We understand a war by relating it to the periods of peace which precede and follow it; and we understand a peace by observing the war into which it leads.

This principle, of course, was not a sudden discovery of Clausewitz' own. It is implicit in occasional historians of much earlier times—Thucydides, for example—and in some 18th century historians who preceded Clausewitz. Moreover, the principle should not be regarded as a "timeless truth." It does not really hold for many wars of the past. In more primitive or more feudal times, wars often were, from a general historical point of view, largely accidental. The personal whim of a king or baron or bandit could start and carry on wars which had no very coherent relation to peacetime social processes, and no very deep effect on social structure. Many wars have been fought to avenge a personal insult or to relieve boredom or to get a pretty wife. Even such extensive wars as the medieval Crusades cannot be fully explained as the continuation, by other means, of peacetime politics.

The concrete historical data from which Clausewitz was chiefly generalizing were the wars of the French Revolution and Empire. His central principle was a summation of the nature of those wars and wars like them: in particular, of the wars of our own historical period. The nature of the wars of the French Revolution and Empire was prefigured in some but not all respects in the commercial and imperial wars from the 17th century on, and was reproduced in the important wars from 1815 until our generation.

Prior to the late 18th century, the wars of Western civilization,

with the exception of some civil wars, were the concern of a limited
section of the population: either of a special, often hereditary caste,
or of a few leaders who employed relatively small mercenary armies.
The weapons and equipment, also, were made by a special, relatively small class of artisans, and did not represent a very large proportion of social capital or energy. Wars could be a temporary
inconvenience for some of the nonwarring majority, because of food
or housing that might be requisitioned, or fields that were sometimes laid waste. But for the most part, wars were fought on the
social surface. Except that they were part of the general cost levied
on the exploited majority by the ruling classes, they did not make
a great deal of specific difference to the majority. The economic and
social and religious systems were not altered by the wars, and the
political change of one baron or prince to another was not of much
moment except to the barons and princes. Societies were loosely put
together. What was done by the war-making social section had,
often, only minor repercussions upon, just as it was little influenced
by, the rest of the social structure.*

The wars of the French Revolution and Empire, upon which
Clausewitz' studies were concentrated, showed the following major
contrasts to such earlier wars:

1. The armies were no longer small, and confined to a special
caste of the population or to mercenaries. They were mass armies,
drawn, often by conscription, from the citizenry as a whole.

2. Weapons and equipment had become much more substantial.
There were hundreds of thousands, even millions, of muskets, and
the powder and shot which they used; heavy artillery and naval
cannon; many more vehicles; and all the incidental equipment
which mass armies require merely to keep eating and moving. This

* Much of what is said in this paragraph would not hold, or would hold only
partially, for a number of the civil or social wars prior to the late 18th century: for
example, the Hussite Wars, the German peasants' and the French religious wars of
the 16th century, or (in some respects) Cromwell's revolutionary wars. Moreover,
even certain "international wars," such as the Children's Crusade and the Thirty
Years' War, would have to be partly excepted.

meant that the proportion of social capital and energies required for the maintenance of the war machine had greatly grown, and—as in the case of foundries and wagon works—had become less specialized, more closely linked to industries and occupations which also had general peacetime functions.

3. The loose feudal structure of society, elaborately hierarchical, in which men's political loyalties were primarily personal—to suzerain above or to vassal or serf beneath—had been replaced by the centralized modern nation. All inhabitants of a given region had become alike transformed into "citizens" of "the nation," and had become subject to its laws and taxes. "The national interest" was asserting itself over group, sect, and class interests. Thus, what happened to any one section of the inhabitants—such as the army—affected more intimately than before the entire community.

4. The increasing strength of the ideology of nationalism, and the democratic ideologies of the "general will" were also serving to bind together the whole national population, and to project the nation as a unified and continuous enterprise through time.

These changes, each of which was intensified during the 19th century, provided the concrete content of Clausewitz' theoretical conviction of the interrelationship of peace and war, and of the historical continuity of the struggle for power. The development of the modern nation as the major form of political organization, of modern industry and technology, and of modern ideologies, had in fact altered the nature of war by reducing its personal, episodic, and accidental elements, and integrating it far more closely into the social process as a whole.

Parallel to his theoretical analysis of the changed nature of war, Clausewitz advocated changes, or changed emphases, in the conduct of war. It followed from his principle that a nation ought to include in its peacetime organization a permanent staff charged with the detailed planning of the wars into which the peacetime policies would sooner or later lead. Moreover, these plans ought not be confined to a narrowly military field, but must be broadened to cover armament industry, transportation, communication, and so on. Correlatively, there ought during wartime to be a close interdependence between the military direction, the economy, and the political leadership; and attention paid even to psychological and morale factors. These conclusions have of course become commonplace, and are accepted practice in all nations.

Nevertheless, though Clausewitz' principle recognized the continuity of the struggle for power, it still implied a sharp demarcation between the two phases of that struggle: peace and war. War and peace were related by underlying causal factors, but they were distinct. Each was a means of conducting the struggle for power, but the means were of a different order.

The sharpness of the distinction between peace and war was, and continued to be, expressed in political practice, in law, custom, and morality. A war did not exist until it was at a particular moment of time formally declared to exist, by recognized constitutional procedures. A war suspended its existence, at a particular moment, by the signing of an armistice; and ceased altogether by the signing, under known conditions, of a treaty. The nationally and internationally recognized rights and privileges of peacetime differed entirely from those of wartime. "Military objectives" were plainly distinguished from the "non-military." In wartime, a "combatant" was a being of another order from a "noncombatant." International laws, rules, and conventions were designed to indicate the respective behavior appropriate to the one or the other. In internal policy, what was considered permissible for governments in wartime was considered tyranny in peace. From the point of view of personal conduct, what for a combatant in wartime was patriotism was identical with peacetime villainy and dishonor.

2

The changes in the nature of war which led to Clausewitz' generalization did not come to an end at Waterloo, or with Clausewitz.

Each has progressed in the 20th century to extremes which would have seemed fantastic to Napoleon as well as to St. Louis.

Uniformed armies in our day have come to be numbered in the tens of millions, drawn from every section of the population, and even from the women. Within the armies, it is to be remarked that only a small percentage of individuals is now expected to perform what was formerly considered to be the distinguishing function of the military: namely, to wield weapons against the enemy. The greater part has functions identical with "civilian" or "peacetime" functions—engineering, repair, communications, research, transportation, mathematical calculation, construction, and so on. In addition to the uniformed armies, there is an immense army without uniform making up the fifth columns, irregulars, partisans, spies, saboteurs, propagandists, and the rest.

The weapons, equipment, and supplies required by contemporary armies have become immense in quantity and staggering in their technological intricacy. In the Middle Ages, the armament industry meant a handful of individual artisans. Today the armament industry is virtually identical with industry as a whole. Armaments make use of, and are dependent upon, almost every kind of material and product. Fractional horsepower electric motors are as necessary as gunpowder. Delicate gauges and electronic tubes play a bigger part than rifles. DDT, as well as bombs, is needed to win battles. Aluminum and steel and copper and electric power, nylon and sulphur and sugar and penicillin, almost anything that can be named, is a part, and most things an essential part, of the military machine. The "war economy" is equivalent, simply, to "the economy."

Political centralization has advanced everywhere in the direction of the monolithism that is already realized in the totalitarian states. The nation regards every citizen as a subordinate unit to be harnessed to the yoke of "the national effort." And across and through the national boundaries and the powerful nationalist ideologies stretch the new doctrinal ideologies of our time.

Under the pressure of these and related changes, the old distinctions become blurred. What is a "military objective," and what "non-military"? Is a fort or a battleship military, and a steel plant or a power distributing center not? But all are alike essential to contemporary war, and the formal distinction is a real absurdity. Who is a "recognized combatant"? A man in military uniform, following specific orders? a guerrilla or partisan in rags? a saboteur in a business suit? a fifth columnist running a factory or editing a newspaper? a short-wave broadcaster?

When is a nation "militarily prepared"? When it has a large trained army? Or when it has efficient steel mills and reserve stocks of strategic materials? When it can turn out skilled captains, or turn out on rapid notice tanks and radar?

Who is a "military man," who a "civilian"? The general who has won battles and studied tactics? or the scholar who has mastered nuclear physics and biological chemistry? the expert in naval gunnery? or the expert in propaganda, who can unify the national will, and break down enemy morale? Is naval strategy a military field, and the construction of filters for uranium fluoride a civilian occupation? Is the businessman who reports on the chemical industry abroad a spy? Is the general in charge of psychological warfare a soldier, and the educator who teaches the errors of foreign ideologies a man of peace?

The confusion is still more profound. When does war begin? Was it war when Italy invaded Ethiopia? No war was declared. Was it a war that happened in Spain? If so, between whom? Who were the combatants? Was it peace when Hitler marched into the Rhineland? into Austria? into Czechoslovakia? Has it been war since 1937 in Manchuria and Korea and China? No war was declared in 1937, or in 1947. And who has been fighting those wars— or that peace? Is the war against Germany and Japan still going on? There have been no treaties. Is it war in Greece? in the East Indies? in Indo-China and Malaya? When will it finish—if it has begun? Was it peace in Prague, in February, 1948? Was the Berlin airlift a peacetime operation?

From the facts themselves, the necessary conclusion emerges. We must, in order to remain in accord with the facts, revise Clausewitz' principle, carry it a required step further. In our day, partly through general social and technological developments, and partly by the deliberate plan of the totalitarian movements, the distinction between "military" and "civilian" has been obliterated. The line of demarcation between "peace" and "war" has disappeared.

3

In *The Struggle for the World* I wrote that the Third World War had begun in April, 1944, the date of the communist-led mutiny in the Greek naval forces stationed at Alexandria. Even those reviewers who otherwise favored that book were inclined to object to the "extremism" of this statement, or to explain it as exaggerated rhetoric, a metaphor or figure of speech. I want to make clear that, in intention at least, the statement was the most literal of prose.

The exact date selected was perhaps somewhat arbitrary. However, facts which only recently have become plain do seem to mark the spring of 1944 as a turning point. By then the communist leadership felt certain that Hitler was going to be defeated, and therefore Hitler was no longer the sole or even the main enemy and problem. From the viewpoint of communist strategy, it was then necessary, with the Hitler onslaught in the process of liquidation, to go on to the next step in the struggle for world communist domination: the contest with the United States and its potential non-communist allies. We find, accordingly, that the communist strategy throughout the Balkans was altered during the spring and summer of 1944. The communist-led partisans virtually ceased their operations against the Nazis, and concentrated their efforts against the rival, non-communist resistance movements (Zervas in Greece, Mihailovitch in Yugoslavia, the Zogists and republicans in Albania). The Western High Command, not understanding the nature of the war and not believing that the resistance was an important military phenomenon in any case, not only permitted but aided the communists in their liquidation of their opponents. At the same time, the communists dropped their 100-per-cent anti-German attitude, and began to woo "good Germans" through propaganda and the operations of the Free Germany movement. The communist forces in China had all along been staying out of fights with the Japanese, in order to prepare for the time when they would move toward the conquest of all China.

The exact date is not important. For that matter, it is only in the case of wars of the traditional type, the beginnings of which are formalized by declarations, that we can assign exact and unambiguous dates.

In spite of the objections made to my statement that the Third World War had begun, the phrase "cold war" was coined and became rapidly accepted within a few months of the time of publication of *The Struggle for the World* (March, 1947). If this phrase is taken seriously, not as slick journalism, it sufficiently makes the point. It is not, as a rule, taken seriously.

During the Big Four Foreign Ministers' Conference in the spring of 1949, I received a letter from a man who, though not publicly known, was a founder and formerly a leading member of the Communist party of the United States. He wrote, in part, as follows:

> It is high time that the question of political warfare (cold war) be understood in its proper stature in the total complex. This type of warfare made Stalin's conquest of China possible at an expense which I would estimate as not more than half a billion dollars to the Kremlin over a period of 23 years.
>
> This type of war is cumulative: that is, whereas 23 years ago, the resources of the Kremlin were small as compared to now, and whereas there were then massive counter-forces like Germany, France, Japan, Italy, etc., they all have been laid low and Britain weakened, while the Kremlin's weight in the total picture has immensely grown. . . . Political war as carried on a generation or so ago (Marxism-Leninism) has grown up from a more

or less serious annoyance to Stalinism, a potent arm of conquest
of the Soviet Empire.

The trouble with us is that although we talk about cold war,
we have not yet recognized juridically and otherwise this type of
warfare *as war itself,* and we deal with it as the Kremlin wishes
us to do, as a nuisance, the parentage of which is taken cogni-
zance of under the table, but not recognized as actual warfare
on the part of the Kremlin proper. . . .

Stalin's Empire, which is carrying on a total war (by the new
method) against us and our allies all over the world, now will
meet us on the diplomatic table again, not to call off the war as
a whole, but to make, with our help, a partial retreat on only one
part of the far-flung front, namely, Germany: retreat in order to
better advance, as Lenin said. . . .

If we continue to meet Stalin on his terms of temporary, one-
by-one bargains, we will remain on the defensive and he will
retain the initiative. . . .

These are not the abstractions of a theorist, but lessons learned from
direct and participating experience.

The phrase "cold war," however, even if taken seriously, contains
a deceptive adjective. By describing a war as "cold," it is presumably
meant that, though conflicts occur, blood does not flow and shots
are not fired. But if so, then the present war, the war that is now
going on, is by no means "cold." Much blood is flowing, and many
shots are being fired. The war has been at least warm in Greece and
in China, in Costa Rica during 1947, in the East Indies and Malaya
and Indo-China, in the Philippines during the struggle against the
communist-led Hukbalahaps. In the Baltic states or throughout
Eastern Europe, it has not seemed cold to the hundreds of thousands
who have been shot or sent to the slave camps of Siberia, nor has it
been cold for the Ukrainian Insurgent Army which from its woods
still holds out against the troops of the MVD and the Red Army
detachments.

It is of course true that the present stage of the war is not identical with the stage of the war against the Nazis which was reached from 1942 to 1944. The principal organized mass armies of the chief direct contestants are not now committed to overt action. (Though it should be remarked that elements of these armies, under the names of "occupation forces," "observers," "liaison officers," "trainers," and the like, are committed.) The war is not yet all out. It may be added that it is desirable that it should not become so.

Even in traditional war, as traditionally understood, all forces and weapons are not employed at all times. In fact, all are very seldom employed. Was it war in the early months of 1940? Less killing and shooting were going on than much of the time since 1945. Mass armies were not committed in Western Europe during 1941 and 1942; but it is generally agreed that a war was then, and there, going on. At no time during the Second World War was every possible weapon thrown into the contest. Poison gas and biological weapons were never used, though they were available. On some fronts (in the Pacific, for example) tanks and heavy artillery did not appear. Often, most of the time, the bulk of the mass armies was not directly fighting.

In any war, an intelligent commander, out of the forces and weapons available to him, uses those that are appropriate to the given stage of the war and the given concrete situation. He does not send heavy tanks into an impenetrable jungle, or 16-inch howitzers into guerrilla warfare in desolate mountains, or battleships up a shallow brook.

It is ambiguous even to call the present war "limited." True enough, the means now being used are selected and limited, though we have just noted that this is the case in all wars at all times. The ratio of more or less novel means—political, ideological, and subversive—to fighting is higher at present than in a conventional war. It would, for this reason, perhaps be convenient to call the present stage of the war "psychological-subversive," so long as we did not consider this to mean that this stage is exclusively so. Nevertheless, from another point of view, from the point of view of the objective of the enemy, the present war is unlimited. His objective, openly proclaimed and never varied, is a communist monopoly of power in the entire world: what he calls the "World Federation of Socialist Soviet Republics." As defined by objective, it is hard to imagine how a war could be less "limited."

The battles and campaigns of this war, far from being minor local episodes, are gigantic in scale. Let us suppose that the American public, and its newspapers and radio announcers, recognized the truth: that we are at war. Let us imagine, then, how, in headlines, bulletins, dispatches, and editorials, some of the events since 1945 would have been presented. In 1943, a single bombing raid on a single city could be the major news of the day. What, then, would we make of the conquest of China? The 1948 consolidation of the enemy position in Czechoslovakia ought surely to equal the recapture of Rostov. Tito's break meant a collapse of a whole section of the enemy front. It is the allies and potential allies of the West who are chiefly purged and deported in the Baltic states and the Balkans. Their numbers are very large—a single new wave of deportations from the Baltics in March and April, 1949, is estimated to have taken 170,000. Under our uncomprehending public view, there is often not a single line in the newspapers, not a sentence on the radio. Suppose the 170,000 were counted, as they should be counted, as divisions of allied troops destroyed?

4

I have tried to indicate, by a brief historical review, that the change in the nature of war, the breakdown of the distinctions between civilian and military, between peace and war, are in part the resultant of a long social development with complex technological, economic, political, and moral factors. However, the objective social development has not been by itself sufficient to bring about the result. In spite of that development, it is still conceivable and possible that there should be peace—genuine peace, genuinely distinguishable from war.

This would be conceivable if there were among men a deep enough moral sentiment to block the exploitation of the material and structural complexities of modern society for the purpose of waging perpetual war: but, though conceivable, that is perhaps not possible. Peace would be both conceivable and possible, if there were in the world a social power able and willing to enforce peace. This, in our interrelated world, would mean a world empire or world government, and such must be, and is, the political goal of those of us who wish peace.

However, though it takes at least two to make peace a fact, one is enough to make war. If my opponent has decided that he is at war with me, then there is war; it will not cease to be because I do not wish it, or do not recognize it. What has made peace impossible for this historical period (which, fortunately, need not be long, but which may be) is not merely the involved course of historical development, but the deliberate plan of the totalitarian movements of our time.

It should by now be clear that the Second World War did not begin in August, 1939, but some years before that, in the Rhine and Ethiopia and Spain and Austria and Manchuria and Czechoslovakia. Moreover, it should also be clear, and is clear to many commentators, that if this had been understood in those earlier years, then the stage of the Second World War which started in August, 1939, or perhaps more definitely in the spring of 1940, and which devastated so much of the earth, might have been altogether avoided. The Nazis and the fascists knew that they were at war. They won all of their preliminary campaigns with little effort, because their opponents did not have the same knowledge, and did not attempt to strike back. The Nazis were thus able to consolidate a position from which they could shake the world. In the days of the early and disregarded battles, they could have been stopped without bloodshed, or with very little.

The present enemy, the world communist movement, has gone far beyond the Nazis, in the logical extension of extreme ideas as in territory and power. We give him, as we gave the Nazis, an extravagant advantage by not seeing the truth. He is at war with us, and therefore war exists; but we do not consider ourselves at war, nor will we recognize that there is a war. In the next chapter I shall consider at some length his manner of conducting this war, but I should like here to cite one or two examples of how he manipulates his advantage.

In the United States, as everywhere, the members of the communist movement function as agents of the Soviet power. They, and their masters, regard themselves as at war with the United States. They work toward the overthrow of the present government of the United States and its replacement by a communist dictatorship. Some of their activities have become so notorious and so dangerous that there are going on now certain legal actions against the communists: some who are not citizens are being deported, and others are being tried on various charges. But these legal actions and the public attitudes toward them show a maximum of confusion and incoherence.

Many patriotic United States citizens, especially those who feel themselves to be liberal (and, whatever the labels, this means a great many, perhaps a majority), are disturbed at the actions taken against the communists. They believe and say that these actions violate the right of the communists to free speech, free assembly, free petition, etc. The communists themselves, and their own and their fellow-traveling press, feed this liberal disturbance by abundant appeals to free speech and the Bill of Rights.

The fact, however, is that the problem of internal communists has nothing to do with free speech or the Bill of Rights, as the communists perfectly well know—they could hardly help knowing so, since their own program is to abolish all these freedoms as soon as they take power. The confusion is due to our thinking about the communists in terms of peace, and their thinking and acting in terms of war. If the liberal public once recognized the truth, that the communists are at war with us and in the war are agents of the enemy, then its disturbance would cease at once. That firm protective steps should be taken against enemy agents is taken for granted by everyone.*

Let us consider another example of a very different kind. Since the communists know themselves to be at war, they are prepared to use, and have used, every expedient means to accomplish the conquest of China. But we, regarding ourselves as at peace, are not prepared to use, and have not used, expedient means which are available to us and possible, to block that conquest. More remarkable still, there are even some among us who are glad that the communists are taking over China—some even who are not themselves communists or fellow travelers but merely politically blind. Or, analogously, we are not prepared to intervene in, say, Bulgaria, even though we have full legal justification under the peace treaty, and even though firm intervention could be expected to bring important results with little risk.

In diplomatic conferences we are prepared to make, and do make, genuine concessions for the sake of peace. The communists seldom make any concession; and when they do, it is in the sense of a tactical retreat in favor of a larger strategy of war. Thus they are inevitably the net victors in every conference.

In the United Nations or the press, communist spokesmen freely and frequently denounce, truly or falsely, anything about us that they choose to mention: our treatment of Negroes or Jews or strikes or Puerto Ricans, our warmongering or oil imperialism or housing or movies. We temper and restrict our criticisms, seldom even referring to the most important matters, because we wish to "reduce tension" and "avoid provocation."

The list might be indefinitely multiplied. In each case, in these chess matches with unlimited stakes, we grant the communist all his men, while we try to play against him with pawns alone.

---

* In Chapter 16 of *The Struggle for the World* I have presented in some detail the democratic justification for the outlawing of the internal communist movement.

This last metaphor is no doubt too extreme. We have placed on the board a few additional pieces—a knight and a bishop, let us say, with our atomic queen threatening from the edge of the table. In this century, all nations, whatever their theories, have had to take practically into account the changed nature of modern war. Everyone knows that wars are no longer a matter merely of armies fighting each other on battlefields. The crustiest soldier understands that the military machine is linked indissolubly to the economy as a whole, to technology and science. The hoariest sea dog will grant the need of psychological warfare, even if it doesn't much interest him. Most staff officers will admit, I think, that wars don't end and begin as neatly as they used to, and that what goes on in peace will have a considerable effect on what happens in war.

All this may be general knowledge, and may be acted upon in practice. Nevertheless, only the communists, so far, have recognized clearly that Clausewitz' principle has become outworn, that the line of demarcation between peace and war has vanished; and only the communists are acting upon that recognition. Only the communist doctrine and practice accepts fully the contemporary reality.

CHAPTER VI

The Communist Conduct of Contemporary War

NO POLITICAL MOVEMENT in history has a career comparable to that of communism. What we now call communism began as an organized force at a conference of the Russian Social Democratic Party held in London in 1903. There Lenin and his supporters formed themselves into a distinct faction, called "Bolshevik" from the fact that they had a majority at that particular conference. Contemporary communism is the historical expansion of that faction. At the beginning, in 1903, the Bolsheviks (or communists, as they decided to call themselves at the founding of the Third International) numbered only a few dozen of Lenin's political friends and associates. Even Trotsky had remained aloof from Lenin's grouping. In 1917, when Lenin was in exile in Switzerland, there were probably fewer than ten thousand communists. Lenin was almost unknown except to the revolutionary circles in Russia and central Europe. The German High Command, which permitted him and Zinoviev to reach Russia after the downfall of the Czar, with the hope that they would speed the disintegration of the Eastern front, were unique among Western leaders in their insight. Even they most grievously misjudged the uncontrollable consequences of their act.

Today the communists are masters of a vast and rapidly expanding empire, already larger in area and in population than any that has heretofore existed. Their forces penetrate deeply into every remaining nation of the world.

I recall this unprecedented achievement, accomplished within less than two generations, in order to warn against the uniform slighting of the communist potential, which has itself been not the least factor in their expansion; and to suggest that we do well to study the methods they have used, even when these seem from a conventional viewpoint to be absurd, fantastic, or childish.

From their very beginning in 1903, the communists have regarded themselves as at permanent war with the entire non-communist world. Their initial premise and axiom was a total rejection of the gradualism and reformism which had crept into the social-democratic political movement. They stated with unambiguous frankness that their aim was not to improve and reform existing institutions, but to smash them; and that this could be done only by violent and total revolution. They proposed to establish "the dictatorship of the proletariat," which, they made clear first in theory and after 1917 in practice, meant the dictatorship of themselves. The period of the dictatorship of the proletariat was begun by their revolution in Russia, and is, they have said, to occupy "an entire historical epoch," an epoch of gigantic wars and revolutions, during which the dictatorship will obliterate every social institution of "the class enemy" until communist world domination is acquired and "the international party will be the human race." In their war, that is to say, as in any war rationally conceived, the communists have a clear and precise objective, to which their intermediary actions are means.

It is surely revealing that most of the terminology and doctrine, as well as the training and morality, of the communists are military in formulation. The leadership of the party is called "the general staff of the world revolution." The centralized, hierarchical discipline from above is more rather than less strict than that of an ordinary army. Deceiving, betraying, lying to an enemy (i.e., a non-communist) is regarded as a virtue. Systematic enterprises in any field are called "campaigns." Even if their immediate business is no more glamorous than selling *Daily Worker* subscriptions or recruiting grocery clerks, they speak of "shock troops," "saboteurs," "victories." Their members are systematically indoctrinated with a military psychology; the most minor dispute in a local branch is utilized as a training ground for "the final conflict."

Since they have declared a perpetual war, they are no longer conditioned by episodic declaration of particular wars, or treaties of a particular peace. Such occasional declarations and treaties are only subordinate incidents in their permanent war.

It follows from their state of war and their unlimited objective that they owe no loyalty to any force other than their own, and they give none. No genuine agreement or alliance between communists and non-communists ever takes place, or is possible. Agreements and alliances with non-communists are defined by communist doctrine as devices for "utilizing divisions within the camp of the enemy." Thus, from 1939 to 1941 the communists had a pact with Hitler; and from 1941 to 1945 they were in a coalition with the Western allies against Hitler. To one or the other of these arrangements, non-communists are likely to apply terms like "treachery" and "betrayal." From the communist point of view, however, there was no treachery, and no betrayal. The communists were never genuine allies of either Hitler or the Western nations. Each arrangement was adopted solely as a temporary expedient, and both were used by the communists solely for their own ends.

Since their own survival depended upon it, they fought, and fought hard, against Hitler; and they were happy to accept all Western aid in carrying on that fight. From June, 1941, to the end of 1943 the fighting was so intense as to absorb almost their entire energies. Even prior to the end of 1943, however, and to a progressively greater degree thereafter—as we have already noted—they began to pursue their own communist aims, which were not only not part of a presumed common war effort against Hitler but were directed primarily against their presumed allies. In this way, they used the latter stages of the war against Hitler to prepare their own imperial conquests in Eastern Europe and in China.

The same principles apply to the ordinary "united front" between communists and non-communists at every level. The united front, which is accepted by the non-communist parties to it as a combined action for a common purpose, is understood by communists as another device—like a treaty or international agreement—for utilizing divisions in the camp of the enemy. The united front serves as a screen or cover under which they can advance their own communist objectives, while they keep non-communists busy attacking each other. It is a stepping stone to a communist monopoly of power. These remarks are true on the small scale of united fronts for civil rights or lower rent or free school lunches; and on a larger scale of the united front governments of countries—as Mikolajczyk discovered in Poland, or Beneš and Jan Masaryk in Czechoslovakia, or Nagy in Hungary. The communists, in their war, are not distracted from their guiding objective.

2

I should like to consider, from what one might call a neo-military standpoint, various of the communist campaigns during the supposed peacetime years since 1945.

Knowing not only the general social strength of the working class in modern society but the further fact that all industry is now directly or indirectly part of armament industry, the communists always seek to dominate the organized working class, that is, the trade union movement. During the last year and a half of the Second World War, while the non-communists were thinking only about defeating Hitler, and during the confused year that followed the Nazi collapse, the communists succeeded in getting control of the chief trade union movements of Continental Europe, in particular of France and of Italy, and also of the small but relatively influential movements in many of the colonial and semi-colonial areas. In this trade union field it may be added that they have more lately suffered important defeats: particularly in the United States, through the defection of men like Joseph Curran of the National Maritime Union and Joseph Quill of the Transport Workers, and by the enlightened strength of such powerful anti-communist trade unionists as Walter Reuther of the United Automobile Workers and David Dubinsky of the International Ladies Garment Workers Union.

The communists exploit any opportunity that happens to arise for increasing their trade union influence. They also deliberately plan campaigns of trade union penetration. It is of the plainest significance that their principal campaigns have almost always a military orientation.

For example, from the beginning of their history, they have had a concentration on the maritime industry—marine officers as well as sailors, firemen, cooks, radio operators, and so on, and the longshoremen and other dockside workers. Their success in this field is not complete, but during 1948 and 1949 there were spectacular demonstrations of how far they have advanced and how directly their maritime position is related to military potentialities. For three months in the autumn of 1948 the great American ports on the Pacific lay idle at the command of the communist-controlled Pacific unions administered for them by Harry Bridges. From the spring through the summer of 1949, Hawaii was virtually isolated from the mainland by the same will—the will, that is to say, of the Kremlin. In July, 1949, England's desperate economy staggered under new blows as a handful of communist agents tied up the docks of London.

Every military man knows the military importance of control of transport. But many military men have not yet realized that there are more means of gaining that control than guns and bombs. It should also be noticed that the communists use their position in the maritime industry for the additional military purposes of intelligence, secret transport of agents and operatives, and capture (kidnapping).

Control of communications is another concept sufficiently familiar in military planning. It is not neglected in the communist strategy, and the communists have devised new ways for gaining and securing it. With varying but notable success, they have undertaken campaigns among those who operate telegraphic, telephonic, and radio communications. It is revealing that their chief efforts have gone to, and the best results been obtained in, international communications. In the United States, they have not got very far among the ordinary telephone and telegraph workers; but their influence is strong in the union at the long lines center, that building in New York where, with a fine disregard for national security, so large a part of the United States' international contact is concentrated. They have also done well among the marine radio operators. In France, Italy, and some other Continental nations, a communist nod can shut tight virtually all mechanical communication; and, in what might be regarded as rehearsals, has several times done so. As a correlated result of their position in communications, the communists gain intelligence listening posts of incomparable sensitivity.

The Second World War proved that among the primary military objectives of modern war are the factories that are essential to the war economy. Many bombs were dropped in order to damage and disrupt the factories. But the communists understand that a well-timed strike or act of sabotage can often slow a factory as much as a bomb. As in all cases, they plan their work among industrial unions in the light of a controlling military perspective.

With the advanced technology of modern war, key technical and scientific positions have become objectives of the first order. We have already noticed that the communists have captured the French Atomic Commission, with a party member at its head, and agents planted throughout its apparatus. The Canadian Atomic Spy Case (recorded in the remarkable and most valuable *Report of the Royal Commission*) shows how determined is the communist concentration on nuclear scientists and technicians. In the United States the communists use every means to gain influence at every level of nuclear enterprise over these physicists who seem many of them cursed with a formidable political stupidity.

During the wars of the past, the maneuver of "envelopment from the rear" has made some dramatic contributions to victory. In the

Second World War, this maneuver was given a new content by the employment of parachute troops, speedy naval craft, and mobile armored forces. However, it is a maneuver that can be executed by means other than cavalry, planes, boats, or tanks. A native fifth column, stiffened by a mission and directives from the external center, can carry out the maneuver while the enemy remains passively "at peace." Along such lines, for example, runs a favorite unabandoned plan of the communists for Spain. The communists believe that they will be able to take over Spain if Franco falls. Toward that end they skillfully manipulate the non-communist anti-Franco sentiment, confident that the non-communists are too muddled politically to block their road once Franco is out and confusion sets in. (At the same time, by what is not a contradiction for communists, they feel their way toward a rapprochement with Franco, just as prior to 1939 they simultaneously manipulated anti-Hitler sentiment, and proposed a deal with Hitler.) Spain in communist hands would mean Western Europe threatened with an envelopment from the rear. It would not be a bad balance for the communists to set against the Atlantic Pact. Similarly the communist operations in Malaya and Indo-China are more or less such an enveloping maneuver in the campaign for China. Even the drive in Chile, which was halted—but not ended—not much short of success, might be so defined in relation to America. Needless to say, all these actions are taken or planned in what is formally regarded as a time of peace.

Early in 1948, a civil war, to which little attention was paid in the United States, was fought in Costa Rica. What had happened was according to a pattern which should have become familiar. Through united front methods, the communists had become ascendant in a Costa Rican government headed nominally by weak grafters. They had engineered the nullification of an election in which the united front had been repudiated. The communists saw ahead the same path to control of Costa Rica that was just then being finished in Czechoslovakia. The Costa Rican anti-communists, knowing what was happening, had, without success, appealed for help to the United States government and to the United Nations. By luck too good to be counted on, there was a man in Costa Rica, Figueres, who was resolved not to permit the subjection of his country. He fought, therefore, and, for the time being at least, he won—though he was compelled, because of his material weaknesses, to make some bad bargains that have since been plaguing him.

At about the same time, a Pan-American Conference was held in Bogotá, Colombia. Using an explosive incident as a starting point, the Colombian communists seized direction of riots which resulted in as much devastation to Bogotá as a major bombing attack, came close to taking over the government, and broke up the conference under the most humiliating conditions.

Let us observe, in relation to these two incidents, a simple fact of geography: Colombia and Costa Rica flank Panama and the Panama Canal from the south and the north. Our military commentators lament the lack of adequate bases, aircraft, and guns for the proper defense of the Canal. They too often forget that there are other means than ships or submarines or planes for closing that vital link in our communications.

In traditional wars of the past, it has often been the case that a major contending power has fought for some time not by the use of its own armies and navies, but through auxiliary forces—of subordinate allies, or mercenaries. The Soviet power has the advantage of fighting in such a way through auxiliary forces during what the rest of the world regards as peacetime, a time therefore when the opponent feels inhibited from taking adequate countermeasures. It is in this form that we can understand the fighting in China, the East Indies, Malaya, and Greece, and the smaller scale fighting in Costa Rica, Iran, the Philippines, and elsewhere. The timing, the political and strategic direction, even much of the tactical direction of these campaigns are under the control of the communist high command, which operates according to its central plan for world conquest.

These campaigns can be carried on at minor cost to the Soviet Union itself and to the core of its manpower and armies. The objective in them is twofold. There is the positive aim of improving the strategic position, and acquiring control of new territories, resources, and peoples. But, where that is not possible, and along with that, there is also the negative aim of draining the resources and energies of the United States and its allies, who react, in accordance with the defensive policy of containment, by trying to stuff the continually reopening breaches.

Few elements in modern war are more decisive than true and adequate intelligence. The communists, by virtue of their methods of infiltration into every sector of enemy society, into industry and labor, church and club, laboratory and government, are in an ideal position for intelligence work: every communist is a conscious, and every fellow traveler an unconscious, intelligence agent of the communist center.

From the time of the First World War, there has been an increasing recognition of the military importance to be assigned to the operation of capturing the mind of the enemy. To the communists no task rates higher. The funds, the personnel, and the ingenuity which they devote to it are almost beyond calculation. Every medium of communication in every language is used, and used massively: personal conversation, radio, newspapers, leaflets, books, pamphlets, magazines, speeches and lectures, classroom and kindergarten, comics, movies, theater and all the other arts, posters, and slogans painted on walls. Great congresses and meetings are supplemented by cocktails or games in private homes; a luncheon for two backs up the short-wave radio; picnics are added to millions of copies of a pamphlet.

There is a product for every taste and interest. Scholars and sportsmen, children and scientists, the religious and the sex-starved, teachers and workers, the rich and the penniless, soldiers and pacifists, neo-Protestants and neo-Catholics, Negroes and bankers, Jews and anti-Semites—there is for them all an ideological dish flavored with the sauce of the Revolution, in admixtures carefully varied from the bland mush for the innocent liberal to the dark and heavy dessert for the inner party member.

Throughout, the ideological offensive pursues the double aim of breaking the enemy's will to resistance, and of bolstering the morale of the communists themselves and their supporters.

3

To stir up strife behind an enemy's lines is a stratagem as old as war itself. Until recently, however, Resistance—as such action has come to be termed—was generally regarded as a side-show for amateurs. . . . Resistance is the name which we give to operations directed against an enemy, behind his lines, by discontented elements among the enemy or enemy-occupied populations. (The term "enemy" is used here in its broadest sense. It applies equally to belligerents, opponents in a cold war, malevolent neutrals or indeed to any state against which it is decided to conduct Resistance operations.) The gamut of such operations is very wide. It includes revolt, guerilla, sabotage, terrorism, civil disobedience, strikes, "go-slow" techniques, non-cooperation, the spreading of hostile or diversionist propaganda and the harboring of enemy agents or escaped prisoners. With the exception of the last two, these are all part of the ordinary stock-in-trade of revolutionary action. Resistance indeed differs from Revolution (or Counter-Revolution) only insofar as its operations are supported by an external Power or conform to the general military and political strategy of that Power.*

The phenomenon of Resistance came to prominent public notice during the Second World War. It still remains the case, however, that many military men and many statesmen in the non-communist world continue to regard it as "a side-show for amateurs." Their deprecating judgment of Resistance is proved by the minute place

* Julian Amery, "Of Resistance," in *The Nineteenth Century and After*, March, 1949.

which they assign Resistance in their plans and policies—and budgets.

Their error—and it is a very grave error—has several sources. In the first place, it is due to the inertia of conventional thinking. According to conventional military doctrine, inherited from the 19th century, wars are won by concentrated blows of massed armed force which destroy the armed force of the enemy. In such a perspective, the apparently diffuse, badly organized, weakly armed operations of Resistance appear negligible.

Second, Resistance is thought of primarily as exemplified during the Second World War in France and Italy, and it is recalled that no serious Resistance functioned in Germany, which had to be battered to pieces by bombs and shells.*

Third, the idea of Resistance is limited to those movements which called themselves such during the Second World War, and is not extended in time and in space to other movements which are fundamentally identical.

The first source of error is eliminated as soon as we grasp the fact that conventional military doctrine is no longer adequate to contemporary war, because the nature of war has changed.

What contribution to the defeat of the Nazis was made by the French and Italian Resistance movements is a matter of dispute. There are some, and these naturally include many of the Resistance leaders, who believe that it was considerable and even decisive. General Eisenhower, as Amery observes, once "described the operational contribution of the French Resistance movements as worth six divisions"—though I am not sure that this is his considered military opinion; the remark may have been for politeness, like conferring an honorary decoration. I have talked to many, on the other hand, who were directly involved in the French and Italian Resistance activities, and who have come to the conclusion that they counted for

*A different policy might, however, have fostered a very considerable Resistance in Germany. The nucleus and potentiality were there.

very little, were perhaps even negative in the net—"not worth the bother."

It is not necessary to settle this dispute. In the terms in which it is conducted by Western military leaders and commentators, a vital factor is omitted. They judge the efficacy of the Resistance movements by the sole criterion of contribution to the defeat of the Nazi armed forces. This is not, however, the only or even the principal historical criterion that applies to the Resistance movements. Though these movements are in form, and partly in substance, directed against an occupying authority or a home government regarded as "the enemy," they are also struggling on their own account, or on the account of an external power to which they are subordinated, for power. This was understood perfectly, and planned for, by the communist sections of the Resistance. The accomplishments of the communist Resistance in France and Italy against the Nazis were in communist eyes distinctly secondary. The main objective was to advance the communist power position within these nations. For this, the war and the occupation, and the immediate postwar confusion, gave them incomparable opportunities. They used the Resistance as a perfect cover for recruitment, the assassination of anti-communists, the training of activists and the assembling of arms, intelligence and infiltration, and the seizure of many organizations including the trade union federations of both countries. The communists in both France and Italy emerged as the most powerful single political force. The Resistance, so viewed, does not have to be modest about its accomplishments.

In France and Italy, it is true, the communist Resistance (which, of course, was only one part of the wartime Resistance, and in the fight against the Nazis a lesser part) did not go on to take full power. But in Yugoslavia and Albania, the process was completed in triumph. Tito and Hoxha, starting in 1941 with a handful of followers and a fistful of Moscow-trained advisers, in 1945 took over their countries for communism. That accomplishment is not unimpressive. The mighty Reichswehr had not been able to do it. The still mightier armies of the Western allies had declined the attempt, as too risky. But the Resistance sideshows succeeded. It might seem wise if our leaders should decide to spend on the problem of Resistance a few per cent of the time that they give to super-carriers, super-bombers, and super-atomic weapons.

It certainly would have proved wise in the past. In both Albania and Yugoslavia there was no necessity for the communist victory; the communists won by default. In both countries there were non-communist Resistance movements, in the beginning much more powerful than the communist, which, with proper political direction and sufficient material aid, could have served better than the communists against the Germans, and could have defeated the communists also. Nevertheless, the Western leaders, in their political simplicity and blindness, chose not merely not to obstruct but most actively to aid the communists. " 'As you know,' " an Albanian anti-communist remarked to a British mission in 1944, " 'there are three parties in Albania: the agents of Germany, the agents of Russia, and the agents of England. That is quite natural, but what none of us can understand is why the agents of Russia are paid in English gold.' " *

The third source of error is the most deluding of all. In our time, Resistance is not a phenomenon only of formal war. The failure to see the continuity of Resistance before, during, and after declared war is a derivative of the larger failure to understand that the line of demarcation between peace and war has disappeared. For example, the Chinese communist organization, from its beginning shortly after the Russian Revolution, can be defined without distortion as a Resistance movement. Mao Tse-tung is a Resistance leader. The Chinese movement conforms exactly to the description, or definition, of Resistance which I have quoted from Amery. Though Mao has not disposed of great bombers or ships or tanks, who will belittle the accomplishments of the Chinese Resistance? We should not judge the results of war by the noise of the explosions.

* Julian Amery, *Sons of the Eagle* (London: The Macmillan Company, Ltd., 1948). This is the best book on the wartime Resistance with which I am acquainted.

More generally: since the time when the communists won a central territorial base (by taking power in Russia), almost the entire communist activity external to the base directly held can be subsumed under the idea of Resistance. Outside the Soviet boundaries, the communist fifth columns, with their attached allies and dupes, are Resistance armies, fighting a Resistance warfare by all the typical means of the Resistance, from subtle persuasion to direct terror and full scale battles. This warfare is continuous, day and night throughout the world. Its objective—world communist power—is never lost sight of. No treaties, declarations, agreements, or charters are allowed to interrupt its course; these are all utilized as instruments in the struggle. And this warfare has not been in vain: though its prosecutors have suffered more than a few temporary reverses and defeats, the net gains are solid and wide.

In a conventional war, military commanders are trained to watch hourly on their maps the changing positions and strengths of the opposing forces. Alas, in what Western staff offices today will we find a map with its colored markers showing the shifting progress of the battle for the world?

4

It has not been my intention in this chapter to survey, much less to analyze, all of the communist tactics and procedures. In Chapters 5, 6, and 7 of *The Struggle for the World,* I have made a somewhat fuller, though far from complete, review—many books, and much experience, are needed for a sufficient description. My narrower aim here has been to present certain typical and major examples in order to show the military or "neo-military" significance of the communist methods.

The communists, where and when they consider them appropriate, employ methods which everyone can recognize as military: that is, fighting and destroying and killing by formally organized groups of men that we call "armies." Many of their other methods, however, have not in the past been ordinarily thought of as military. Nevertheless, when we analyze them in the concrete, we can quickly discover that they are implementing objectives the strategic nature of which is as unmistakable as that of ordinary battles or campaigns. The methods which the communists use in seeking these strategic objectives are often more effective and more successful than conventional methods like shells and bombs.

Marx was himself a close and admiring student of Clausewitz. After reading Clausewitz, he sought to adapt to the purposes of the revolution Clausewitz' strategic principles. Lenin and Stalin have, in what communist theoreticians would call "a dialectical leap," gone a whole phase beyond both Marx and Clausewitz. They have developed independent principles of revolutionary struggle, and in turn applied these to the refinement and extension of military strategy in its narrower sense.

It would, of course, be a mistake to oversimplify the conclusion, and to hold that communism is *only* a military force—partly open and partly secret, or that its actions have *only* a military significance. Communism is also a complex social movement, and a secular religion. It is misleading, however, to separate the various aspects, which are in reality indissolubly united. Again we confront the fact that in our day the military and the civilian, peace and war have become confounded.

If we do oversimplify—and the shorthand of simplification is often hard to avoid, we shall be closest to the truth if we understand communism in military terms. The goal of communism is not an idea or an ideal, but world power: a strategic goal, militarily understandable. Communism uses ideas and ideals, as it uses drugs and guns and airplanes, as instruments in the advance to this goal. I have found by experience that, among those who have had no direct experience of communism and have made no lengthy study, it is easier for a military man than for a civilian to grasp the nature of communism. Even though the military man has been trained in a narrow tradition that has stuck to the direct problems of conventional war, he senses more quickly the kind of reasoning that communists use, because it is fundamentally his kind of reasoning, strategic reasoning. The content is unfamiliar and perhaps fantastic to him, but he grasps the approach, the method. The civilian, on the other hand, especially if he is a liberal or a "progressive," recognizes much of the subject matter with which the communists seem to be dealing. After all, much of it—exploitation and race and class and capitalism and rights and peace and labor organization and ideas and art—seems identical with his own. But it is very hard for the civilian to see what communism is "all about." In his own "two sides to every question" approach, he has never encountered the communist *kind* of reasoning, he has never used a comparable method, and he really doesn't believe that there can exist "the sort of human being" that the qualified experts tell him a communist is. The experts, he usually concludes, are the paranoid victims of a phobia.

It has been my further aim in this chapter to motivate, again by concrete illustration, the statement that the communist war for world control is not limited by formal declarations, but is continuous. Since the communists are at war, then, no matter how peaceful may be the actions and attitudes of non-communists, war exists.

Let us finally reflect on this question: what chance does a defensive (containment) policy, which ignores many of the principal methods of contemporary warfare, have against the continuously aggressive policy, on a literally world front, of a dynamic enemy who is willing to use, and who uses, all methods?

CHAPTER VII

United States War Plans

ALL CONTEMPORARY NATIONS maintain permanent establishments to elaborate what are called "war plans." These war-planning staffs are a comparatively recent innovation. They express in practice the recognition, so often denied in theory, that wars are not accidents, but an integral part of the historical process.

In effect, the staffs have operated on Clausewitz' principle, and to their functioning Clausewitz devoted much attention. They have assumed that wars are continuations of national politics "by other means"; and they have further assumed that there is a clear demarcation between peace and war.

During the phase of peace, with the advantage of the leisure and lack of distraction which peace provides, the job of the staffs is to work out plans suitable for the conduct of the war phase. Such plans, however, cannot be developed very far unless it is known what opponent they are to apply to. In the past this has seldom, during peacetime, been altogether clear. It has therefore been necessary to have a number of alternative plans, dependent upon what possible opponent or combination of opponents would actualize as the wartime enemy. As a rule, the significant choice has been limited. Major powers do not have to exhaust much time on planning for wars with weak nations. These can be handled well enough with inferior or improvised plans. The more probable enemies among other major powers have usually been fairly well marked some years in advance of open hostilities.

Modern military doctrine, reasoning on the basis of the historical experience of wars, has been able to define a clear objective of war considered from the military standpoint, and thus of war planning. This objective is usually stated more or less as follows: the destruction of the armed force of the enemy. This does not mean the destruction of every individual who has functioned as a unit in the enemy's armed force, but the destruction of the enemy's armed force as an organized group capable of carrying on effective struggle. Thus, the German destruction of the French armed force in 1940 was accomplished in conjunction with a (relatively) small destruction of individual soldiers. Once this military objective is attained, then the enemy can no longer resist the imposition of the victor's geographical or political objectives, or for that matter of his social and religious objectives, if the victor has any.

It may be remarked that, though modern military doctrine has been clear in this definition of military objective, it is only the "great captains," the commanders of genius, who have in the conduct of wars pursued it without deviation. Secondary objectives, of territory, prestige, and sentiment, have usually interfered to one or another degree with the defined primary objective.

Though the primary objective seems in definition to be both unambiguous and narrow, the change in the nature of modern war has introduced multiplying complications. Modern war is a function of the whole economy and the whole society, not of a small and clearly distinguishable section. Consequently, the destruction of the armed force of the enemy requires, on the positive side, the mobilization of the entire society. On the negative, the destruction is contributed to not merely by armed assault on the enemy armed force proper, but in all manner of indirect ways, by the weakening of his industry, finance, morale, and so on. Account must be taken in the war plans of these various complications.

A review of the complications at the degree which they have now reached might suggest that they are modifying the primary objective. The traditional doctrine allows for the fact that intermediary measures contribute causally to the achievement of the final objective—the destruction of the armed forces of the enemy. After all, one's own army has to be at least supplied, transported, and equipped. But traditional thinking has always conceived that these contributions are secondary in importance, and that the final decision is made, directly and openly, in battle. However, the complicating factors in modern warfare indicate the possibility that the "primary" objective (of traditional doctrine) might follow, automatically one might say, from the successful achievement of some of the "secondary," contributing means. The armed forces of the enemy might be destroyed, that is to say, without battle. They might, for example, collapse as an organized and opposing force, if their supporting industry were sufficiently smashed, the enemy economy thrown into chaos, or sufficient political and ideological pressure brought to bear.

This is not only possible. This is what happened in Austria in 1938 and Czechoslovakia in 1939. Hitler took command of these nations—and destroyed their armed force insofar as it was an organized force opposing the Reichswehr—without a battle. In Czechoslovakia, this happened once more in 1948, when the communists assumed full sovereignty and destroyed any autonomous Czech armed force without an open battle.

We confront here developments which demand a re-examination of the primary objective as defined by orthodox military doctrine. That doctrine implicitly accepted the traditional division between peace and war, and between the military and the civilian. The military section of society could concentrate on its own military objective, which was relevant only to a "state of war," and had no role in peacetime. But the military objective was not, from the point of view of the social process as a whole, an end in itself. The destruction of the armed force of the enemy was sought in wartime in order to make possible the achievement of certain political or social objectives which were judged desirable from the "normal," that is peacetime, point of view. The North, for example, sought to destroy the Confederate army in order to preserve the Union and to abolish chattel slavery. England sought in 1914-18 to prevent the domination of the Continent by Germany, and the growth of German seapower and empire. Today, however, the civilian and military, peace and war, the military, political, and social objectives have become so intermixed, that we perhaps can no longer designate a special military objective which can be pursued by a single section of society (the military) in independence of the historical context. On the other hand, a military objective can today, at least under certain circumstances, be attained by what are traditionally regarded as non-military means.

2

In at least one very important respect, the problem of war planning for the United States is simpler at present than it has ever before been for this or for any other nation. There is no doubt whatsoever as to the principal enemy. There is, in fact, only one other major power, and consequently only one possible major war to plan for. There could be minor wars to discipline a small nation here or there, but these would not be serious military efforts. There can still be some doubt about the exact lineup of secondary nations, but whatever the lineup, the chief and deciding opponent can only be the Soviet Union—more exactly, world communism with its primary base in the Soviet Union. There is thus no reason now for the waste of time and effort which was always heretofore caused by the uncertainty about the opponent, and the consequent need for a number of alternative plans, only one of which could in the end be applicable.

So evident is this situation that it requires no acquaintance with secret information to know that the war-planning abilities of the United States government and military establishment are concentrated today on the problem of a war plan to be used against the Soviet Union (and whatever satellite and allied nations may be attached to it).

So far as we may infer from what has been publicly discussed or indicated, the development of United States war plans accepts two fundamental assumptions:

1. The possible war, the Third World War, will be of the same basic kind as the wars of the past several generations, and will differ only in scale. New weapons, with different physical characteristics and with vastly greater destructive power, will be used. New tactics will have to be worked out for the effective employment of these weapons. The war will be bigger, though not necessarily longer. Such differences, however, do not involve any sharp discontinuity. Each major war, during the past couple of centuries, has used new and more destructive weapons, and has seen at least some important tactical changes.

The testimony given to Congress by General Bradley, the Army Chief of Staff, in connection with the debate over the Atlantic Pact, was perfectly in line with this assumption. At the beginning of war, it would seem from his words, he envisaged strategic atomic and other bombing operations against the Soviet homeland. The Navy's initial role would be primarily defensive: keeping sea lanes open against Soviet submarines. The Red Army would attack Western Europe. With the help of the Atlantic Pact and the rearming which he believed should implement it, the Red Army would be held somewhere, and a bridgehead maintained in Western Europe. Just exactly what would happen after that was not made clear. Nowhere was it suggested by his testimony that the Third World War would differ in any fundamental respect from the Second, or the First.

2. The second assumption is, simply, that the beginning of the Third World War is a possible event in the future. There will be (or would be) a day in the future, a particular moment of time (designated by "D-Day" or some such symbol), when the Third World War will begin; subsequent to this moment it will have begun; prior to it the war will not be—that is, there will be peace.

Reasoning from these assumptions in terms of traditional doctrine, the problem of war planning for the United States is the direct one of preparing an armed force capable of destroying the armed force of the Soviet Union; and of deciding on a strategy and on tactics whereby the U.S. armed force can accomplish that objective. It is well understood that this planning cannot be military in the narrowest sense. It must take account of economic plans, both technical and structural, plans for general political, social, and psychological mobilization, and so on.

This planning is being done, under the assumptions, in a time of peace, even if an uneasy peace. The peace is secured, at least for a temporary and sufficient period, by the national policy of containment.

Meanwhile, advantage is taken of the peacetime phase in order to improve the position from which the United States would begin the possible future war. This, too, is done in traditional ways. Diplomacy is used to strengthen ties with friendly nations, and to build up a system of treaties, alliances, and informal understandings. Arrangements are made that look toward the use of strategically important naval or air bases beyond United States boundaries. Some strategic materials are stockpiled. Protected access is sought to key natural resources like petroleum and uranium.

The public reasoning seems to be more or less of this sort: We are now at peace. We aim to "preserve peace." Nevertheless, there is an "aggressive power" loose in the world that may start a war. Therefore we must prepare against that war by that aggressor, and be ready to defeat him if and when the time comes. There is no immediate urgency. Meanwhile, just to keep our fingers crossed, we will, more or less haphazardly, try various moves that will help preserve peace, and various others that may give us a better start in the possible war of the future. We will try an alliance here, economic aid there, a protest to that country and a hundred million dollars to this, a strengthening of the United Nations one week and a military mission the next, a withdrawal of troops from one locality and a rearmament in another, a friendly conference of foreign ministers and a denunciation by the Voice of America, a speech now about the sincerity of Stalin and a speech then about the communist scheme of world aggression—in short, whatever comes into our heads as appropriate to the immediate situation that happens to arise.

Lying back of this behavior and this reasoning, there lurks in some minds the curious militaristic bias to which I have already referred. As a nation, we are not unlike a very strong man, who, at a bar or a racetrack, is most of the time good-natured, careless, even stupid, and who allows himself to be kidded and pushed around and cheated; but who does so partly because of his strength, and his confidence that when things go really too far he can whip any man or combination of men in the crowd. So, in international affairs, the United States has often acted as if it didn't really much matter what was done in peacetime, whether policy was intelligent or stupid, whether we let other nations get away with this or that grab, whether, forgetting all about foreign policy, we concentrate on domestic votes. When the time for war comes, no matter what has meanwhile happened, we can whip them all. Thus it has so far been in our history. Quite the contrary of the usual opinion, many democracies, in comparison with dictatorial countries, are bumbling in peace but terrible in war.

This attitude is militaristic not because it means a militarization of ordinary social life—it means rather the opposite; but because it puts its final reliance on military measures. It doesn't matter how many mistakes are made, how many sins of commission and omission. In the last analysis, so the half-conscious feeling of many runs, we've got more atomic bombs, and they can solve all problems. We've never yet prepared sensibly for a war, and we've never lost one. So why should we this time? But this time, after all, may be different, like that final morning before Thanksgiving when the turkey comes for his breakfast corn.

3

Experience has begun to teach us the inadequacy of traditional planning and traditional diplomacy. There is no diplomatic precedent for the Marshall Plan. Our intervention in Greece under the Truman Doctrine is a remarkable departure from historic ways, especially remarkable for what we continue to think of as peacetime. Perhaps even more startling was our intervention in the Italian elections, which went somewhat beyond what was publicized. Here and there our representatives and our friends are beginning operations which are even more novel and irregular. We are learning to think and act in terms of the new condition of the world.

If this were a generation ago, our present war planning could be rated as very good. Our general diplomacy and foreign policy could be judged, compared to our past performances, reasonably strong and intelligent. Even as matters stand today, our planning and policy are not so much wrong as incomplete. The direction of development during the past three years is correct, but the journey is not finished. From appeasement, we have reached the uneasy turning point of containment. But containment, as we have seen, cannot be a stable equilibrium. From containment, we must either drop back to appeasement, a deal (or what would seem to be a deal), or go forward to the offensive.

Our present planning and policy, with no changes except in details, can probably prevent the military defeat of the United States for several years yet to come, can in fact probably ensure that there will be no total war during those several years.

However, our present planning and policy cannot stop the communists more than temporarily, nor can any other plan or policy which is essentially defensive, and which fails to take into account the nature of contemporary war. The communists will not stop until either they are defeated, or they win; and what they aim to win is the world.

What is called "the Party" is *an army which accepts no convention of any sort as common to its adversary and itself*. Such a Party, or rather the general staff of such a Party, does not recognize any declaration of war or even any distinction between a state of war and a state of peace. The mere existence of such a Party reveals and signifies a state of war which can end only with the definitive destruction of all pre-existing social structures

—a destruction which is the Party's reason for existence. This special type of army, adapted to the conditions of the 20th century, is committed to a war far more total than the total war of which Ludendorf made himself the theoretician, since its war is not limited to periods of military operations. It is not conceivable that it can stop itself, short of conquering the planet. It is a Protean war of unlimited duration. . . . Such an Enterprise [the communist movement] wants to be *alone on earth.**

The inadequacy of the present policy and planning is summed up in the fact that it leaves the *timing* to the communists. They have the initiative; we "react." The reaction is sometimes effective, but the pace, the control of direction is theirs. Our policy, as a consequence, is subordinated to, determined by, theirs. This follows, even though our policy is or is supposed to be diametrically opposed to theirs, because they select the issues, the field, and even the mood of combat.

The dependence of our policy on theirs has been continuously proved during these years since 1945. While their diplomatic rhetoric was friendly (in form), ours was wooingly effusive in both form and substance. After they turned to denunciation, we, reluctantly and long after, began introducing a few harsh adjectives about them. They invade Greece, and we try to defend Greece. They break off foreign ministers' conferences, and we cease holding them. They ask for a new foreign ministers' conference, and we attend. They carry on a war in China, and we "review our Far Eastern policy." They say that we are warmongering imperialists, and we reply apologetically that we want only peace and friendship. They demand half the Austrian economy, and we beg them to be content with the oil fields, the Danubian shipping, and enough reparations to keep Austria permanently bankrupt. They say that we have a "kept, hireling press," and we draw up jointly with them (in the United Nations)

* Jules Monnerot, *Sociologie du Communisme* (Paris: Gallimard, 1949). Pp. 30-31. (My translation.)

a document on how to keep the press free. They suggest that they would like to do business, and we announce that they are "sincere"; they declare that "imperialism" must be destroyed, and we discover a "split in the Politburo." They carry out programs of genocide in the Baltics, Bessarabia, and Soviet Georgia, and we beat our breasts over the Negro problem. They exterminate, within their borders, all suspected sympathizers with the West, and we, in the United States or Japan or the American Zone of Germany or Hawaii or Puerto Rico, grant communists full democratic rights. They provoke a situation in the East Indies that could only be handled by military action, and we shut off credits to the Dutch. They stage great strikes in France and Italy, and we pay for them.

If the pattern continues, we will have granted them the decision and the timing on the shift to a total armed war. Presumably they would not select the moment that would offer their opponent his most favorable chances for winning.

In this same connection, there is for the United States a curious difficulty which leads to a grave dilemma. We have seen that present United States plans entail the assumption that we are now at peace, and that a possible war lies in the future. This in turn involves the conception of a D- (or some other letter) Day which will be the moment when peace ends and war begins.

Let us then ask: How will we recognize that D-Day? how will we know that it has occurred?

In the past, such days were recognized by the issuance of formal declarations of war. The history of totalitarianism makes it certain that the Soviet Union would not start with a formal declaration, but with a blow. The staggering proportions of such a blow have been sufficiently described by the experts on atomic and biological warfare.

The dilemma, then, is this. Granted our present ideas, including the idea of a D-Day, we must either await passively such a blow, or we must ourselves strike it—begin, that is to say, what is misleadingly called a "preventive war." * Our present defensive policy of containment would guarantee that the first half of the dilemma would be the one to eventuate in fact.

It is not a strong recommendation for a war plan and a policy that they should guarantee, in advance, a colossal and perhaps catastrophic initial defeat, timed by the enemy, and so timed as to be of the maximum advantage to him.

Let us use an analogy. Suppose that there were two contiguous ranches, of vast extent, located in frontier country where there was no police force and no functioning governmental authority. The two share a long fenced boundary which runs along all kinds of terrain from flat meadows to cliffs and canyons. One of them, the X Ranch, is much the more prosperous, with fat pureblood cattle, many fine buildings and corrals, and much first-class equipment. The other, the Y Ranch, has poorer animals and inferior, shoddy equipment and buildings. Both employ many hands.

The policy of the Y Ranch is constant attrition. Every night, fences are cut and heads of X cattle driven over the line. Disguised Y employees are planted in the X working force, and in its management. They, or their colleagues from across the line, frequently damage X equipment, dynamite barns, burn fodder, dismantle pumps and contaminate water holes. The infiltrated Y agents nurture discontent among the cowhands, and spread mythical stories about utopian conditions on the Y Ranch. The Y agents in the X management give regular reports to the Y bosses, and manipulate contracts to favor Y interests. Every now and then, the Y Ranch carries out wider operations. Miles of fence are torn down, a new fence is put up around sections of heretofore X land, including all cattle, buildings, and men found there, and Y signs are posted.

---

* Misleadingly, because you obviously do not prevent a war by starting one. What is really meant by the phrase, "preventive war," is: a war which you deliberately start in order to have, in your judgment, a better chance to prevent not war but defeat.

Both managements know, in addition, that the complete Y plan is to take over the entire X property, after dynamiting the central buildings and shooting up most of the leading personnel.

The X management was trained in more settled parts of the country, where legal, rather than violent, methods were in practice. It counters the Y actions by hiring numerous lawyers, and getting certified copies of its deeds and titles. It is disturbed about the fence cutting, and tries to develop repair crews to rush each morning to the latest breaks. It strains its resources to try to put the fires out, save its fodder, repair the pumps, and test and decontaminate the water holes. Occasionally it dismisses one of the more blatant Y agents around the property; but often the other agents, and those they have influenced, raise such a howl that the job, or another, is given back again. When parts of its land get absorbed by the shifted fence into the Y Ranch, the X lawyers file formal protests. But the X management has always had a great respect for fences. It keeps its wire cutters in the storehouse (from which they are often stolen by the Y agents), even though the Y-built fence is so slipshod that it could almost be pulled apart by hand.

The X land shrinks; its cattle diminish; its loyal employees lose confidence; its supplies are exhausted and its equipment deteriorates with the never ending repair jobs, and the rushing about. The exhausted watchmen cannot properly guard the buildings and corrals and endless miles of fence. The Y management, well informed, observes, guiding its own decisions and its own timing. The Y management is even, at times, a little puzzled. For it knows its own immense weakness compared to X. It knows that most of its own men are dissatisfied, only waiting for a lead to go over to X. It knows that it has no firm title to any of its acres, and not even the counterfeit of a title to the lands which it newly fences off; and that it would have to yield on one section after the other if the X Ranch merely walked in and asserted its rights. It knows that its whole operation, in spite of its bold front, is so shaky, functioning so badly, that it is in danger of toppling over at a single firm push. But the push doesn't come, and the Y management concludes that it has been right all along in believing that there is an endemic disease, spread throughout the X organization, which paralyzes its power of decision.

4

The primary difficulties in the present war plans and the present policy of the United States do not arise from their technical execution, or the details of their practical operation. Though there are agents of the enemy even in high places, the overwhelming majority of those who are concerned with plans and policy and their execution are loyal, and as intelligent and hard-working as there is any reason to expect a large group of men to be.

The source of the chief deficiency is in the basic assumptions which I have made explicit: the assumption that the possible Third World War is of the same general kind as the previous world wars; and the assumption that the beginning of the war is an event of the future.

We have seen, on the contrary, that the Third World War is not future but now, is already taking place. And we have seen that it is not a conventional, formal war, a war of organized massed armies hurling themselves at each other in total armed conflict (though this may be a later phase of the present war), but a kind of war for which we have no name—a political, subversive, ideological, religious, economic, Resistance, guerrilla, sabotage war, as well as a war of open arms.

The two assumptions, in short, are false. Not only are they false. Experience has already proved them dangerous. The traditional, conventional war anticipated in present United States war plans may never take place. If the communists can win their objective of world domination without conventional war, why should they start it? With the United States preparing for a conventional war that may not happen, and believing that victory or defeat depends on, and only on, that conventional war, the United States meanwhile loses in the actual war that is actually going on. Thus the United States runs the risk of being defeated before it is fully aware that the battle has started. Even short of ultimate defeat, the failure to prosecute the present war consciously and effectively can only mean that the conventional war, when it came, would have been made progressively more difficult to fight and win. Every step we lose in the political-subversive war is that much more of a handicap to make up if the starting gun fires for the total race. By not recognizing the fact of the present war, and acting appropriately, we fail to use our opportunity to make the possible formal war of the future easier, surer in outcome, and less destructive.

The human cost of these false assumptions is still higher. So long as we cling to them, we are prevented even from trying for the best possible variant, which, if once we made up our minds to it, could become not only possible but likely. These assumptions eliminate our chance, which is an excellent chance, of winning the world struggle against the communists by winning the present phase of the war *without* the need for fighting a total armed mass war. Is this a chance to be abandoned lightly?

The communists are committed to a struggle for world domination. They will continue their struggle for that objective until they either reach it or are defeated. At the same time, it is certain that the United States will not passively accept communist domination. The question is merely, how will the United States fight, and when?

The real effect of the assumptions that underlie the present United States plans is to make a total armed war inevitable. The communists will continue their present informal war, which a policy of containment can delay but not block. Sooner or later, the United States will judge that its security is intolerably threatened. This judgment would result from a super–Pearl Harbor engineered by the communists; or it might come from a communist coup in a West European nation, or simply from a sufficient change of mood in United States public opinion or military leadership. At that point, the United States would fight an all-out war by arms.

This outcome may be unavoidable in any case, but we ought surely to set a policy which offers a chance of avoiding it. We can do so only by abandoning the two assumptions. We must realize that the war is already going on, in a political-subversive-Resistance phase. We can then adopt plans seeking to defeat the communists in this present phase of the war. If these plans succeeded, as there is good reason to believe that they could succeed, then the present phase of the war would be the last. With its strategic objective—the defeat of communism—obtained "by other means," there would be no need for all-out armed conflict.

I stated in the preceding section the dilemma which, under our prevailing conceptions, arises out of the problem of recognizing "D-Day." This dilemma is not, however, irresistible. We can escape it, and the lamentable conclusion to which it leads, as soon as we recognize that the D-Day of the Third World War is an event not of the future but of the past.

CHAPTER VIII

The Vulnerability of the Communist Empire

IN MILITARY PLANNING, there is a stressed and valuable precept against underestimating the strength of the enemy. Many battles have been lost from the wishful optimism of eager commanders who have persuaded themselves that the enemy was stupid or slow or undermanned at the decisive spots. It is no less important, however, to know the enemy's weaknesses. The most telling stroke is at the holes in the armor, not at the thickest plate. Every boxer understands that if his opponent has a strong left and weak legs, then he should keep clear of the left and try to run him ragged. If battles are lost by wishful optimism, victories are also foregone by a failure to strike at the time and place of weakness, and entire wars have ended in needless defeat from the hesitation of a captain who, seeing only the enemy's power, overlooks his vulnerable heel.

The communist empire is weaker, potentially weaker at any rate, than the non-communist public now generally believes. The communists themselves know how to play on the fears even more effectively than on the hopes of their opponents. Their myth of the inevitability of communist victory spreads its influence beyond their own ranks— is perhaps more convincing outside their ranks than within them. Part, at least, of the communists' strength is a reflex of the fact that non-communists think them to be so strong. In Europe, this is quite plain. If a worker or peasant in France, for example, believes the communists to be in the end invincible, then, unless he is a hero, which few men are, he will not have much stomach for the struggle against them.

In order to discover where we can thrust most effectively, moreover, it is not enough to estimate the general weakness of the communists. We must specify just where and in what they are weak.

There are a number of weaknesses of the communist empire which are characteristic and well known. These I shall only mention here, since I have analyzed them elsewhere,* and they have been studied at length by others. The most conspicuous of these are the economic weaknesses. In spite of all the propagandized triumphs of all the Five Year Plans, and in spite of the addition of the conquered satellite territories, the Soviet economy remains backward both quantitatively and qualitatively. Its output is low, the quality of almost all its products is poor, and its real costs are excessively high. Structurally the Soviet economy is out of balance, so that it cannot realize its theoretic economic potential. It does little net good to overfulfill the plan for crankshafts if the plan for magnetos collapses and there is no adequate transport to get the crankshafts to an assembly plant, or warehouses to protect them from physical deterioration once they get there.

Correlated with the economic backwardness is a cultural deficiency expressed in the lack of skilled workers, technicians, engineers, able foremen, and so on. This lack was immediately apparent to the many American soldiers and officers who, during and just after the Second World War, came into contact with large numbers of Soviet soldiers (liberated prisoners, Soviet soldiers who had been impressed into—or said that they had been impressed into—the Reichswehr, and others who were used as forced labor by the Nazis). The simplest mechanical problems about internal combustion engines or plumbing or locomotives or electricity, the solution of which is almost second nature for most Americans, were beyond the Soviet capabilities. Even where individuals were supposed to have been trained as mechanics, it would turn out they were acquainted only with some small element of a mechanism—a carburetor, say—and had no comprehension of the whole.

* Cf. *The Struggle for the World,* Chapter 8.

It is also, by now, well known that the majority of the people within the Soviet empire hate and fear their communist masters. The inference to be drawn from the mass slave-labor camps, the purges, internal passports, prohibition of foreign travel, and suppression of opposition opinion, as well as the reports of the hundreds of thousands who have in recent years escaped from the Soviet prison-society, is too clear to be denied any longer by any but fanatics or deliberate liars.

These three weaknesses which I have just cited are well enough known, but it is not always realized that from this knowledge there are practical conclusions to be drawn for a plan of action in the struggle against communism. For example, it should be immediately obvious that in our trade policy toward the Soviet empire we should aim not to alleviate but to increase the economic troubles; that we should encourage the escape to our lines of the maximum number of skilled workers, mechanics, and engineers; that we should strive to stimulate further the discontent of the Soviet masses, and to give them hope and leadership. I shall, however, reserve to Part Three of this book the discussion of these and other practical consequences.

2

The weaknesses which I have listed in the preceding section are familiar and long term. There are others, not less important, which have not been so publicly stressed or which have become only recently acute.

We can be much surer today when we write about Soviet conditions than we were before the Second World War. The war opened up the Soviet Union to a much closer examination than it had ever before received. Several million persons—German soldiers, Polish, Baltic, and other citizens who were first seized by the MVD and later released or who later escaped—have traveled almost everywhere within the Soviet Union, and can now report from firsthand observation. Soviet soldiers have been directly observed beyond their own boundaries. During and since the war, hundreds of thousands of persons from the Soviet Union itself and from the satellite nations have escaped into voluntary exile, and can also report. In addition, the news and speeches and reports from official Soviet sources, even when most heavily propagandized, are, when analytically interpreted, very revealing.

1. At the present time (1949) there are signs of an economic crisis of considerable severity within the Soviet Empire, particularly within the satellite nations. One political expression of this crisis was the 1949 Soviet effort to increase the trade of the satellite nations with the outside world.

Few items of the communist myth are more widely believed, among non-communists, than their boast that their economic measures "solve" the problem of the business cycle and of economic crises. This item is, however, as false as all the others. The communist measures do not eliminate economic crises, but merely change, in part, their form. By the use of slave labor and compulsion, they avoid mass unemployment (though not all unemployment); and by suitable subsidies they can prevent mass bankruptcies (as capitalism has also learned, perhaps unwisely, to do). But major economic dislocations have been nevertheless characteristic of the Soviet economy. These have been particularly obvious in fiscal affairs, with a series of intense inflations and sudden, arbitrary deflations. The lack of economic balance, to which I have referred, slows or shuts off factory operations as effectively as a lack of orders. Livestock and crops have disappeared as a result of the Politburo's agricultural policies even more quickly than they do from the vagaries of the "free market." Black markets, free and controlled stores with totally different sets of prices, barter—all permanent features of Soviet economic life— are not symptoms of economic health. The only sense in which Soviet communism has eliminated the business cycle is by keeping the economy in a nearly continuous crisis.

At present the economic condition of the satellite nations is particularly critical. Their inclusion within the Soviet empire has meant the sudden disruption of their entire economic life and tradition. Their trade with the West, upon which their economies have depended for markets, for manufactured products, and for capital, has been cut to less than half of what it has traditionally been. Soviet industry cannot supply what they need as imports, and is a market for their goods only in the sense that a robber is the market for his victim.

At the same time, the internal economic relations of the satellite countries are being disrupted by clumsy nationalizations, and by the subordination of national industries to Soviet trusts. Equipment has deteriorated, and cannot be replaced; manpower output is low. The trained and able personnel is being purged, and replaced with economic incompetents. The attempt to win support from the workers by raising nominal wages combines with the low technical efficiency, the high police, military and bureaucratic expenses, and the Soviet looting to maintain heavy inflationary pressure. The severity of the crisis seems to differ in the various satellites, and to be particularly marked in Czechoslovakia and Rumania.

2. The Soviet Union has not yet succeeded in integrating the satellite nations into the communist system. The great public expression of this failure is Tito; but potential Titos and potential Titoism have been widespread throughout the satellite nations. Purges, liquidations, mass exilings to Siberia, trials, denunciations, have had to continue and multiply. Vice-premiers, generals, ministers, party members and non-party members, as well as cardinals and priests, have had to be dismissed or tortured or imprisoned or shot. Agricultural policy has had to tack and veer in trying to hold its course against the stubborn and sullen peasants.

The importance of Tito's defiance of the Kremlin, even if in the end Tito is liquidated or capitulates, can hardly be overstated. The communist enterprise requires a monolithic centralism from which no deviation is permitted. There cannot be, without endangering the entire structure, even the potentiality of future opposition, much less an active and functioning opposition. Tito, in relation to the communist movement, has been compared to Trotsky. In fact, the implications of his break go beyond those of Trotsky's in both theory and power. Trotsky (until 1933, when the issue had become academic) was unwilling or unable to break with the Party. His faction was cut to pieces before he attempted to organize it seriously. Until the end of his life, he made "the defense of the Soviet Union," even Stalin's Soviet Union, a cardinal principle of his own politics, and he denounced as a counterrevolutionist anyone who differed on this issue by a hair's breadth. But Tito is openly organizing not only an opposition faction and party, but an independent nation which could, if the development continues, become an enemy nation. He is openly defiant, and his agents operate at the heart of the communist movement itself, as well as in public. The long continued existence of a Tito with an established power base would create an almost intolerable strain within the communist movement and empire.

Tito is unique only in having been, so far, successful. We know from what has happened in East Europe since his expulsion from the Cominform that potential Titoism is present in all of the satellite nations, and doubtless also within the Soviet Union proper.

Markos, head of the Greek guerrillas, Gomulka (since recanted) in Poland, Rajk in Hungary, Xoxe in Albania, Kostov in Bulgaria, conspicuous leaders in all of the Balkan states, have had to be lopped off for Titoist tendencies. There has been a corresponding purge throughout the lower ranks of the various parties.

From the point of view of the communist high command, there is this peculiarity to the Tito issue. If Tito succeeds in maintaining his independent position (which he can do only by aid from and links to the West, and a correlated wider political separation from the Kremlin), and if other Titos arise, then the communist plan for world domination cannot succeed. If, however, the Kremlin does solve the Tito problem, then it will quite probably have derived a positive addition of strength from the controversy, just as it did from the fight with Trotsky. This follows because, although the long-continued existence of an independent Tito would be dangerous and even fatal to the communist enterprise, a relatively short existence can be turned into an advantage. Tito in the open is used by the Kremlin as a stalking-horse to uncover possible Titos throughout the communist movement, just as Trotsky was so used from 1927 on. Throughout the Party, the MVD can observe what members display any slight sympathy for Tito, or fail to sound convincing in denunciation; and the names of these members can be entered in the appropriate files. To give a chance for this maneuver is perhaps part of the explanation for the comparative mildness of Stalin's counter-Tito measures during the first year after the break. Stalin is patient; and his patience has so far always been rewarded. But if he does not succeed in the end, the maneuver itself will add to the extent of the disaster.

Whatever may prove to be the outcome, the 1949–50 fact is this: that not a single one of the satellite nations, not even the three tiny Baltic states which were the first pupils, is as yet a reliable "fortress of the revolution."

3. The communist party and youth, within the Soviet empire and to some extent throughout the world, seem to be going through a grave theoretical and, one might say, moral crisis. The evidence for the existence of this crisis comes from escaped Soviet refugees, party members from non-Soviet nations, intelligence that leaks through the Iron Curtain, and from the analysis of published reports of Party discussions, decrees, speeches, and so on.

This crisis has nothing to do with the supposed "split in the Politburo," about which there has been so much speculation and publicity. Such speculation is a bitter deception of the non-communist public. No one, absolutely no one except its own members, knows what goes on in the Politburo. Conceivably it may be split into factions. From an a priori point of view, and in the light of the experience of human nature in complex historical situations, this may seem likely. However, there is not the smallest shred of positive evidence that the Politburo is in fact split. It is a frequently used communist tactic to suggest to their enemies that there is a split in the communist leadership. The story is built up that X or Y or Z, Litvinov or Thorez or Mao or Gromyko or Zhukov—or Stalin, is a "good" communist, not like the other "fanatics," and that we can get somewhere by dealing with him. We may even be able to help him against his fanatic opponents. The catch is that the whole business has been planned in advance. X or Y has been deliberately picked for his warm smile or his quiet voice, and has been specifically instructed to be conciliatory in his manner.

We know nothing about any split in the Politburo. But there is evidence, both direct and indirect, that there is trouble in the minds of Party members.

All human beings exhibit a powerful tendency to verbalize their action. They seek to discover an ideological structure—philosophical, moral, scientific, or religious—which can be put into words, and which will serve to "explain" and to justify what they do.* Moreover, when we perform an action which does not fit into one of the established verbal systems at our disposal, we are made uneasy; "our conscience troubles us," or we break out in neurotic symptoms. Thus, men and women are not content to regard easy divorce and remarriage as a simple transfer in the object of lust. They require a "scientific" utilitarian philosophy which explains the superstitious basis, or agrarian economic determination, of "old-fashioned morality." Similarly, an industrialist can battle against a wage rise with a much more peaceful mind when he is able to show to himself and others the dangers of "the welfare state." And a terrorist, after throwing his bomb, can digest his dinner more readily if he is fortified with the essays of Bakunin and Nechaev.

---

* These verbal structures have been elaborately examined by Vilfredo Pareto (Cf. Part VI of my book, *The Machiavellians*). They are called "rationalizations" by some psychoanalysts.

This is a universal human tendency, and it may be that it is especially strong in Russians. The characters in Russian novels, at any rate, are remarkably prolix in their verbal elaborations of their own behavior. They are likely to go crazy, or to commit suicide or give themselves up to the police, when they cannot find the redeeming words.

However it is with Russians, it is certainly the case that communists develop a hypertrophy of this verbalizing function. In communist terminology, it is called "the union of theory and practice." They boast and believe that only Marxism totally provides such a union. "The union of theory and practice" means, for a communist, that every action undertaken must be correlated with a verbal explanation and motivation expressed in the terminology of "dialectical materialism," and illustrated with texts drawn from Marx, Engels, Lenin, or Stalin. All those who have at any time belonged to any branch of the communist movement will have observed this tendency in constant operation. No issue, no matter how trivial, is ever presented or discussed on its mere empirical merits. It is always encased in theory and quotation. The theory is often very ingenious. For example, communists frequently use and counsel violence in strikes. But this violence is always "self-defense": because, historically, the exploiting class is engaged in a continuous offensive against the laboring masses. Or: The dictatorship of the proleteriat, executed by the Communist party, is, no matter how terroristic, the most democratic form of government that has existed because it is exercised for the majority against the reactionary minorities; whereas bourgeois democracy, no matter how free and easy, is actually a tyranny because it represents the class rule of a minority over the great majority. And so on.

The theoretic-moral crisis arises at the present time in the minds of communists precisely because their union of theory and practice has partially broken down. Their theory has not been able to provide adequate coverage for this "stage of the revolution." They do not have the words to justify to *themselves* what they feel they have got to do. As men, as communists, and many of them as Russians, they are therefrom troubled in spirit. To those who do not understand the nature of the communist movement, it will doubtless seem a scholastic waste of time to linger so insistently on this point so remote from atom bombs. But in the struggle against communism I am not sure that the unraveling of atomic secrets greatly outranks in importance the enquiry into these secrets of the communist soul. Certainly the results of this enquiry can have a more immediate and direct application to the daily tactics of the struggle, and such application I propose to make in Part Three of this book.

By their coup d'etat in 1917 and the years of civil war that followed, the communists took and consolidated state power in Russia. Russia, prior to 1917, was an empire. This empire had been built through the expansion of the Duchy of Muscovy during more than four centuries of conquest. Within the Russian Empire, the position of primary power and privilege was held by the descendants of the original conquerors, the Great Russians. Many of the other peoples of the Empire had not been assimilated to the Great Russians, but differed in language, culture, religion, and social development. In many respects, they were colonial subordinates of Great Russia. Nevertheless, in the eyes of the world, Russia was not an empire in the sense of the British or French Empires, where the imperial relation and distinctness between, say, India and Britain, or Indo-China and France, were obvious both socially and geographically. Russia was looked upon as a single nation, with a single state power extending over a continuous territory.

In the confusion of the last year of the First World War, and under the dynamic impulse of the Revolution, the Russian Empire tended to fly apart. A number of the earlier non-Russian peoples within the imperial boundaries set up independent governments of their own, the most notable of which were Georgia and the Ukraine.*

* The most notable, that is to say, of those that were subsequently reduced by the Bolsheviks. Finland, Estonia, Latvia, Lithuania, and Poland were also among the nations liberated by the collapse of Czarism. They managed—at that stage—to retain their freedom.

The communists, with their base like that of the Czars in Muscovy, reconquered these independent states—by war—and subjected them to their own monolithic dictatorship. The expansion of the communist empire during recent years is, thus, by no means a novelty; it has its precedents in the years from 1918 to 1922.

The need for the union of theory and practice required that a verbal accounting should be made for the real structure of the communist state. This was done by calling the state not Sovietica, but the Union of Socialist Soviet Republics, and by elaborating a constitutional myth according to which the actually monolithic state was a free federation, freely dissolvable, of autonomous units.

Thus, at the very beginning of communist state power, the communists confronted serious difficulties in both theory and practice over "the national question." They could, in terms of their own ideology, justify the conquest of Georgia and the Ukraine (as of anywhere else) by the fact that these nations did not have communist governments, were therefore counterrevolutionary, and were merely being liberated by the entry of the communists. But once Georgia and the Ukraine had communist governments, then they must presumably be regarded as the brotherly equals of every other communist state, including the Great Russian. Therefore the "free union."

From the point of view of the non-Russian peoples of the former Russian Empire, however, the communist state continued to look like an imperial tyranny of the Great Russians. The difficulty was eased by the super-state character of the Party—the real ruling power, and the presence of non-Russians in the Party: Stalin is of course not a Russian but a Georgian. Nevertheless, the difficulty was not solved even within the pre-1939 boundaries of the Soviet Union. Periodically it has been necessary to carry out gigantic purges and liquidations in the sub-republics. Millions were killed, exiled, or starved to death in the Ukraine in 1931–32. In the master purge of 1936–38, the entire leading apparatus of all the lesser republics was overturned.

The Second World War proved how far the communists were from complete success. They had to begin fighting by liquidating entire several of the small supposedly autonomous regions (an act now called "genocide" when carried out by non-communists): Chechen-Ingush, Kalmuck, Crimean Tatar, Volga German, Karachayevt. Millions of Ukrainians were ready to welcome the Reichswehr as a liberating army (they were finally repelled only by the insanity of Hitler's Ukrainian policy); and the Germans were able to enlist, under General Vlasov, a large Ukrainian army. After the war, the communists had once more to try to subdue the Ukraine. Even today a Ukrainian Resistance (the Ukrainian Insurgent Army) is still operating against the communists.

In handling the national problem within the boundaries of the Soviet Union, as consolidated after the civil wars, the communists were immeasurably aided by the fact that the Russian Empire had been a unified historical entity. Though the comparison was far from exact, fighting between Great Russia and Georgia or the Caucasus or the Ukraine could be presented as a purely "internal affair," like the Civil War in the United States. Almost all of the non-Soviet world, except for a few exiles, scholars, and specialists, looked upon the Soviet Union, as they had looked upon the Russian Empire; as "one nation." In the eyes of that outside world, if not in the eyes of their own subjects, there was one, and only one, "communist state."

The question then arose: What is to be the relation of the non-Soviet "masses" (i.e., foreign communists) to the Soviet state? Combined theory and practice, though not without travail, produced an answer which was unambiguous, satisfactory, and complete. The Soviet Union is not like other nations, which are only political devices for the deception and exploitation of their subjects for the benefit of the bourgeoisie. The Soviet Union is the true "fatherland of *all* toilers." It is the supreme achievement, the bastion and the fortress of the world revolution. It is therefore the *first* duty of all workers (i.e., communists) to *defend the Soviet Union* against any and all forces hostile to it. The communists of other lands must be prepared to sacrifice their means, their countries, and their lives, if necessary, to the defense of the Soviet Union. This answer, granted the premises of Marxism-Leninism-Stalinism, is logical and convincing.

Now, however, the problem has radically changed. Communists hold state power in a number of nations which were never part of the Russian Empire, and which (with the possible partial exception of Bulgaria) have been in all respects distinct from Russia as historical entities. The question now becomes: How are relations to be regulated among a number of separate communist states?

To this question, Marxism-Leninism-Stalinism has not yet succeeded in providing an answer.

Communism in the past never had to face the problem except as a speculation about the future. The traditional doctrine did have something to say. The conflicts, rivalries, and wars among peoples and nations are caused, the doctrine declared, by the contradictions of capitalism and class struggle. When states become communist, the contradictions will disappear with the disappearance of capitalism and classes; consequently, the conflicts will end. All nations will live peaceably and cooperatively side by side in communist brotherhood, just as all individuals within each communist nation.

This vague and pious formula is not, however, a concrete answer to the concrete problem. The communists themselves, living in the midst of the real conflicts, know that it is not.

On the practical side, the Russian communists, with their dominant position in the world communist movement, have been attempting to devise an answer in terms of unadorned power. They treat the satellite nations as subordinate colonies which are to be manipulated for the exclusive benefit of the original Soviet state. That is, they demand that the communist leaders of the satellite nations follow exactly the same policy that applied when these nations were still in capitalist hands. But even at the level of pure power, the practical solution has been muddied by Tito's defiance.

Even, however, if the practical solution worked for the time being, it would not be satisfactory to the communists.* The communists must have their union of theory and practice, words which justify to themselves what they are doing. It is of prime significance that Tito, in so many of his speeches and documents, hammers away at this point: We are in a new situation; Marxism-Leninism-Stalinism does not provide the answer.

The communists cannot openly say that the satellite nations are merely colonial dependencies, and that the master-nation exploits them by right of superior power. To become just one among other "imperialist exploiters" would be to give up communism, and would hardly be an attractive approach to new candidates for liberation. But to admit these nations to full equality would be to threaten the monolithic unity of the communist political structure, lacking which the whole machine might fall apart. The communist theoreticians try to temporize with jerry-built theories, hoping that a revelation will soon be made manifest somehow. The satellites properly aid the Soviet Union now because they were liberated by the blood and exertions of the Red Army and the Soviet Union † . . . but communist doctrine teaches that there is no gratitude in politics. The satellite nations are not "communist states" but "people's democracies," a more primitive stage of the revolution. And to make this syllogism more complete, the theoreticians are beginning to declare that the Soviet Union, which they pronounced "socialist" fifteen years ago, has now reached the stage of "communism" . . . but communist doctrine teaches that under communism the state "withers away," a process not yet very noticeable in the Soviet Union. If all, the Soviet Union and also the new nations, are "building toward

---

* It goes without saying that it is far more unsatisfactory to the non-communists of the satellite nations. But I am analyzing here only the crisis as it appears to the communist mind.

† To this Tito replies that he and his Yugoslav party and army, not Stalin and the Red Army, liberated Yugoslavia. It is a relevant reply, though it happens to be false. Without the Soviet training of himself and his associates, the guidance and aid from the Soviet Union, and above all the political deals put over by Stalin on Roosevelt and Churchill, Tito would certainly have failed.

communism" under the monolithic leadership of the national communist parties, why in the name of Dialectical Materialism is one
to be preferred over the rest?

It should be noted that this "Titoist" problem, though related
to problems of the past, is genuinely novel. It arises in acute form
only after several states are brought under communist control, and
it arises acutely only for communists who are within those states.
It is politically almost impossible for Titoism to make great inroads
among communists of the non-communist nations. The problem of
the latter is to gain power, and for this they need the help of the
communist state best able to give it: that is, of the Soviet Union,
which at the same time has much greater resources for influencing
and controlling foreign communists. It is for this reason, no doubt,
that the official communists have not had much trouble with Titoism outside of the Iron Curtain. Even in Trieste, on Tito's border,
the Cominform without difficulty won the great majority of the
local communists.

Titoism is a specifically communist problem. It is quite true that
nationalism in the traditional sense is also an important disintegra-
tive force in the Soviet Empire; and true also that Titoism derives
a good deal of its "mass base" and social dynamism from nationalist
feeling. Nationalism, however, undergoes a subtle transformation in
its passage through the communist furnace. It is a mistake to reduce
Titoism merely to nationalism, and a mistake which, if persisted in,
will diminish the effectiveness of any Western tactic designed to
exploit Titoism in the struggle for the world defeat of communism.

A doctrinaire mind that becomes, for whatever reason, troubled
by one problem, is more easily disturbed by others. Besides this
complex question of the interrelation of several successful communist states, the evidence of refugees and of the Soviet press itself
suggests that other questions related to the present stage of the
revolution are bothering the spirits of at least some communists.
Among the most sincere, those not corrupted by bureaucratism and

power, the conflict between communist ideals and daily practice seems to be making an impression stronger than at any time since the early days. They know that there is always less freedom, always more terror, and some of them, at least, begin to wonder. There are others—this is clear from what some of the military refugees have said—who begin to ask themselves: Is our victory perhaps not inevitable? are we going to lose? They, after all, know their own weaknesses better than we do. There are few men who are not troubled if they believe in advance that they are going to lose.

There is still another very important problem, not of today but of the possibly close future, for which Marxism-Leninism-Stalinism has no satisfactory solution, either in practice or in theory. What is the mechanism of succession? How, and upon what verbal grounds, will X replace Stalin? Stalin's position as leader is itself "illegitimate" in Ferrero's sense: there is no generally accepted formula (such as the hereditary or democratic formulas) which justifies the power which he in fact wields. He gained power in fact by building an inner-party machine, and destroying his rivals and their supporters. But what when he dies? To repeat the same process again, with no single outstanding candidate, and with the heroic days of the original Revolution far in the past, would threaten full civil war. Internal struggle, even if much short of civil war, might weaken the Soviet Empire disastrously in the face of its world opponent. Therefore, a communist must reason, either we unite around one man, or we are lost. So, all can understand in the abstract, as all can understand in Congress the need for "reducing the budget." But around which man? why not around me, or my man? There is no theory, there are no words, which can justify the selection of this man *rather than* that man. This void is a fearful chasm.*

* I believe that what I have here called the "theoretic-moral" crisis explains in part the shakeup in the communist high command which occurred early in 1949. It is noteworthy that several of the highest Party leaders were replaced in their principal *public* jobs by routine second-raters like Vishinsky and Gromyko. In some cases at least, this does not seem to have been a "demotion" of the older leaders. Rather, in accordance with communist evaluations, they were cutting down on less

4. The totalitarian structure of Soviet society is centralized to the highest possible degree, and rigidly controlled from the top. All persons must behave in accordance with a single, monolithic "general line." Spontaneity and initiative at the lower levels are prohibited. The Nazi as well as the Soviet instances have shown in our time the imposing power of such a social organization. The leadership is able to concentrate social resources on selected key objectives, and, relatively immune from the influence of public opinion, can change or reverse policy much more rapidly than in a looser type of society such as our own. The full flow, directed into a single surging channel, gives to outsiders the impression of being able to carry every obstacle.

It seems probable, however, that the strength of the rigid totalitarian machine is gained only by the sacrifice of other qualities that are in the end more decisive for survival. The centralized, incredibly bureaucratized, mechanical society is less flexible, less resilient than the looser, more disorderly, more spontaneously creative society. The totalitarian machine is built of a heavy cast-iron that has a ponderous and crushing strength but that will crack and break from well-directed blows, rather than from a steel which can yield and recover. We know that in 1942 the Soviet Union was close to dissolution not merely from the impact of the Nazi armies but from the disruption of its own internal apparatus of control. Military analysts have told me that the Red Army, an analogue of Soviet society as a whole, provides demonstrations. They say that when contingents of the Red Army were defeated during the Second World War, they were more thoroughly defeated than in the case of the British, American, or for that matter the German armies. They needed a

---

important work (the public jobs) in order to concentrate on what the communists regard as primary: the inner-party problem. Specifically, they are no doubt trying to prepare for the convening of a Party Congress, which has not met in Russia for more than a decade. It would, however, be most awkward, if not impossible, to hold a Party Congress before the theoretic-moral crisis is "solved"—i.e., before there is an ideologically acceptable answer, which can be unanimously voted, to the new problems. The fact that the Congress has not been held is, thus, an additional proof of the existence of the crisis.

longer time and more space to regroup and recover in order to be able to make another stand. I am not sure of the accuracy of the military illustration, but it seems to me likely, from its very nature, that the communist system can collapse fast once it starts collapsing.

3

During the course of the Second World War, world public opinion made a full reversal in its estimate of Soviet military capabilities. The contemptuous view that the Red Army was "butter," a clumsy laughingstock, was turned upside down into the opposite view that the Red Army is as great a fighting aggregate as has ever existed.

I advance a judgment on such a matter with a humility proper to my own technical ignorance, but I cannot avoid believing that we now incline to overestimate the Soviet military potential even more grossly than we underestimated it in 1940. After all, the 1940 judgment was based upon a solid, indelible fact: the miserable performance of the Red Army in the Finnish War. The Finnish War, moreover, was a very direct and unmixed military experiment. Moscow made a feeble attempt to proclaim a free Finnish government under Kuusinen, but political influences were of negligible importance, on either side. There was no second front to worry about. It was just a straight fight between minute Finland and the gigantic Soviet Union. And the Soviet Union fought badly.

We are told that the Finnish War was a trivial episode. Didn't the Red Army defeat the Reichswehr, and is that not sufficient proof of how good the Red Army is? The problem is not so easy. We should not accept without examination even that apparently self-evident statement that "the Red Army defeated the Reichswehr." It is certainly true that the Reichswehr was defeated. Just why and how was it defeated? Is it really true that it was defeated by the Red Army?

We must naturally recognize that military operations by the Red Army were part of the cause of the defeat of the Reichswehr. They were surely not the entire cause (as Soviet propaganda since the war proclaims), and it is doubtful, to me at any rate, how great a proportion of the cause they add up to.

The German Army, in the first place, was never able to make a full concentration of its forces on the Russian front. Even in 1941, some of its best troops were in Africa, some had to remain in the Balkans, where they had more trouble than had been expected, and there had to be large occupation and defensive detachments in Scandinavia, the Low Countries, France, and Italy. The Luftwaffe had taken severe punishment in the Battle of Britain, and had to retain a considerable part of its forces for the continuing air war. Soon the threat and later the actuality of invasion in Africa, Sicily, Italy, and France were pinning down, and then using (and destroying) more and more of the available troops and equipment; while the Allied bombing was smashing the Luftwaffe and the German industries and cities.*

Secondly, it is doubtful that the Red Army could have kept going without the massive material aid which it received from the West. Quite apart from combat weapons, it would have been starving and frozen without the food and clothing, and crippled without the tens of thousands of trucks.

Perhaps even more crucial in defeating the Reichswehr within Russia were Hitler's errors. Beginning with his disastrous blunder in ordering the assault on Moscow in the early winter of 1941, Hitler time and again overruled his generals even in relation to purely military operations. Still more fatal were his political directives which transformed large sections of the Soviet population—and army—from indifference or even positively favoring inclination into total enemies.

Finally, we should record that Germany in 1939, just as Germany in 1914, simply didn't have what it takes, in manpower and material

---

* It is often overlooked that a principal strategic result of the bombing of Germany was to deprive the German armies in the Soviet Union of adequate air support

resources, to carry through a program of conquest on the scale that it had projected.

The belief that the Red Army defeated the Reichswehr, though it has considerably more substance than the equally unmodified Soviet declaration that the Red Army defeated the Japanese Army, would seem to be at least an oversimplification. We do not have to be communists to find some point in the Marxian theory (unmentioned by the Soviet propagandists) that an army cannot rise too far above its economic and cultural base. An army is not formed out of ideas alone. The relative weaknesses of the Soviet economy and the Soviet culture must necessarily be reflected in the Soviet army.

The announcement, in September, 1949, that "an atomic explosion" had taken place within the Soviet Union indicates that the technical inferiority is less absolute than it was prior to that occurrence. Nevertheless, there is still some distance between an atomic explosion and the ability to conduct a nuclear war. There has never been anything "top secret" about the way in which General Motors and Ford produce automobiles. The Soviet automobile plants, however, remain a quarter-century behind.

4

Whatever may be the truth about the military potential of the Red Army, it seems reasonably clear that its military role is conceived of by the communist leadership as that of the strategic defensive. A defensive strategy for the Red Army (in relation to the over-all world struggle) is motivated in part by a realization of all the various Soviet weaknesses which we have surveyed in this chapter. It follows also as a consequence of communist doctrine and tradition.

The strategy of the communist movement as a whole, in its indissoluble and complex unity, is that of the continuous offensive. Its retreats are always considered to be tactical—"in order better to advance"; when it retreats in one area of operations, it always maintains the offensive in other areas. But the weight of this continuous offensive is sustained by the political (ideological, subversive) phase of the movement, not by the military. The function of the military is to supplement and complete the political work, not to replace it or substitute for it.

This relationship between the political and military arms is expressed in the structure and administration of the communist movement. It is the Party, the organization of professional revolutionary politicians, that runs everything, and the Party is run by the supreme politicians in the Politburo. The organizer and first commander of the Red Army was not a general but the politician, Trotsky. The Supreme Commander of the Second World War was the politician, Stalin. To have great power, a soldier must be more than a great commander in the narrowly military sense; he must be a "Bolshevik general," a political general. The communists have thoroughly absorbed Treitschke's principle that war is simply a violent type of politics.

Communist doctrine has gone much beyond the pre-1917 belief of many communists that the masses within each nation would make their own revolution in their own way at their own time. Revolutions now are planned, organized, and directed from the Soviet center. It is still believed, however, that the nation concerned must be made "ripe for revolution," both negatively by the effects of capitalist disintegration and positively by the political, ideological, and subversive operations of the organized communist movement. The Red Army can then step in to finish the job, like the undertaker who closes the lid of the coffin that other hands have made.

Meanwhile, the Red Army remains "eternally vigilant," ready "to defend the conquests of the revolution." Thus the Red Army waited to receive Hitler's attack, even though this wait was most doubtful from a military point of view.

The only exceptions to this rule of the strategic (military) defensive would be in cases where the communist leadership judged that there could be no risk of a serious war, where victory would be easy and certain. The Finnish War was perhaps such an exception (though that war was not so easy as the communists judged beforehand). More probably, however, the Finnish War should be regarded only as a tactical offensive, within the framework of a strategic defense against the possibility of the German War to come. So also in the case of the Red Army's 1939 invasion of Poland—which was besides a necessary consequence of the treaty with Hitler, and involved no military risk. The Baltic states were taken over in 1939–40 without fighting, by a combination of diplomacy, political pressure, and military threat.   .

The one genuine exception may have been the Polish War of 1920–21. The Red Army did, certainly, invade Poland. Nevertheless, this seems to have been brought about by a political miscalculation. Lenin and Trotsky believed that the Polish workers were ready to revolt. If the slogans of the revolution were raised, it would be necessary only for the Red Army to appear; the Polish masses would rise up, overthrow their "exploiters," and Poland would be added to the Soviet Republics. The Polish masses proved a grievous disappointment. The licking that the Red Army then took was a rough lesson for the future, and a reinforcement for the defensive doctrine.

In analyzing this issue, which has so direct and so critical a relation to anti-communist perspectives, we must not omit reference to what we know about Stalin himself, since Stalin is the principal leader not because of personal peculiarities but because he so typically embodies the traits of the leading communist stratum. Stalin is a prudent and a patient man. He has never shown any tendency to act hastily, rashly, or impulsively; he has never taken a big chance, unless he was compelled to. In 1923, this very problem of the function of the Red Army emerged dramatically in connection with Germany. There were at that time in Germany major civil disturbances, and in some areas virtual civil war. Defeat, inflation, misery, governmental breakdown had produced a "revolutionary situation." But it was clear to the Communist International that the German

Communist party could not, without external help, carry through a German communist revolution. Trotsky and others demanded that the Red Army be sent in to make the German revolution. Lenin and Stalin opposed and defeated Trotsky's proposal. They did so because they believed that it might precipitate a more general war which would endanger the Soviet Union itself (though they had additional and fancier ideological arguments). They were not prepared to risk what they had already won for the sake of something which, according to their theories of inevitability, they were going to get in the long run anyway.

This has always been Stalin's attitude, in his inner-party struggles as well as in his world policy: Why risk what we have by an over-hasty move to gain what we shall in any case achieve later? Let us prepare the victim first, and strike openly later. In such a way he cut the ground from under his party opponents before he hauled them up on charges. He undermined their factions and their positions, until they were left exposed, ready to collapse at the final quick, sharp blow. These methods never failed in the past. Why should they be abandoned in the future?

Boris Souvarine (the author of the great biography of Stalin, and probably the world's leading authority on the personal and political history of Stalin), with whom I have discussed this point, believes that it is even relevant to note that Stalin and his principal associates are now old men. Does it seem likely that they, at their age, with so much already, would voluntarily choose to cast the final die? Above all, when they believe that they have in their communist arsenal better methods, of which they believe themselves to be the unchallengeable masters, and by which they are confident that they can gain their objective?

For the Red Army to take the offensive now would mean, they know, the immediate entry of the total armed force of the United States into the struggle. And with that, they know that their risk would be of nothing less than all.

Communists have a very shrewd way of combining "peace propa-

ganda" (i.e., propaganda to persuade others to be militarily unpre-
pared) with "scare propaganda" (propaganda to terrify others into
submission by threatening what the Red Army will do to them if
they are anti-communist). In parallel columns of their press, they
shout for peace and sing the colossal and irresistible might of the
Red Army.*

It is almost universally believed that if a total armed conflict
should break out, the Red Army would immediately strike west.
It is also believed that, at present and for at least several years to
come, the Red Army, meeting no effective opposition, would succeed
within a few weeks in overrunning Western Europe and reaching
the Atlantic and the Pyrenees. Military men have shown me on the
map how simple the maneuver would be, with the divisions now
at Soviet disposal. Nearly all that is written about the strategy and
conduct of the possible war presupposes that all Europe will be
occupied. The objective of European rearmament under the Atlantic
Pact, as this has been publicly discussed, is to try to organize and
equip a West European force which could delay the Red Army's
advance, and hold temporarily, perhaps on the Rhine.

I do not wish to deny that this Western offensive is the most
probable Soviet move, or even that it could not probably be carried
through successfully and quickly to the line of the Atlantic and the
Pyrenees. What concerns me is the psychological attitude revealed by the universality of the belief that this is unquestionably
so. A proper estimate of the Soviet weaknesses suggests to me that
it is quite possible that the Red Army, far from mounting an offensive to the west in Europe, would, as its first major move, fall back
to the east.† The reasons for this would not include any opposition

---

* This is a favorite juggle of that most contemptible of the breeds of contemporary men, the fellow-travelers, those souls in Limbo, despised alike by Hell and
Heaven. I have several times, for example, heard that most able apologist for Soviet
policy, Professor Frederick V. Schuman of Williams College, curdle the blood of his
audience by the tone of threat in which he suggests the dread fate in store for all
those who might dare to cross swords with the Red Army.

† There are specific reports of Soviet actions that indicate preparations for such a

which they expect either in the near future or for many years to come from the formal West European armies. That opposition they believe that they could crush with little difficulty. But, in addition to the grave logistical problem of maintaining large occupation and defensive forces in the West, they have reason to ponder the effect of having the still unreliable satellites astride their lines of communication.

If meanwhile we had pursued a policy, adapted to the present phase of the actual war, which had aided and developed to a maximum the resistance spirit of the satellites—perhaps even succeeded in liberating some or all of them, and which had helped in preparing, against the possibility of its need, a West European Resistance, then a Red Army operation of mass advance to the west would have become still more untenable. Much more would have been accomplished toward the defense of Western Europe, and much more quickly and cheaply, than can be expected from the conventional approach of the Atlantic Pact.

Whatever may be the probabilities of Red Army moves once a total armed conflict began, the defensive military doctrine of the communists combined with their present vulnerability make it exceedingly unlikely that they will in the near future begin that kind of conflict.

From the entire analysis it follows that the United States, for a few years to come, is relatively secure in a strictly military sense, and is almost completely secure from the possibility of military defeat.

The supreme significance of this fact is the following: for two or three years we are free to act in almost any way that we choose in relation to the Soviet Union and to communism without a serious risk of total armed conflict, and with no risk of military defeat.

The rather widespread idea that we might "provoke" an armed conflict by pursuing an offensive anti-Soviet and anti-communist

---

move rather than a western advance. I am not in a position to evaluate adequately these reports.

policy is at variance with the facts of the situation, and is above all absurd in the light of the experience of communist behavior and attitudes. The Red Army would certainly move if the communist high command believed it sure to win: after all, though the communists are willing to wait a long time in achieving their objective, they are not unwilling to gain it more quickly. Today, the relative weaknesses of the communist empire prevent the Red Army from moving. Tomorrow, if we had increased those weaknesses by a vigorous offensive plan, the Red Army would be still more rigidly inhibited.

Communists are *never* "provoked"; if they sometimes *seem* provoked, that is only a rehearsed bit of acting for the sake of psychological effect on their opponents. Their training includes a careful study of the art of provoking *others* while they themselves remain "objective." The rantings of Vishinsky in the United Nations, like the courtroom ravings of a Judith Coplon or the loud contempts of the communist defendants before Judge Medina, are all of them acts, put on and off like greasepaint.

Experience uniformly proves that communists are always emboldened to further aggression by friendship, conciliation, or appeasement. Such attitudes their doctrine interprets as signs of "bourgeois weakness" and degeneracy. It is from firmness and power that they yield and retreat, and offer concessions. Arthur Young, the inventor of the helicopter made by the Bell company, once told me a perfectly illustrative story. One day near the end of the war, he was demonstrating his machine to a Soviet general. The general, looking over the controls while the helicopter rested on the ground, began to press certain buttons and switches. Young asked him politely to stop, explaining that he might damage the machine and even wreck it and themselves. The general paid no attention, and continued. Young made his request sharper, with no effect. He then shouted, "No!" still without results. Finally, very much concerned over what might happen, he hit the general's arm a hard blow that knocked it away from the control panel. The incident was with that ended; the general became all smiles and affability.

It would be absurd to hold that all risk of a Soviet armed attack can be eliminated. There is such a risk, of course—no matter what policy and plan we adopt or fail to adopt. That risk, however slight, must always be allowed for. It is not intelligently allowed for by predicating the activization of military forces on some distinctly marked D-Day that may well never occur. Rather, the United States must be continuously ready to commit whatever military force is required by the development of its own plans and the given situation.

5

I have in this chapter stated and analyzed the weaknesses, or some of the principal weakness, that in their combination prove the communist empire to be exposed and vulnerable. The communist leadership, we can be sure, is more acutely aware of these weaknesses than we can be. Some of these weaknesses have characterized the communist regime from the beginning, and are not likely soon to be remedied. However, others of them, and among these some that are most crucial to the success of the struggle against communism, are episodic, and can be overcome.

To cite the most obvious example: We have been informed that in the late summer of 1949 an atomic explosion occurred within the Soviet Union. There is no reason why this knowledge should be the occasion of panic. The development of nuclear weapons as a significant military arm requires a good deal more than the ability to produce an atomic explosion. There must also be solved the problems of the delivery of the weapons, their physical control, their detonation (or release), and the manufacture and stockpiling of all components on a sufficient scale. "Sufficient," moreover, must mean to the communists a nuclear armament which, when combined with their other weapons, they would think *sufficient to defeat the United States and its allies*. When we recall the enormous advantage in this field of the United States—by virtue of the temporal headstart, and of technical, scientific, and industrial superiority, such sufficiency is quite an order, even for the Politburo. Nevertheless, the possession by the communists of even a few nuclear weapons, together with the means of employing them, appreciably reduces the military odds in favor of the United States; and the possession of a considerable stockpile (even if still much inferior in quantity and quality to the American stockpile), while it would not assure communist victory, would make communist defeat also a catastrophe for the non-communist world. Given time by a conciliatory or merely defensive policy—and a few years is probably enough, the communists will have that stockpile. That is why they followed up the announcement of the atomic explosion by an intensification of the "peace offensive."

There is, again, every reason to suppose that, given time, they will succeed in solving the problem of the satellite nations—the problem of the relations among several successful communist states, and the correlated theoretical-moral problem. On the practical side, the communists are systematically destroying those individuals and groups in the satellite nations who are potential sources of opposition. It is not a work that can be finished in a day. But in the end, if they are allowed to, they will succeed. We must never forget that the communists are capable of anything: no means whatsoever are prohibited if they are thought to be for the end of the revolution. They will, if necessary, kill, torture, and exile to the slave camps of Siberia tens of millions of East Europeans.

It is necessary to understand that the communist empire is today vulnerable, more vulnerable by far than it is generally believed to be. It is necessary also to insist that tomorrow—three years or even two years from now—it may be much less vulnerable, both from having corrected present weaknesses and from having gained additional sources of strength. A survey of the communist weaknesses must not make us complacent. On the contrary, it should prove to us both the opportunity and the need to decide and to act now, while action promises results both victorious and assured.

Part Three

PLAN

CHAPTER IX

The Turn to the Offensive

NO MATTER WHAT may be the defects of present United States foreign policy, there can be no doubt of the extraordinary change which has taken place since 1946. At the end of 1946, the United States was still acting toward the Soviet Union in terms of cooperation and appeasement; it was demobilizing and disintegrating its armed forces; it seemed to be abandoning the claim to international leadership; and the bulk of its citizenry seemed concerned only to get the war aftermath over with, and to return to seeking money and pleasure. A continuation of that policy might quite probably have caused before now the loss of all Europe to the communists, and would certainly have led in the end to total defeat.

By 1949 the wheel had turned the half cycle to containment. Cooperation and appeasement, though they were still attractive to many in wish, had been laid aside by almost all except the communists, their hangers-on, and the self-deluded. The armed forces were being strengthened, not dissipated. A daily increasing percentage of the population was becoming aware what was at issue.

To bring about these changes, there had been a sharp break with the tradition of American foreign policy. There was now open intervention in the affairs of other nations; entangling alliances and agreements with Europe; and in the Marshall Plan a deed of economic diplomacy for which there is no precedent in the history of any nation.

All this had happened in the United States without the imposition of dictatorship, without a governing class unified in its point of view, and under the critical scrutiny of a many-hued opposition which had full access to the means of public communication and to the ballot-box.

We have studied in the earlier parts of this book the reasons for which the present policy must be regarded as inadequate. But inadequate rather than simply wrong. The direction has been right; it is necessary only to go further on the same bearing. The present policy needs not to be superseded, but, rather, to be surpassed. What is required is to carry through to their full consequences the implications of the policies and plans already adopted. From retreat we have passed to the defensive policy of containment. What remains is to go from the defense to the attack.*

The general nature of a policy both correct and adequate is clear enough.

There is first the correct estimate of the situation, and of the enemy, his capabilities and weaknesses, and his objective. We know the enemy: the world communist movement, with its Soviet base; and we know his objective: monolithic world domination. The situation we discover upon analysis of the evidence to be: a continuous war of a new kind, a political, subversive, ideological, Resistance war which is also a limited war by arms, and which may develop into an unlimited war by arms.

If this is the situation, what we seek is properly described as a *war plan*: a plan, however, not of the conventional variety (though inclusive of the conventional variety), but for this new kind of war. If a war is going on, and if we are, whether we wish to be or

---

* It cannot, unfortunately, be excluded that, instead of completing the cycle, we shall slip back from containment to appeasement. After all that has happened during the past fifteen years, I am unwilling to believe that such a retreat would be more than a brief vacillation. If we as a people once more try to appease a totalitarian aggressor, an aggressor moreover toward whom we have already once tried appeasement and tasted the fruits, then we deserve to be destroyed.

not, a party to it, then, unless we are ready to quit, we must seek to fight it and to win it.

The first step in fighting this war is to recognize that it exists. Next must come the definition of our own objective. This definition, to be a serviceable guide, must be made precise and narrow. It is dictated by the nature of the situation, the enemy, and his objective, and can only be: the destruction of the power of Soviet-based communism.

It is advisable to make a double comment upon this definition of objective. In the first place, it will be noted that the proposed objective is political, not military. In a conventional war plan elaborated according to modern (non-communist) military principles, the specific objective is always, as we have seen, the destruction of the armed force of the enemy. In this case, therefore, it would be: the destruction of the Red Army. However, the conventional objective is selected on the implicit assumption of a conventional, formal war. In the new kind of war in which we are now engaged, the relevant political objective must be considered primary to the narrower military objective. Of course, if the political objective is attained, it would automatically follow that the power of the Red Army as an instrument of the Soviet Union or of communism would also have been destroyed. By stating the military objective as the primary and central aim of our plan, we would obscure the fact that we may be able to destroy the Red Army by, for the most part, non-military means, as a by-product of the destruction of the communist political power. In addition, we would tend to give less emphasis to those non- and semi-military means by which we may be able to achieve our aim, and which at the very least would immeasurably simplify the conventional military problem.

If a total armed conflict did begin, we might then have to reverse the order of priority. The destruction of the Red Army might have to be made the primary practical objective, as the only means for breaking the political power of the communists. But that problem belongs to another phase.

Secondly with reference to this definition of objective, it is plainly by no means broad enough to cover the full international social aim of the United States and the American people. It is formulated in a deliberately narrow and negative manner, in order that it may be precise enough to be definitely accepted or rejected and, once adopted, to constitute a directing concept to which subsidiary proposals can be unambiguously related as means and methods. This restriction is justified because the attainment of this objective is the necessary condition for the attainment of any other objective, or any wider objective. If we do not smash the communist power, we shall cease to exist as a nation and a people. A youth may hold as his highest ideal the wish to be a scientist; but if he has typhoid fever, he has to be cured first. Whatever kind of future world we want for ourselves and our children, we must first make sure that we or they will be there to have it.

In *The Struggle for the World* I have argued for the positive objective of a democratic world order, led in its beginning by the United States, as a stage in the building of a genuine world government and world society. I shall not repeat that discussion in this book, but shall remain within the limits of a specific plan of action.

2

We must keep in mind that the war for which a plan is required is not a possible war of the future, but the actual war of the present. The plan, however far its perspectives may extend into the future, must be of such a sort as to coordinate and guide daily actions, now and continuously until its objective is reached.

Given the estimate, the statement of objective, and a knowledge of our own capabilities and resources, the problem of the plan is to state those methods of implementation by which the objective may be reached. The implementation can, from an abstract point of view, be roughly divided into "internal" and "external." Each of these can, in turn, be broken down into a number of fairly evident categories. For example, the internal implementation is concerned with measures in such fields as the military, the economic, the ideological, and what might be called the social or structural. In the external implementation, a distinction might be made between the more or less traditional measures, both diplomatic and economic, and those more informal, novel, and unstandardized measures specifically designed to answer the challenge of the ideological, subversive, Resistance war that is now being fought.

It is primarily with these last that I shall be directly concerned in the subsequent chapters of this book. I have already discussed the others, in Part III of *The Struggle for the World,* and I see no reason to alter what I there wrote. I shall make at this point only a few incidental comments:

Internal implementation. A plan of military rearmament and development is at present going forward in the United States. Economic plans have also been formulated, and are being worked on. To some degree, economic war plans have been put into internal operation, in connection with rearmament, the stockpiling of strategic materials, the allotment to industry of a small number of "pilot" orders, the maintenance of synthetic rubber and other plants not normally needed in peacetime, and so on.

With respect to both the military and economic planning, particularly with respect to the latter, there is a large arena for technical discussion and dispute, and such discussion and dispute are in fact taking place. Disregarding these as irrelevant to my present purpose, there is nevertheless one general observation, closely related to the central thesis of this book, to be made. The military (and the economic) planning is predicated, we have already seen, on the assumption that the war is in the future, that it will begin, if it begins, on some definite D-Day. We have also seen that this assumption is false. With the recognition that in reality the war is already taking place, it becomes necessary not so much to alter details of the military planning as to reorient our way of thinking about the military phase of the struggle. In correlation with the offensive strategy of the over-all plan, the attitude should be one of willingness to commit, in the present and not merely in the future, whatever military forces are or might become necessary to the support of measures undertaken in non-military fields. This means that both direct military preparation and its attendant economic measures should be advanced con-tinuously, day by day, rather than allowed to wait on paper, for the most part, until the starting-gun of the phantom D-Day of the future.

To some extent, this point of view has already been forced on the United States by experience. If we disregard legalisms, it is apparent that the United States has already been fighting, on a considerable scale with armament and on a small scale with personnel, in Greece, Iran, China, Korea, southeast Asia, and the Philippines. The arms and officers sent to Turkey, and participation in the rearmament of Western Europe, by men as well as by armament, are hardly normal peacetime activities. It is conceivable, as I shall later discuss, that there could be much more open but still limited fighting without any certainty that this would lead to a total armed conflict.

On the ideological side of internal planning, a good deal has been done, but much remains. The prevailing anti-communism of the American public is still on the whole superficial; it is not an in-formed anti-communism. In a democratic nation, the effective con-duct of national policy needs and should have the understanding and voluntary support of the people. For this, in the present case, the truth should be told, over and over again, about the Soviet Union, the nature of communism, and the condition and aims of the struggle against communism.

I have listed also, as part of the internal implementation of an over-all plan, "social or structural" measures. By this I mean to refer, on the one hand, to such elementary requirements as the outlawing and suppression of the internal communist movement; and, on the other, to what changes or developments in governmental or other institutions may prove necessary to the effective pursuit of the plan's objective.

External implementation. Under the policy of containment, the United States has already made new departures in diplomacy and international economic maneuvering. Many of these are equally appropriate to a policy of the offensive, and many others readily suggest themselves as soon as we begin to order our reasoning from an offensive point of view. Granted the central objective, it is easy to agree that our foreign economic policy should be designed to aggravate further, never to alleviate, the economic crisis within the Soviet Empire; that we should never allow ourselves in international conferences or meetings—as we have done a number of unfortunate times in the past few years—to be jockeyed into a position where we vote with the Soviet states and against our allies or potential allies; that we should use every economic and diplomatic device to encourage the breakup of the satellite system, and the solidarity of the non-communist sections of the world; etc. I am only incidentally concerned with such measures as these.

I propose, in the remaining chapters of this book, to discuss, very practically and concretely, the kind of external measures which have little precedent in traditional American diplomacy, but which are peculiarly and specifically related to the kind of war in which we are now engaged. I shall concentrate on this area of operations for a number of reasons. In the first place, measures of the kind to which I refer (there is unfortunately no single name to cover them) are neglected both in discussion and in practice, whereas the other methods of implementation (rearmament, diplomacy, economic relations, and so on) receive full recognition in both planning and action. Moreover, if the estimate of the situation at which we have arrived is correct, then the novel, untraditional measures have a great and perhaps a crucial importance for the successful conduct of the war, and the achievement of the objective.

It is a mistake, to which Americans are habitually inclined, to judge the importance of an object or action in purely quantitative terms of size or cost. The Marshall Plan, it is felt, *must* be supremely important in the contest with the Soviet Union, because it costs about 5 billions a year; the United Nations must count for a great deal because it too costs a lot of money, employs or concerns so many people, has so many committees and meetings, and gets such a lot of space in the newspapers; and it goes without saying that armed forces which draw down 15 billions or more yearly must be supremely significant.

Many of the untraditional measures are relatively cheap, sometimes very cheap, in cost, and little publicized (indeed, in the case of some sorts the effort is to avoid all publicity). This is another reason for their neglect by Americans: what is so seemingly small in scale *cannot* be very important. What these untraditional measures require is usually not great quantities of money, but imagination, firmness, intelligence, and sometimes heroism.

Nevertheless, comparative results are by no means properly judged by money or display. We have already observed that the only objective evaluation of moves made in the struggle against world communism is in terms of the effect on the relative power balance. On this balance, an action initiated by billions of dollars and thousands of speeches and editorials may count for much less than one carried through by a few thousand dollars, a handful of men, and not a single line in the public press. Indeed, if the grandiose action is in pursuit of a false policy decision, its net effect will be all the more negative from its size.

For example: Whether or not one agrees with the policy evaluations made by the State Department's 1949 White Paper on China, it is a fact that between 1945 and 1949 several billion dollars were spent on Chinese affairs. It is a further fact that these billions not merely were wasted, but quite probably, from the way in which they were used, contributed to the Chinese debacle. Contrast this with the following: In the early 1920's, Moscow sent a few agents, with a little money, into Albania. There, with great difficulty, they managed to gather a few native Albanians around them, principally dissatisfied intellectuals of the towns. In 1940, the Moscow-directed group still numbered its members in no more than dozens. At the end of 1944, still having received only a minute amount of material aid from their masters, they took over control of that strategically most important country. Or again: Which would be more important, to spend a billion dollars to rehabilitate German industry with no political result except to make the Germans feel again their nationalist oats, or to spend a million dollars on a thoughtful plan that would strengthen the political, moral, and organizational ties of the German trade unions with the West? Or to put it even more strongly: It is more important to win over a single communist party member than to sign an elaborate treaty with, and spend billions on, a major nation, if that nation cannot be trusted. To strengthen France's Atomic Energy Commission under the communist, Joliot-Curie, is a defeat, not a victory; to keep even precariously alive a small detachment of the Ukrainian Insurgent Army is an unalloyed victory, the consequences of which might prove of almost incalculable weight in the final outcome.

Another motive for concentration on the "untraditional methods" is that *only* by the large-scale use of these methods do we have a chance to defeat the communists without a total armed conflict. The communist power is not going to fall apart merely because we wish it to. The traditional methods (armament, diplomacy, trade maneuvers) cannot lead to a decision. If they are evaluated properly, in the light of past experience, they must be understood simply as a preparation for a war by total arms, through which the actual decision would be expected to come. But modern history has proved that the untraditional methods (which may include, of course, a limited use of arms) are, unlike the traditional methods short of full-scale war, capable of bringing about a *decision*.

By concentrating attention on the untraditional methods, I do not, however, want to suggest that conventional methods should be abandoned. The objective of the general plan is the defeat of the communist power. The attainment of the objective requires implementation in all relevant fields. Though we do not need, and should not seek, a rigid interlocked blueprint of the totalitarian mode, our action ought to be so scheduled that each line of operations is consistent with and supplements all others. Moreover, there is inevitably a good deal of overlapping.

3

The adjective "untraditional" is not very satisfactory in application to the kind of measures in question. Such measures—ideological, subversive, guerrilla—have, in truth, a very long tradition which goes back into ancient and even pre-history. What gives them their novelty in our time is their greater quantity, scale, and continuity, and their greater relative weight as a determinant of social struggle. Their changed and magnified role is a consequence of the change, which we have surveyed, in the nature of modern war. Some writers refer to these measures in general as "subversion." If this word is understood broadly enough, and stripped of its moral associations, it is probably as good as any.

From the beginning, "subversion" has been a principal and continuously used field of communist action. In making our own plans, we have the communist experiences and even some of the communist personnel (former members who have broken with the Party) to learn from. During the Second World War, each combatant, whatever its theory of warfare, found it expedient to make considerable use of these methods, and, in the case of most combatants, advisable to create organizations specializing in them (the United States Office of Strategic Services, and the British so-called "SOE" and "D" Organizations are examples). This source, too, is rich in lessons both positive and negative.

The non-communist powers largely broke up the specialized organizations after V-J Day. But again during the last year or two, direct experience has led to the occasional and increasing use of the subversive methods. What is called for is a great expansion and a more conscious direction of what has already begun.

In order to illustrate these methods, and in order to be concrete, I shall refer to specific instances from the recent past, when the methods might have been effectively used but were not or were used insufficiently; to instances of the present when they could be; or to instances which will probably arise, or could be made to arise, in the future. My specific references, however, are intended only as examples, illustrations. Others, as apt or more promising, could without doubt be found by anyone who tried to work out a program of action with the same orientation. The main point is not this or that specific action, but the general plan, the central objective, and the basic methods of implementation.

4

Before, however, considering the specific content of a plan for offensive political-subversive warfare, it would be well to drag into the open a question which, ordinarily, lurks secretly in the background. Why should not the United States launch an all-out armed attack at once, and get the whole business over with? If the Soviet Empire is weak but may well overcome many of its weaknesses, if it does not yet have nuclear weapons in usable quantity but within a few years will have, if the issue of communist world domination has got to be settled some time, then what are we waiting for? Why not start what is usually (though, as we have noted, wrongly) called a "preventive war"?

This question is too serious to be left, as it now is, to closed and private debate. The answer is neither self-evident nor easy.

In the United States, the idea of striking the first armed blow is morally repellent to most people. I believe that this moral attitude arises out of intellectual confusion. From a strict pacifist standpoint, it naturally follows that it is morally wrong to start the fighting in a war. It also follows that it is morally wrong to fight back if someone else starts. Pacifism is, therefore, irrelevant to the issue, since pacifism condemns all fighting on every occasion.

The general, non-pacifist public seems to feel that a "defensive" war is morally superior to an "offensive" war. The distinction here, however, is not based on objective fact but only on subjective sentiment. From a military point of view, a successful strategy in modern war is always offensive; a defensive strategy is never more than a temporary bridge to the offensive. In terms of historical causation, everyone recognizes that modern wars do not start with the firing of the first shots, but have their source in a whole series of events that mark the developing conflict between two nations or sets of nations. Thus the question of who fired the first shot could not possibly answer the deeper question of who was, historically speaking, the "aggressor."

The fact is that both sides in a modern war are both "defenders" and "aggressors." Each is defending what it takes to be its own interests; and, necessarily, offending, attacking, what the other side takes to be its own interests. Otherwise they would not be fighting. It is because of this fact that the great majority of the people on each side—no matter what has gone on in the military sphere—genuinely and sincerely believes that it is "defending" itself against the "aggressions" of the other side.

These characteristics hold for all modern wars, but the usual distinction between "defensive" and "aggressive" is especially absurd at the present time for the plain reason that the war is already going on. It is no longer a problem of starting a war, but of winning it, or losing. The communists have the objective of world domination. From the point of view of the non-communist nations, they are therefore already the aggressors. Of course, from the communist point of view, the situation is reversed: it is those who interfere with the attainment of their objective who are the aggressors.

Assuming the rejection of absolute pacifism, the question of where and when to shoot is a matter of expediency. If there is good reason to believe that a sudden, massive armed blow would in the net result, as compared with waiting for such a blow from the enemy, save many lives and goods, result in less destruction and social disintegration, give a better chance for building a workable world polity, then to strike such a blow, far from being morally wrong, is morally obligatory. If there is to be war in any case, it is hard to comprehend why a war is morally better because it is more difficult, longer, more cruel and costly and bloody. A quick war, it seems to me, is better than a long one; an easy war, than a hard one.

The problem is not abstract. There are few today who would not agree that when Hitler's troops marched into the Rhineland, it was those—few alas—who urged an immediate attack who were morally, as well as militarily, superior to the deciding many who waited for the offensive against Poland, and Pearl Harbor.

In the present case, moreover, we can be almost certain that if the United States launched an immediate full-scale attack, it would be able to win a military victory. This too is morally not unimportant. That the Confederate leaders attacked Fort Sumter was not their worst crime; what was morally most reprehensible was to take their people into a war in which they had no reasonable expectation of victory. They condemned their people not merely to die and suffer, but to die in vain.

So much for the historical and moral issue. Whether or not to begin a full military war is a problem of expediency. If so, we must determine whether such an act is in truth expedient, now. It seems to me that it is not, for the following reasons.

In the first place, it is an obvious duty to hold off from a total armed conflict so long as there is a reasonable chance, even a very small chance, that the crisis may be solved, and the necessary objective attained, without that conflict. It is the thesis of this book that such a chance is offered if the United States undertakes the prosecution of an offensive political-subversive war as the means for gaining its objective.

Second: even if we cannot thereby prevent an eventual total armed conflict, we can, by intelligent and vigorous action before its onset, make victory both easier and less destructive, materially and socially.

Third: the people of the United States itself, and of the world as a whole, are at present confused about the nature of the contest with communism, and badly prepared both for conducting that contest and for utilizing, in a fruitful and positive manner, the future defeat of communism. Political war against communism, if properly waged, is a method not only for weakening and perhaps defeating communism, but for educating non-communists. The methods of prosecuting the political war are also methods of preparing the personnel, minds, attitudes, and structures which can fill the vacuums that will be left by the collapse of the communist empire, and which can serve in the organization of a workable world order. Political-subversive war against communism now, rather than immediate all-out armed attack, thus not only assures victory, but assures also that the victory will be worth winning.

These are the three arguments that today seem to me sufficient to call for a decision against an immediate total attack. But though sufficient today, they may not be as the situation changes tomorrow. If, for example, the Soviet Union should devise a way of making quickly and on a mass scale nuclear or other weapons of mass destruction; or if the Soviet Empire should be driven through to the Atlantic, or should get and begin to enlarge an important foothold in South or Central America; then the decision might have to be sharply reversed. Such possibilities will be lessened if we adopt and carry out a plan of offensive political warfare. That is another and a powerful reason in favor of such a plan. Such a plan is, indeed, the only rational alternative to immediate armed attack.

CHAPTER X

A Deal with Russia

LET US SUPPOSE that tomorrow a large plane (an imitation B-29, let us say) flaunting a Red star should land at the National Airport at Washington, and that Stalin should descend from it. Let us suppose that he asked to see the President, that he was escorted to Blair House, and that, after a double toast in vodka and Bourbon, he spoke as follows:

"Mr. President, I am here as emissary of the Politburo, and thus of the Soviet Union. After a careful review of the entire situation, we have come to the conclusion that we are licked. To continue our present course can mean only that we shall be completely defeated, and our State and ourselves annihilated. If we are going to have to surrender in the end anyway, we might as well surrender now. We have always been realists, and we approach you now not as equals, but as the vanquished approach the victors. What are your terms? We are ready to meet them."

There is no public evidence that the President, or any other person or agency in Washington, would, on this supposition, have an answer.

It may be objected that this supposition, even understood as a fable, is impossible. The objection is justified. Neither Stalin nor any of his immediate colleagues will ever make that trip or ask that question, either literally or figuratively. They are irrevocably committed.

But if Stalin will not, Comrade X or Y, representing not the Politburo but perhaps a fraction of the Central Committee or the industrial commissariats or the kholkoz directors or even the MVD slave camp administrations, might. It is conceivable. If Comrade X would hesitate to come on his own initiative, he might be induced to respond to an invitation, properly worded.

If Comrade X asked for terms, what, then, is the reply?

2

Most of those who are concerned, either as executants or analysts, with policy toward the Soviet Empire, are aware that a careful distinction must be made between the Soviet rulers and the masses whom they rule. To be against communists and communism does not mean to be against the people of Russia or of the other now Soviet territories. It means quite the contrary, since the Soviet masses are the chief victims, not the accomplices, of the communist rulers; and the defeat of communism means the liberation, not the enslavement, of the Soviet masses. The slave camps, the purges, the desertions and surrenders during the Second World War, the prohibition of foreign travel, the pervasiveness of the secret police, as well as the direct evidence of those who have escaped, all prove beyond reasonable doubt that the majority of the subjects within the Soviet Empire does not identify itself with the regime.

The strategic significance of this distinction between the Soviet rulers and masses is evident enough. Potentially, at least, the masses are our allies, not our enemies. Our aim should be to make this continuously clear, and to widen, not heal, the internal Soviet breach.

The possibility of defeating communism without total war depends, in the last analysis, upon a sufficient internal breakup of the Soviet empire by revolutions of one kind or another—by political upsets which, whatever their social content and by whomever made, would at least crack the hold of the monolithic Kremlin machine. This is recognized by many of those in the United States who defend and explain the policy of containment. They argue that a firm containment of communist expansion will give the Soviet people, who hate their rulers, a chance, somewhere along the line, to revolt.

This perspective of internal Soviet revolt, and the distinction between the Soviet rulers and people upon which it is based, are vitiated, however, by a confusion typical of the sentimental liberalism which governs so much of American political reasoning. "The people," "the masses," not only in this case but in general, do not exist as an effective social force unless they are organized, articulated. So long as they are anonymous, amorphous, the masses are capable only of sporadic movements that may result in temporary disturbance, but can have no decisive outcome. In order to *act* on history, the masses must acquire a backbone and a head. The backbone: some degree of organization; the head: a leadership. (The two organs are, it would seem, a simultaneous creation, since it is the leadership that organizes.) Lacking these, the masses, the people, are protoplasm, steam without pistons, electricity without a circuit.

Among the laws of politics—and we know more of these laws than we choose to recognize or use—none is more firmly established than this: that within any established group, an internal revolution is impossible unless there is a division of the ruling élite. The élite is superior in power to the masses precisely because the élite is organized, *is* the leadership. It makes no difference how seemingly "intolerable" the condition of the masses may be. The condition of the Temple slaves of Egypt was dreadful almost beyond comprehension, but that did not prevent them from remaining slaves for century after century. The American Negroes, before 1860, were living under what were from a 19th century point of view intolerable conditions; but these conditions could not be basically altered until the American ruling classes divided. The lamentable condition of the French peasants and workers was not enough to bring about the French Revolution.

The communists understand this law perfectly, and they make it the first axiom of their method of maintaining themselves in power. The communists within the Soviet empire do deliberately what other ruling groups have done only half-consciously. They aim to include within their own monolithic machine all actual and potential leaders, and the controlling echelons of all organized social structures. Conversely, they aim to destroy all potential leaders whom they are not sure of being able to absorb into their own machine, and at the same time to destroy not only all organizations that are or might be opposed to themselves but even all organizations which have any independence or autonomy (since independence *might* evolve into opposition). The history of the revolution in Russia might be written coherently in terms of the pursuit of this double aim. We can see its operation in the day-to-day news from the nations taken over during recent years.

These considerations bear directly on the strategy of the struggle against communism. The idea that within the Soviet empire "the people" as such, the masses, will revolt successfully is an illusion. They will revolt only if they acquire a leadership, and through that leadership some measure of organization. Where will that leadership come from?

In part, the leadership can come from without. That is to say, a combination of exiles with representatives of the Western nations (in particular of the United States) can, if it succeeds in establishing some sort of contact with persons inside the Soviet empire, constitute at least part of the leadership which must be found if opposition movements are to develop seriously. But an external leadership is as a rule not enough. Leaders, at any rate of the second and third ranks, must be found internally.

Within the satellite nations, the communists have not yet succeeded in pulverizing the masses, and absorbing within their own machine all of the potential opposition leaders. Indeed, the party purges in the satellites are proving repeatedly that many of those who have joined the Party, for self-protection or from ambition, are not by any means reliable Kremlin-communists. The satellite regimes are still unstable. "The people" within them can revolt because there still exists an internal nucleus of leadership and opposition organization. The example of Yugoslavia shows, in fact, that such a "revolt," resulting in a profound modification of regime, can take place even without a mass civil war, and without external assistance (assistance, that is, from the West).

Yugoslavia had the advantage of its geographical position, the absence of the Red Army, and the presence of a strong and experienced army of its own. (Even these advantages, however, will not suffice to maintain Yugoslavian independence of the Kremlin, unless there is Western pressure and support.) It is doubtful that the Yugoslavian example can be followed exactly in other satellites. Help from the outside, in one or another degree and form, will be needed even for a successful beginning. The terms of the solution to the satellite political problem are, however, reasonably clear.

Within the pre-1939 boundaries of the Soviet Union, the situation is presented differently. There the communists have had thirty years to put their theories into practice; and there they have come much closer to their political ideal of an amorphous mass, without autonomous organization or articulation, confronted by a monolithic élite. Except in scattered spots here and there, in some sections of the Ukraine perhaps or in outlying areas, there is not even a potential leadership outside of the presently privileged strata: there is no "out-élite." * How then is an internal change of regime even possible? The unorganized, unled masses cannot revolt, cannot become a serious opposition. There can come from the masses waves of discontent that could include shapeless uprisings, disturbances, strikes, and sitdowns. Without leadership these can have no permanent issue. But if serious opposition requires leadership, where can that leadership be found when all leadership, including all potential leadership, is monopolized by the Party?

The answer is implicit in the analysis. The leadership in the first stages (except for what can be supplied externally) can only come

---

* The Soviet élite is wider than the Soviet communist party. It includes several million non-party members in economic management, the officer corps, etc. The Party, however, is the sole political articulation of the élite as a whole.

from *within* the Party itself, by a division in the Party. This fact is the master key to the overthrow—or even the serious weakening—of the Soviet regime from within. Therefore, since the overthrow of that regime is the supreme objective of United States policy, it is one of the master keys of correct United States strategy—one of the keys, not the sole key, because there are alternative means for entering that door.

The possibility of a division within the communist élite unquestionably exists. On a world scale, this is proved by Tito. For the Soviet Union proper, it is proved by the now continuous escapes and attempts to escape of Party members from the Soviet into the non-Soviet world. It is indirectly demonstrated by the fierce self-purging of the Russian party. The Soviet weaknesses which we surveyed in Chapter VIII are, we might say, the objective bases for a division within the Soviet party. Their combined effect is to generate doubts, fears, and conflicts. Each weakness is, in effect, an occasion for conflict: if Tito breaks away from the Kremlin, then there cannot but be a conflict of opinion within the party over what policy to follow toward Tito; if Stalin dies, then, since there is no "law of succession," a dispute over who should follow is inevitable (even though it should be kept within bounds); if a satellite economy is in crisis, then a difference over the solution of the crisis cannot be avoided.

Any division in the communist élite, of whatever kind on whatever subject, is an advantage to the struggle against communism. The maximum that can be expected from a division is the attainment of our objective without total war. Even a minimum simplifies the struggle, and cuts its cost. It must therefore be a general principle of our plan of action, penetrating throughout the plan, to promote, widen, exploit, and if possible guide such divisions.

There is little doubt that fear is the primary stimulus to communist division: fear that the communist enterprise will fail, a fear, induced by a knowledge of internal weaknesses, that could be augmented by an awareness of the growing strength and determination of the enemy, and by actual defeats—if actual defeats should be administered. Fear is not the only stimulus, and not in itself sufficient. At least some individual communists are troubled and divided within themselves by the frightful disparity between their nominal ideals and their real practice, a disparity which could be accepted by sincere men when they could think it temporary but which they are finding to be permanent and deepening. To this stimulus—of the "ideal"—I shall return in the next chapter.

There could also be the stimulus of hope. Within the communist movement, even the thought of opposition is dreadful: even thoughts seem to find their way into the files of the MVD. But if thoughts of opposition are dreadful, how much more so are the smallest opposition acts? I, as an individual communist, may be guilt-ridden through the dirtying of my ideals; I may be convinced that the communist enterprise is going to be defeated; I may be, subjectively, opposed to the regime; I may be ready to run the 99-per-cent risk of the MVD terror; but I still may not be prepared to turn to action. Unless I am a saint or a masochist, I will want a chance, however slight a chance, of a positive result. If I know in advance that, whatever I and any others like me do, the war and the atom bombs will still certainly come, and I and all like me will still be certainly annihilated, then I do not have an adequate motive for action.

An internal change in the Soviet regime depends upon the development of an internal opposition. The development of that opposition depends upon a division in the communist party. That division cannot take place unless those individuals who might bring it about have a positive perspective, have, that is, something to gain. Such a perspective can be offered only by the United States. To those individuals, the members of the potential opposition, the United States must say, in effect: We are ready to settle without war. Here are our demands. Meet them, and you may live.

3

It is a curious feature of the present world crisis that no one can be sure just what it is that the United States wants. Everyone who wishes to know can find out what the communists want: they want an absolute monopoly of world power. What exactly, in contrast to the communists, does the United States want? The policy of the United States is anti-communist; that much is apparent. What precisely does it object to in the communists?

Let us look at this question from the point of view of an imaginary communist party member who is subjectively ready to go into opposition, ready, in other words, to become part of the leadership of a movement against the present communist regime. Might not his meditations proceed somewhat as follows: "The way things are going, atomic war looks like a certainty before many years, and it looks as if we were the ones who are going to get atomized. I am not sure whether the United States is an imperialist aggressor, the way Stalin says, or a defender of peace, the way Truman says. Whichever it is, if Stalin and the Politburo go on as they have been, the United States is going to start fighting one of these days, because it is not going to stand by forever to be liquidated by stages. There must be many others in the Party who feel the way I do, and certainly the masses don't want Stalin's war. With help, we might be able to get rid of Stalin and the Politburo, and take over ourselves. Suppose we did? Have we any guarantee that that would stop the war? Wouldn't the United States still feel that it had to fight, Stalin or no Stalin, communism in the Kremlin or no communism? They demanded unconditional surrender from Germany, Hitler or no Hitler. Nobody representing the United States has ever made clear just what they are after in our case. If we've got to fight anyway, what is the use of risking my neck ahead of time, and weakening the country by an internal struggle? I'll keep my mouth shut, take plenty of vodka, and have a few more years, maybe, before I'm turned into a fission by-product."

Our imaginary communist is asking for a deal. In order to change his negative conclusion, or to have a chance of changing it, we have got to offer him one.

In order to list the terms of a deal with Russia—for that is what it amounts to—we must first state exactly and clearly just why we are against communism. However, not all of the reasons why we are against communism are relevant to a deal. We may not like Russian dances or caviar or painting, but Russia would not from such dislikes be judged an enemy. Politically, we have the right and necessity of being against any regime, against it to the extent of fighting and destroying it, insofar as it endangers our own security and our basic interests. This qualification is strict. We may be morally repelled by the religion, customs, political system, penal practices, and so on of another nation. If so, as human beings we would, and I think legitimately, try by peaceful means of education, persuasion, example, and perhaps even commercial advantage, to alter what repels us. Nevertheless, we would not have the right in such matters to intervene by force, unless the consequences of these beliefs, practices, or institutions were such as necessarily to threaten our own security and interests.

On the other hand, a deal with Russia would be meaningless if conceived as a detailed settlement of "the German problem," "the Austrian problem," "the Korean problem," "the Chinese problem," and all the other thousand "problems." If each and all of these detailed problems were settled, and to our satisfaction, another thousand would promptly arise. What is required is a general settlement.

Now the reason why the United States must be against the Soviet communist regime, must (whether American leaders are conscious of this or not) have as its objective the destruction of that regime, and must seek this objective if necessary by total war, is because Soviet-based communism seeks to rule the world, and to destroy, among all other non-communist powers and interests, the United States. This is not merely the communist aim (if it were merely the aim, it would have only a psychological interest); the aim is powerfully and uninterruptedly implemented in action. This aim is implemented along the following primary lines:

1. Throughout the world, communism directs an enormous fifth column, infiltrated into every social level. This fifth column has as its sole reason for existence the overthrow of all non-communist governments and institutions, and their replacement by the communist power monopoly.

2. The communist-controlled Soviet Union, from its home area and by its agents throughout the world, conducts a colossal and constant propaganda in furtherance of its aim of world domination.

3. The Red Army has operated, and continues to operate, both with uniformed troops and by undercover agents, beyond the Soviet borders, in order to further the subjection of new nations to the communist rule. Personnel of the MVD and of other Soviet institutions also operate in the same manner.

4. The Soviet Union has already taken over, by force and subversion, a whole series of nations.

5. The internal organization of the Soviet Union is on a complete war footing. Moreover, the militarization of Soviet society is, from the point of view of the rest of the world, irresponsible. This is true not only because the Soviet regime refuses to accept any explicit international inspection or control, but because the Soviet interior is sealed against the implicit control and surveillance that result from free intercourse with, and travel by, diplomats, journalists, students, tourists, and businessmen. It is not a mere matter of internal "tyranny," which could be dismissed as no business of outsiders. Granted the size and population of the Soviet sphere, and the nature of modern technology, the sealed and militarized totalitarian internal structure of the Soviet Union (and progressively of the added areas of the Soviet Empire) constitutes a permanent and uncontrolled threat to the non-communist world.

These are the five principal expressions, in action, of the communist aim of world domination. The elimination of these five, therefore, is the minimum basis of a deal with Russia.

4

Let us state again, in a positive formulation, the five principal clauses of a deal with Russia:

1. The liquidation *de facto* of the communist fifth column. What the deal must provide is not a formal declaration of "non-interference" such as was contained in the Roosevelt-Litvinov agreement of 1933, or a change of address, as in the fake dissolution of the Comintern in 1943. The form is of no importance; it is the fact with which the deal must be concerned. The world-wide communist fifth column exists. It is politically directed and organizationally controlled from and by the Soviet communist center. This control is not exercised, as sentimental liberals believe, by "fraternal relations" and a "community of ideas." It is assured in a most material way, by subsidies and terror, and rests upon a secret *apparat,* of direct professional agents * of the Kremlin, which constitutes the core and skeleton of every communist party.

The deal is not for a promise to liquidate, but for actual liquidation, for the performance. Needless to say, the performance would have to be proved, checked, and demonstrated in a wholly convincing manner.

It may be objected that even after the liquidation of the Soviet fifth column, communism would remain. It is true that there would still remain individuals within most countries who believed in one or another version of communist ideas, and enough of them in some countries to continue to form national communist parties. There would no longer, however, be a unified world movement, directed and sustained from a single powerful base. Communism would split, as did social-democracy in its day, into a variety of local sections. These, if they were still problems, would be local and domestic

---

* Ruth Fischer states, from direct experience in the inner Party, that *paid* Soviet functionaries made up one-twelfth of the large Party membership in pre-Hitler Germany. The *apparat* functions, of course, outside of as well as inside the Party; and there is at least one professional agent assigned to every front organization.

problems, to be solved—or not solved—in accordance with domestic ability and intelligence.

2. The cessation of Soviet-directed propaganda in furtherance of communist world domination. Here also, as in all its terms, the deal must call not for promises but for performance.

3. The total withdrawal of the personnel of the Red Army—uniformed or undercover, the MVD, and all other related Soviet institutions, from all territory outside the pre-1939 Soviet borders.

4. A free choice of government, after suitable preparation, by the peoples of all the territories and nations which have been submitted to *de facto* Soviet control since 1939. The suitable preparation would include the three measures already stated; the return of all those who have been imprisoned or sent to slave camps; the return of exiles; a period of education and discussion; and internationally supervised elections.

5. A sufficient modification of the internal Soviet structure to guard the world against its secret and irresponsible militarization. This would seem to require, as a minimum, two primary steps: the opening up of the Soviet Union to normal intercourse with the rest of the world—that is, the right of entry and unrestricted travel for visitors, journalists, diplomats, businessmen, students—and magazines and books; and, second, the prohibition of the manufacture of atomic and other weapons of mass destruction, together with the safeguarding of this prohibition by some such system of international inspection as is provided by the so-called "Baruch Plan."

These five measures (but nothing short of these) would be enough, I believe, to solve the present international crisis. They would not guarantee peace forever; no human measures could give that guarantee. But they would make unnecessary the total war that now so closely threatens our generation and our decade. We are not able to stop war "in general"—that is the illusion of pacifists. We can, sometimes, prevent *this* war—the specific war which specifically approaches. And that, after all, is enough.

The terms of this deal fall very far short of what we should, and do, desire with respect to Russia. This is particularly true in the case of the internal modifications that would be demanded. Ought the deal include integrally, for example, measures to guarantee a minimum of political freedoms within Russia—the right of political opposition, free speech and assembly, habeas corpus, and so on? Ought it to include provisions for a free choice of sovereignty not only by the recent satellite areas, but also by other areas within the Soviet Union, of which the Ukraine is the most important example, which are also historically "subject nationalities" and which retain today both an independent ethnic character and an aspiration for freedom? Ought it to provide for the suppression of slave labor?

Certainly we wish that these things should come to be. The question, however, is whether they should be included as parts of a deal which would be proposed as a substitute for war. (There is no doubt that, from expediency as well as from moral-ideological motives, these would be included among United States war aims, if it came to full-scale war.) I have given the objective criterion which legitimizes the demands that are incorporated in the proposed deal: we rightly insist on the elimination of those actions or patterns of action which, directly or through their consequences, are a genuine threat to our security or basic interests. By this criterion, the five measures which I have listed are all both justified and necessary. This is not so clear in the case of such additional demands as I have cited in this paragraph.

It may be added, however, that an actual carrying through of the five measures would result indirectly in many further internal Russian changes, among them, almost certainly, some degree of democratization, and at least an opportunity for the Ukraine and the slave laborers to acquire freedom. These demands do not, therefore, imply an "abandonment" of the Ukraine and of the slaves, but on the contrary a method, more favorable than that of total war, for their liberation.

This proposed deal with Russia is not to be thought of as a *bargain*. The five measures are not points to be haggled over, or to be "paid for" by "equal concessions" from the Western side. They are minimum demands, to be accepted, unilaterally and *in toto*.

Not as part of the deal, but as a purely voluntary appendix to it, the United States could, and should, offer an inducement, a compensation. The compensation should, it seems to me, consist of the following:

1. Implicit in the idea of a deal is the greatest possible gain for the Russians: namely, the United States would not, and would not need to, go to war.

2. Through the Baruch Plan, the United States has already freely offered to submit its own atomic installations and weapons to international inspection and control, and in the end, under proper guarantees, to international ownership.

3. Finally, it would seem both possible and wise for the United States to offer to Russia, contingent upon acceptance of the deal and the actual performance of the five measures comprised in it, most generous economic aid. Credits of twenty-five or even fifty billions of dollars would not seem excessive when compared to the costs of a new total war. This economic help would not merely be an inducement to the acceptance of the deal, but could be expected to have a transforming influence on the Russian people and their society.

5

It may well be objected that the whole idea of proposing "a deal with Russia" is silly. It is unlikely enough, it might be argued, that the United States government would ever be so undiplomatic as to put forward such a flat and plain proposal; but, if it were by some chance put forward, it is impossible that the communists would consider accepting it.

I readily agree that official communist acceptance would be so unlikely as to be all but impossible. The truth is that by accepting such a deal, the communists would in substance cease being communists. (That, indeed, is just the point.) Nothing, though, is quite impossible. A minutely long chance is worth taking, if success would mean no total war.

The motive for advocating a deal is not predicated upon the likelihood of the present regime's accepting it. A proposed deal can become, whether acknowledged or not, a chief part of the platform of an internal opposition to the regime. More than that, to propose a deal can be the signal for creating an opposition, for calling an opposition into existence. It gives an opposition a rallying ground, a *reason* for existence; it gives sense and point to opposition activity.

It is believed by many that a successful opposition to the regime cannot arise within the Soviet Union proper. Let us grant that it is unlikely. But we cannot know in advance that failure is certain. We cannot estimate the exact effect which would be produced by a shift of United States policy to a dynamic offensive, especially if the United States proceeded *as if* a successful opposition were possible, and planned its moves to aid the formation and growth of an opposition.

Even if a successful opposition is impossible, any opposition at all, even an embryonic and hidden opposition, even a growth of subjective opposition sentiment, would weaken the regime, and prepare some of the steps for its overthrow and replacement.

Quite apart from its relation to an opposition the leadership of which would include dissident members of the present élite, the proposal of a deal would have other and significant positive results. It would, for example, be a way, far more convincing than by abstract repetition of the principle, to show the Russian people that we regard them as our friends and allies, not as our enemies; and from the point of view of the Russian people, the deal would promise immense benefit and no loss. The specific measures comprised in the deal would make unmistakably clear to the peoples of the satellite areas that the United States holds the perspective of their liberation and freedom. Throughout the world, the publication of the deal's proposals would help to solve that puzzle which gnaws so persistently at so many minds: what does the United States want?

This proposed deal, and its specific provisions, are not a subject-matter for confidential conversation between ambassadors-at-large and deputy foreign ministers. They ought to be loudly and con-stantly proclaimed, in every public forum. Perhaps, if, in spite of all that is done or neglected, the armed showdown looms close, the proposed deal should become a final ultimatum.

CHAPTER XI

The Propaganda Attack

THERE IS NO LONGER any debate over the general question whether propaganda * is important in the modern world. Everyone knows and grants its importance, and translates this knowledge into practice: the businessman budgets his millions for advertising and public relations, governments their tens or hundreds of millions for "Agit-props" or "Ministries of Information," and armies establish their bureaus of "psychological warfare." Propaganda has always entered into the conduct of human affairs. In our time its role has been monstrously expanded by the invention of new techniques of communication, by the increase of mass literacy, by advances in psychological knowledge, and by the enfeeblement of fixed traditional beliefs which leaves the human psyche more exposed to manipulation.

The strategists of modern warfare have all come to accept, though with varying emphasis, the use of propaganda as a supplement to arms. The communists for two generations, and more recently many non-communists, have also understood the use of propaganda as a substitute for arms. Experience shows that in the present phase of

---

* I am using the word "propaganda" in a broad sense: any means of inter-human communication used for the accomplishment of an external practical end—political, religious, social, economic, etc., as the case may be. I am concerned chiefly, of course, with political propaganda, and more particularly with political propaganda as it relates, positively or negatively, to the supreme American political objective—the overthrow of the communist power. In the broad sense, propaganda is not in itself either good or bad, true or false. Propaganda may, and often does, employ lies; but it may also employ truths, or affective symbols which are, strictly speaking, neither true nor false.

the present war propaganda can be a primary weapon in the attainment of strategic goals.

The subject of propaganda is so complex and so vast that it would be ridiculous to suppose that anything very significant could be said about it in a single chapter of a single book. It can hardly be omitted, however, in the outline of a plan for political-subversive war. I shall limit myself to a series of comments on the four major questions concerning any propaganda program: how much? by what means? to what audience? with what content?

2

I have stated that many of the measures of subversive warfare are relatively cheap. Propaganda measures are not, unfortunately, among these. When the arena is, as it is, the world, a small, cheap propaganda program is no better than none at all. It cannot accomplish anything. Therefore, a cheap campaign is also the most expensive, since the money that has gone into it is altogether wasted. It is like buying an icebox on time, stopping payments a third of the way through, and losing both box and money. Propaganda must be massive, sustained, continuous, if it is to have effect.

The chief official (foreign) propaganda instrumentalities of the United States are at present the Voice of America (radio propaganda) and a certain amount of printed material, much of which is distributed through the United States Information Service. Many persons, including many Congressmen who must vote the appropriations, consider these instrumentalities to be extravagant luxuries. In a sense they are right: but not because these are so costly; rather, because they are isolated dainties, like a minute tin of high-priced caviar offered as a complete meal; because they are not an integrated part of a full-course plan of propaganda, which would cost ten or twenty times the present sums, and which would be in turn an integral part of the general war plan.

The need for massive propaganda is demonstrable. Without it, other measures taken in the struggle against communism often lose, in whole or in part, their positive effect in shifting the power balance. Through propaganda, moreover, independent results, counting heavily in the balance, are possible. This, surely, the communists ought to have taught us. The communist conquest of the Balkans would quite probably have been impossible without the aid of the propaganda campaign through which they deceived public opinion in England and the United States from top to bottom—all the way to the highest level of military and political leadership. Not the least, and perhaps the chief, factor in their conquest of China has been the brilliant and systematic propaganda offensive whereby they confused, disarmed, and sterilized American counteraction. Even our own more limited tests can teach us how positive and concrete the results can be. The accomplishments of the Berlin radio station of the American Occupation (RIAS) in the struggle over that fateful city is a recent and striking proof. Can Americans, who invented modern advertising, have any doubts?

I wish to cite, from direct experience, an example to show how necessary propaganda is to measures undertaken in other fields. In terms of money and national energy, the Marshall Plan has been the major postwar undertaking of the United States in international politics. It is a fact, which I discovered directly on the scene, and which can be confirmed by those other observers who have no motive for denying it, that hardly anyone in Western Europe understands the Marshall Plan. Many, very many, have never heard of it. What those who have heard have heard is usually an utter fantasy. The ignorance is not found merely among the rural populations and the uneducated; the ignorance, and above all the fantasy, extend right through to journalists, editors, deputies, and ministers. No one, or hardly anyone, knows whether the Marshall Plan aid is a gift or a loan; whether it comes in money or food and goods; whether it is building up or buying out European factories; whether Europeans have anything to say about what comes over, or whether it is all decided in Washington (or Wall Street); whether it was forced on Europe by rapacious American finance-capitalists, or sought by Europe. In this jumbled confusion, the only clear word —clear, and omnipresent, sounding even to the tiniest village—is that of the communists: the Marshall Plan is a conspiracy of American imperialism to enslave Europe, and to use the European peoples as cannon fodder in their war.

These are the psychological facts, when there has perhaps never been so favorable a basis for honest and straightforward—and at the same time immeasurably favorable—propaganda as has been created by the operations of the Marshall Plan. Whatever may be its motives and incidental aspects, the Marshall Plan has permitted Western Europe to live. The food, clothing, jobs, machines, trains, trucks, electricity of Western Europe are, in the most literal physical sense, Marshall Plan compounds. This should have been said plainly to every West European, and to the world. And that kind of talking takes money.

To the question, how much propaganda? the reply is: as much as possible, to the limit that the resources will sustain. There cannot be too much.

3

Americans, when they are considering the problems of international propaganda, are likely to assume short-wave radio to be the sole or by far the principal means of communication. In practice, the Voice of America has been our major official propaganda instrumentality. I certainly do not wish to deprecate either the use of short-wave radio in general or the Voice of America particularly; I wish to urge the expansion of both the general and the particular. At the same time, we should note important limitations in short-wave radio as the medium of propaganda, and stress the potentialities of other media.

Radio, especially short-wave radio, is strictly limited in the audience that it can reach (an obvious fact to which I shall return in the next section). Moreover, it utilizes only the single sense of hearing, whereas we know that communication is more effective and lasting when it occurs through two or more modes of perception. Propaganda can be communicated through any physical signs which are capable of expressing or stating meanings (feelings, sentiments, ideas, etc.), and it is unwise to neglect any feasible means. In practice, the rich variety of visual media should be more abundantly added to the aural.

This means, simply: books, magazines, newspapers, pamphlets, throwaways, posters, cartoons, maps, charts, pictograms, movies, plays, stickers, labels, matchbox covers, stencils, and scrawls on walls . . . there is hardly any limit to what ingenuity can devise. In every country of the world, there ought to be at least one newspaper, magazine, and publishing house defending the point of view of the world anti-communist offensive. Where such do not exist, they ought to be created. Personal letters, for another example, have more than once proved their propaganda efficacy—they served rather well in the 1938 Italian elections, to cite a publicized case. Our propaganda field, it must be remembered, is the world. The struggle against communism is not something that goes on against an enemy confined within definite geographical borders. He is everywhere, and his influence is to one or another degree within nearly everyone. We must wish to speak to everyone in Europe, Africa, Asia, Australia, Latin America, and in the United States, as well as to everyone within the communist empire.

To penetrate the Iron Curtain, radio is no doubt—or seems to be—the easiest solution. But we learned during the war (and much of what we have not learned the communists can teach us) that there are techniques by which printed words (or their equivalents) can be sent almost anywhere to almost anyone. Groups of exiles from the satellite nations and from Russia have found it possible during these recent years, even with their meager material resources, to maintain liaison with their homelands, and to send in words even so elaborate in form as books and magazines. These words are better to drop, and can sometimes be more effective, than bombs.

It should not be thought that all propaganda must be "official," governmental. On the contrary, much of what is propaganda in effect, whatever it may be in intention, does and ought to come, in the case of a non-totalitarian nation, from private individuals and organizations. However we may qualify our own appreciation of the European edition of the *New York Herald Tribune,* the *New York Times* overseas air edition, the air editions of *Time* and *Newsweek,* the foreign editions of *Reader's Digest,* these are eagerly and thoroughly read and re-read in other countries. The net result is not in the communists' favor. The peoples of the world today rather generally understand that there are now only two great powers. These two powers are mysterious, and awesome. There is an immense curiosity. Again and again I have been asked by Europeans: is there no way whereby we can get more American books and magazines? The dollar crisis makes it impossible to import them through normal trade, but can't some arrangement be made so that they will be available, at least in every town of any size? They do not mean "propaganda books," but the books and magazines that the American public itself reads, and through which they will be able to feel that they are coming closer to the mind and reality of the strange Western Power. There is no reason why private individuals, clubs, and foundations cannot act to answer this wish and need without waiting for a law by Congress or an official decision by the State Department.

4

All those who have had experience with any sort of propaganda—advertising, public relations, religious or political propaganda—know that the specific audience aimed at is an important determinant of the forms, techniques, and even the content of the propaganda instruments. You do not discuss the tensor calculus with the presumed clientele of a soap company. There is no use distributing pamphlets to those who cannot read, nor do you recommend Cadillacs to Bulgarian peasants. Nevertheless, there is always some method, if only we are ingenious enough, for communicating with anyone: the human is a communicating animal.

At what audience do we aim in the propaganda offensive of the war against communism? In a sense, we aim at all human beings, though not at all on all occasions. Therefore we must have a propaganda program operating at every level, from cartoons to treatises.

There is one particular audience which we have so far neglected, but which, I have tried to show in previous sections of this book, is both of the highest importance and also, now, accessible. That audience is composed of the communist party members themselves and their close associates, throughout the world and especially inside the Soviet Empire, above all within the Soviet Union proper.

Indeed, within the Soviet Union, and to a lesser but increasing extent within the satellite countries, the communist élite is, from a plain practical standpoint, the only audience there can at present be for radio propaganda. Within the Soviet Union, the masses have access to only two kinds of radio receivers: weak, inexpensive sets able to receive only the closest local station; and centralized more powerful sets, as in most collective farms, villages, and many city apartment houses, parks, etc., which, connected with a number of loudspeakers, and under the control of a functionary, provide approved collective listening. Even most of those who, in the cities, could afford more powerful sets (which are made only in small quantities) would not dare to use them for foreign reception, since they live crowded together with other families in a flat where they always are, or fear that they are, spied upon. Only the party élite and the affiliated non-party section of the privileged élite have both the money and the privacy required to own and to use sets capable of getting the foreign broadcasts.

Technical advance may make it possible to reach the others, but meanwhile it is absurd to try to address "the Russian people" with a communication which it is physically impossible for them to hear. (I omit further reference to my own conviction, motivated in Chapter IX and elsewhere, that it is at present more important to reach the communist élite: a superfluous reinforcement of the conclusion to be drawn from the physical facts, which are themselves decisive.) Though this is, or would seem to be, obvious enough, it is not always remembered by the Voice of America.

Upper-level communists, who are the potential Soviet listeners, constitute an audience which is in most respects, and certainly in politics, highly sophisticated. There is no use in talking to them as if they were peasants, or ten-year-olds who didn't know the facts of political life. There is little point in informing them that Russia is a dictatorship or has slave-labor camps: they know such things much better than we do. Nor is there anything, I think, to be gained by "sweetening" programs to them by music or humor or "drama." We must enter—can only enter—their minds and feelings through routes that are familiar to them. They, or some of them, want information, facts, genuine news—which they cannot get and which they know they cannot get from their own press and radio. This can be supplied amply and without adornment. They would be, or could be, interested in thorough, high-level theoretical discussion of what are for them the burning problems: Titoism, war, the conflict between their ideals and their practice, Stalin's successor, productivity and technology, and so on. The problem is quite different from that of selling Wheaties.

5

There is a theory of propaganda, widely though as a rule implicitly held in the United States, that might be called "Propaganda for Propaganda's sake." Propaganda is thought of as an independent field, a "thing in itself" which can be "good" or "bad" without reference to anything beyond itself. It is this implicit theory which may explain the way in which propaganda divisions of the government tend to be set up. Experts in the techniques of propaganda—from advertising, public relations, journalism, social psychology—are brought together to staff and run a propaganda division. Since they genuinely are experts, as skilled in the techniques as anyone in the world, they are expected, on the basis of the theory, to turn out first-class propaganda. Often they do not.

Propaganda is in reality not a thing in itself, but an instrument. It exists for the sake of something other than itself, for the objective which it is the business of the propaganda to serve. As Hitler correctly insists in *Mein Kampf,* no propaganda is either good or bad except in relation to its objective. We are concerned here with political propaganda: that is, propaganda designed to serve a political objective. Such propaganda can be significant and effective only as an integral part of a policy which is as a whole significant and effective—that is to say, a policy which has made a correct estimate of the situation, has clearly defined its objective, and then takes those measures—of which propaganda measures are one category—which do in fact lead toward the achievement of the objective.

When we ask, what should be the content of American propaganda in the present war against communism? the answer is: this is not an independent or separate question. The content of the propaganda is simply the war plan as a whole, the plan of action. The function of the propaganda is to reinforce, supplement, further the actions decided on in pursuit of the objective. If the policy is vague or self-contradictory, then the correlated propaganda will be futile no matter how "expert." If the actions are wrongly conceived, then the most skillful of propaganda will only make their results all the worse. For these reasons, it is quite wrong to think that the *direction* of propaganda should be turned over to technical experts. The direction is a political task, and a task for the highest political leadership. The practical execution should of course make use of technical experts, and of the most qualified experts available. In the present war, a propaganda division headed by persons who understand communism, the nature of the present war, and the issues of contemporary world politics, but staffed by inferior technicians would show net results far superior to one manned by the finest technical experts in existence but run by political incompetents. In

the Soviet Empire, it is the Politburo that is the Directorate of Propaganda.

Not only should propaganda be correlated with the general plan
as a whole. Propaganda is almost always most effective when it is
tied specifically to specific actions and projects. Propaganda which
does not connect up with action is a ruffling of the surface which
leaves the substance unchanged. This was interestingly shown, in one
sphere, during the Second World War. All of the armies conducted
propaganda in the field, by various methods, to induce soldiers of
the opposing side to desert and surrender. When a given army was
passive in a military sense, or losing, its propaganda to this end had
seldom any effect. Only when it began fighting hard did the deserters begin to respond. This did not prove that the propaganda
was useless; propaganda did, in many battles and campaigns, bring
important results, but only when it was an adjunct of action of
another kind.

It follows that it is impossible to draw up in advance a blueprint
for the content of propaganda in the present war. The content is
properly determined by the actions that are successively undertaken.
If we launch, say, a Marshall Plan as a major action, then a major
propaganda campaign to explain, recommend, reinforce, and capital-
ize on the Marshall Plan is called for. If we wish to promote a
Titoist tendency in China, then *one* of the means for implementing
this wish is to make sure that the Chinese communists know all
about Tito, and to discuss with them constantly, by propaganda, the
issues in the Tito controversy.

There are, however, three methodological principles (as they
might be called), affecting the content of propaganda in the present
war, which I feel require some comment.

1. In discussing these matters during recent years, I have often
encountered the opinion that can be summarized as follows. The
democracies cannot have an effective propaganda against communism until they can offer a positive "world-view" to take the place

of the communist world-view. The communists have a complete, systematic "answer" to the problems and aspirations of mankind. We can't just be "against communism." We have to provide a "better answer."

I have come to the conclusion that this opinion, and the feeling of guilt which usually goes with it, are themselves in considerable measure a by-product of successful communist propaganda. The communists have persuaded many of us who are subjectively non- or anti-communists to believe nevertheless that we have to have a total world-view (*Weltanschauung*) of the same *kind* as that of the communists. Since by the nature of the situation we *cannot* have such a belief, we are insensibly led into attitudes of frustration and passivity.

In the first place, the communists do not have an "answer" to either the problems or the aspirations of mankind. What they have is a totalitarian ideology which is full of internal contradiction and is, much of it, false in empirical fact. Far from embodying the aspirations of mankind, this ideology serves in historical reality as the justification or rationalization of a regime which not only has imposed on men the most complete and total terror ever known, but has also proved itself incapable of bringing either material well-being or any fulfillment of cultural and moral ideals. It has been demonstrated that this ideology, so apt at destruction, is impotent to build. The fact that this ideology has, temporarily, a dynamic that results in part from its rigidly orthodox monism, and an attraction that springs from its disguised appeal to irrational passion and base resentments, should not lead us to wish to imitate it, or to despair of combatting it.

We cannot counter this totalitarian ideology with "our own" ideology of the same total order because such ideologies are an essential part, precisely, of what we are fighting against. We are not against merely the communist totalitarian ideology (which is the symbolic mask of the communist totalitarian enterprise for world domination); we were also against the Nazi totalitarian ideology, and we shall be against any other of the same breed. We will never get, and we ought not want, any such "answer."

It is not true, in the second place, that a war or a social struggle can be successful only if the program and apologetics for it are "positive" in form. The contrary is more often true. In general, human beings understand much more clearly what they are *against* than what they are *for*. Nor is this a mere perversity in human nature. What we are against is ordinarily something limited, concrete, historically present: a specific tax or law or institution or form of oppression that blocks the pursuit of what we regard as our legitimate interests. What we are for is something that does not exist and is therefore not subject to the limits and restraints of real existence; it is an ideal construction, compounded, by desire more than by knowledge, out of the unlimited possibilities of an imagined future. The men who made the French Revolution knew very well what they were against—the restrictions and privileges and interferences that were maintained by the *ancien régime,* and these they got rid of: that is to say, their revolution was successful. But the content of the Liberty, Equality, and Fraternity, which they imagined they were for, was very cloudy in their minds, as the event also proved.

We—and we in this case is the great majority of men—are against the domination of the world by a gang of self-maddened technicians of power. We are against the enslavement of nations and peoples, counter to their will, by corruption, lies, and conquest. We are against the reduction of society to the uniform pattern of a spy-ridden slave camp. We are against the strait-jacketing of science and art and invention in the rigid corset of a banal and degrading dogma. We are against the torture and sacrifice of human beings on the bloody altars of these faceless gods, Historical Necessity and the Revolution. We are against the sapping and mining and sterile smashing of every institution and human relation which men have so long and so painfully fitted together in their never to be ended contest against the darkness of nature. We are against power which is legitimized only by power.

But in knowing what we are against, we are also defining, not exactly but in direction, what we are for. We are for the restraint of power by custom, moral principle, and by law. We believe individual human beings to be of an infinitely higher moral worth than any secular end or goal. We believe in an open, not a closed society, in the right of men and nations to be different—within the limits, at any rate, that are imposed by that very right; and in their freedom to explore varied routes to earthly and eternal salvation. We are, quite specifically, for the liberty of those nations that have been subjected to the communist tyranny, and for the removal of the threat to the freedom of all other nations. We are for the right of men not to be snatched from bed at three in the morning by the agents of an uncontrolled secret police. We are for a world order, based on law, which will permit men to advance creatively, without the threat—and actuality—of perpetual war, and the paralyzing weight of fear and systematic terror.

We have no reason to feel inferior about the potential of our propaganda, or its ability to move men to action.

2. Communism is not only an underground army and a conquering empire, but a secular religion, the systematic dogma of which is the ideology of "dialectical materialism." The communist religion is secular in that its postulated Paradise is of this world, not of a world beyond space and time and the grave. The ideology has this curious feature: it hoists the banner of "reason" and "science"; it claims in fact to be the *only* truly scientific account of reality, and of all reality (a claim which, ironically enough, is in itself sufficient to prove that it is *not* scientific).

From its secularism and from its pretense of scientific rationality springs a weakness of a special and penetrating kind which does not in any such manner affect religions and ideologies which are frankly other-worldly, transcendental. A transcendental religion which has as its goal the Kingdom of God, not of man, and which bases its dogma in key essentials on faith, revelation, or some other transcendental source, is thereby exempt from control by empirical evidence. You cannot refute by empirical evidence that to which empirical evidence is irrelevant. (It was a naïveté of the 18th century rationalists and the 19th century professional atheists to imagine, as they did, that they had "refuted" the Church. In the 18th and 19th centuries, a considerable number of Europeans ceased believing in the Church from historical and psychological causes that had little to do with evidence, and for which the atheists' proofs were only what Pareto calls "derivations.") Communism is also forced to reject the world, and empirical evidence derived from the observation of the world. But in doing so communism is inwardly divided.

Doctrinally, communism is committed to the world and to science. In fact, communism cannot sustain the test of the world, of science, of the evidence. That is why the Politburo must hide the world from its subjects, and its subjects from the world. That is why faithful communists must howl down, and finally exile and kill, every critical opposition: they have no other answer than terror. That is why they cannot permit their own ablest scientists to pursue their scientific work in accord with the evidence which they discover and the interpretations which they would make under the guidance of scientific methods and procedures. And that is why the communist leadership must continually rewrite history, falsify statistics, suppress true news and invent imaginary news, censor and lie. They must do these things because neither their beliefs nor their performance can endure the facts. They cannot, as transcendental religions have often done, simply dismiss the world as maya, illusion, unimportant. Since they profess science and a secular aim, they must *actively falsify*.

The account of reality, history, and society given by dialectical materialism is, in many and key propositions, false. In historical experience, communism, professing the contrary aims and claiming to be the sole and inevitable way of fulfilling them, has without exception so far meant less freedom, more and more rigid class differentiation, an increase in income differentials, a continuous increase in the state and police power, a revival of slavery, an increased militarization, a worsening in the material level of life. Other militant religions have also been full of falsehood, and have also brought increased human evils. But they have not, like communism, linked their destiny to this earth.

This conflict deep within the communist ideology is also a source of unrest and division within the souls of communists, and of others who are or who might be attracted to communism. From an understanding of it there follows a conclusion of strategic importance: truths, plain truths and as many of them as possible, are a wonderfully effective content of anti-communist propaganda, whether directed at non-communists or at the communists themselves. Truthful news, truthful history, truthful statistics, truthful studies of the Soviet Union itself, of Europe, Asia, and the United States. Truth is not enough for a complete propaganda; there must also be a content that will stir feeling and will; and we must not be so hypocritical as to fail to admit that carefully designed deception is sometimes necessary. Nor should we take comfort in the sentimental platitudes that the truth (alone) will make us free, that truth crushed to earth will (unaided) always rise again. There is no evidence that truth has any such magic and sufficient power. Nevertheless, communism and communists are vulnerable to the truth.

Dwellers on the eastern seaboard of the United States, who can begin their breakfast with vast depositaries of news, most of it truthful, in such papers as the *New York Times* or *Herald Tribune* or the Baltimore *Sun,* and who (in this like other Americans) can hear from their radio, every hour, news reports that are reasonably free and uncensored, and read each week any of several fat magazines of news which, however oddly presented, is seldom falsified, underestimate the extent of the ignorance elsewhere about the simplest and most important truths concerning what is going on in the world. All the newspapers combined of Continental Europe do not give a fraction of the facts presented in the *New York Times,* and

they give many times the number of falsehoods. The literate supporters of the present revolutionary movements in China, India,
Southeast Asia, and the East Indies know very few of the truths
about the Soviet Union and communism. If they knew more, they
would be unlikely to turn, as many of them have done, to a force
which is certain to destroy all that they seek. As for the people of
the Soviet Union itself, they are allowed by their masters to know
nothing.

Let the truths then be known, and, without diplomatic niceties,
all the relevant truths.

3. We should learn from the communists, and apply three of the
great practical laws of effective propaganda. First, our propaganda
should not be dispersed in content over every possible subject, but
should concentrate on a small number of the most important matters (I do not refer here to news, which is obviously dictated by
what happens). Second, propaganda should not jump back and
forth, day by day, from one subject to another, but should be organized in sustained *campaigns* that hammer away on a single line for
day after day, month after month. Third, propaganda should always
be offensive, should always keep the initiative. It should never be
diverted by an enemy propaganda attack to a purely defensive
rhetoric of defense and reply. If a reply has to be given, then the
reply should be made the occasion and point of departure of a
renewed attack.

These three laws, verified by all practical experience, are not always easy to obey unless they are consciously and continuously held
in mind. It is, for example, a standardized device of Soviet propaganda to keep making such outrageous and often preposterous ac-
cusations against their enemies that they in turn are led to waste
their energies in defensive protestations and proofs of innocence. It
is as grievous an error to be so diverted on the field of propaganda
as it is to be, on the field of battle, deceived into an improper concentration by a fake offensive.

It is hard also to concentrate on sustained campaigns, especially against an enemy so wily. There seems to be so much to say, but trying to say all about everything only guarantees that nothing will be lastingly communicated. Better to say much about a few things: Titoism (the relation of the satellite nations to the Soviet Union); labor and welfare under communism; the problem of the succession to Stalin; the nature of the communist fifth column; the proposed deal with Russia. . . . The communist ideology, like the communist state, has the weakness as well as the strength of its rigidity. A single wedge, driven deep in the mind, can shatter its structure.

CHAPTER XII

The War in the Labor Movement

ALL SOCIAL SCIENTISTS recognize that one of the principal historical phenomena of the past century has been the emergence of "labor" ("the working class," "the proletariat") as a major social force. This could not happen until a relatively large number of workers, and more particularly industrial workers, existed in society: workers in the formal sense of free citizens who sell their services, their labor power, for wages to employers. Through what we call the industrial revolution, the workers, drawn from the land and from the ranks of the formerly independent artisans, came to be. The mere large number of workers was not enough to make "labor" a major social force. So long as the workers were an atomized and formless mass, labor was historically minor. In order to become historically significant, the workers had to be organized. The conditions for their organization were also provided by the industrial revolution, in that the workers were not left scattered in space, but were brought together in groups into factories and mines and workshops. The actual organization of the workers (not of all of them, but of sufficiently many) was well started during the second half of the 19th century, and has gone on during this first half of the 20th.

Those who succeeded in organizing the workers, or in gaining control of labor organizations forged by others, have, as "labor bureaucrats" or "labor managers," become the leaders of this new social force. The labor managers, disposing of one of the greatest powers of industrial society, become, as could not fail to happen, part of the élite of that society. In any society, the leaders of the great social forces become, or rather are, the élite. In the case of a new social force, if the old élite is unable or unwilling to receive the leaders of the new force, and to find a place for them as part of the "in-élite," then these newcomers constitute an "out-élite." A revolutionary situation arises which, if the doors of the in-élite remain closed, can eventuate only in the overthrow of the existing society or the crushing of the new force.

The advance during the 20th century of the labor managers into the ranks of the élite is plainly marked in all industrial nations. The labor managers have become what Americans call "big shots." Their pictures are in the newspapers and magazines, their names are on the radio, their speeches are internationally reported. When they take a trip, or pay a call, or go to the hospital, it is public news. In one after another nation, they have formed political parties of their own which have rapidly overhauled the older parties; or have, as with the Democratic party in the United States, taken over a sizable share in the leadership of one of the older parties. In many nations—Denmark, Norway, Sweden, Belgium, Britain, Australia, France, New Zealand, Mexico, Germany, and others—they have entered, or become, "the Government."

How could it be otherwise? And how childish are the wishful fantasies of outmoded financiers who think that somehow they will "put labor in its place"! Nor is it correct to say, as many do, that totalitarianism "crushes labor organization." What totalitarianism does, on the contrary, is to complete the organization of labor, to crush not it but its independence, and to fuse its leadership into the monolithic totalitarian élite.

2

The communist ideology (dialectical materialism) prominently includes what can be called a labor *mystique,* a mystique of the proletariat. The proletariat is figured as the Messianic class—savior and redeemer. "The Revolution" is *its* revolution, and the period following the apocalyptic conquest of power is "the dictatorship of the proletariat." The proletarian dictatorship is, however, to lead to the salvation of all mankind in "the classless society"—that is, the earthly Paradise.

All this is an eschatological myth in traditional form, which need not further concern us. In Marx's writings, however, the proletariat is also a term in many statements which are presumably intended to be empirical, descriptive statements of fact. Almost all of the chief of these are false. Their falsity is deceptive, because it consists in asserting, as an unconditioned law, relations which, within limits and in some situations, do hold. For example: It is false that (in any empirical sense) the economic class struggle is the ultimate cause of all historical change; it is false that all interests of labor and capital are always objectively opposed; it is false that the development of capitalism means, as Marx predicted, the proletarianization of the overwhelming majority of mankind (he did not anticipate the growth of "service industries," of the "new middle class" of managers, technicians, professionals, etc.); it is false that the development of capitalism means, as Marx predicted, the pauperization, and reduction to a bare subsistence level, of the workers; it is false that proletarian class consciousness drives out national, race, and religious consciousness; and it is false that the workers are wholly "alienated" in the sense of being "in but not of capitalist society." *

Under Lenin's guidance (theoretically formulated in his fateful book, *What Is To Be Done?*), the ideological medley of myth and

---

* Marx's use of the word "proletariat" to designate the workers in modern industrial society is in reality a subtle begging of the very questions that are at issue. This word was used in late Republican Rome to refer to the crowd of ex-slaves, ex-prisoners of war, small farmers who had lost their land with the extension of the *latifundia,* ruined younger sons of decaying patrician families, debtors, etc., who lived swarming in the Roman tenements, had no jobs or any other positive functional relation to society, and were in fact as well as in feeling "alienated." The analogy from Rome, therefore, is not in reality to the working class proper of industrial society, but to the derelicts, drunks, panhandlers, petty crooks, and gangsters who drift around the streets of modern cities—or to workers (or those from any other class) who become outcast and demoralized from long unemployment.

error changes, or acquires, its practical meaning. The ideology becomes fully transformed into the secular religion of the communist army of world conquest. The Revolution becomes, in historical fact, the task of the Party, a Party of professional revolutionists, with the leaders for the most part intellectuals, not workers. The post-Revolutionary dictatorship becomes the dictatorship of the Party.

The Party is to go into *all* classes and all institutions of existing society, in order to destroy them. In Lenin's perspective, the working class is still given major consideration. It is now viewed practically, as the principal *strategic social weapon* to be *used* by the Party in its drive for the conquest and consolidation of power. And, though the Marxian doctrine of labor is false, there are enough partial truths reflected (and distorted) in it to make possible this strategic exploitation: not because of any historical necessity, but by the decision and action of the professional revolutionists. If industrial society "naturally" tends to raise, rather than lower the workers' level of life (as indeed seems to be the case by the evidence), then the revolutionists will themselves create such economic chaos that the dialectical law of pauperization will be fulfilled. If, objectively, labor and capital have some interests in common (as surely they do: is not what we call "prosperity" good for both?), then the revolutionists will by their action and propaganda incite a subjective class hatred in which the objective facts will be blotted from consciousness. If the workers are not alienated by history, then the revolutionists will alienate them.

The communists, therefore, always, in all nations, strive for control of the labor movement—control, that is, of the organized workers. By brilliant use of their method of "fractions," they can win and hold this control even as a minute minority over the great majority. With control, they have gained weapons which, on command, can cripple or smash industries, transport, mines, communications; they have vantage points for every type of intelligence; they have a concealed entrance into governments and liberal sympathies;

and they have a fruitful garden from which to harvest a human crop apt for their own ranks.

Throughout the world, in Asia, Europe, Australia, and the Americas, the communists have scored great victories in their labor campaigns. Though their labor influence has been weakened in the United States since 1947—primarily by the able tactics of anti-communist labor leaders, aided by a hardening of the American public consciousness against communism—the enormous gains which they made on a world scale during the war and immediate postwar period have been generally held. The communist strength in the labor movement cannot be correctly estimated by a mere quantitative comparison of statistics (number of workers in communist-controlled unions vs. the number in non-communist unions). Even in unions which they do not control, the communists have almost always a party fraction; and the communist unions have often a stronger and more dynamic organization than the non-communist.

The communist labor strength is greater than it seems to be from the statistics, because communist operations in the labor movement are governed, as I have discussed in Part II, by a coherent strategic plan. Let me again emphasize the strategic significance of the great campaign of communist-controlled labor action which started in the autumn of 1948, and continued through the summer of 1949. For three months the western ports of the United States were shut more tightly than they could ever be by naval blockade. The dock strike isolated Hawaii. There followed the London dock strike; the Australian coal strike (which also affected the Australian ports); the Italian maritime strikes; the series of Finnish strikes based on the lumber workers (timber is Finland's chief industry), and the closing of all Finnish ports except those used for shipping to the Soviet Union; and the auxiliary actions of the French communications workers and the Italian farm laborers. This coordinated campaign, directed from the Communist center and brilliantly executed, was not an "economic action" or even, as some observers described it, a "political action," but more exactly a strategic action: it was an actual campaign in the present phase of the war, and at the same time a rehearsal for the fiercer campaigns of the phase of the war which the communists expect to come.

3

The general plan of political-subversive anti-communist war must have as one of its principal implementing objectives the aim of breaking the hold of the communists on the world labor movement. This aim cannot, moreover, be served by those reactionaries who, as if themselves inverse communists, act to complete the alienation of labor by a class struggle point of view no less intransigent and destructive than that of the communists, and who wish to use the struggle against communists in the labor movement as a device for smashing labor organization and pulverizing the workers.

The need for operations in the field of the international labor movement * has been increasingly recognized by the United States during recent years. Labor attachés and specialists have made their appearance on the staffs of embassies and missions. International labor organizations and conferences have been activated. The Occupation governments in Japan and Germany have had their labor divisions. The United States labor movement has on its own account expanded its international operations. The International Ladies Garment Workers Union intervened ably in the 1948 Italian general elections. The American Federation of Labor has maintained Irving Brown as its permanent representative in Europe, and has recently sent a representative to India. The Congress of Industrial Organizations had James P. Carey as its representative in its ill-starred dalliance with the communist-controlled World Federation of Trade Unions (an offshoot of the appeasement period), and has had Elmer Cope for some years in Europe. Both federations have sent individuals or missions to most parts of the world, and have welcomed foreign labor representatives in this country.

* I am excluding reference to the internal labor movement.

We have, then, precedents. What is needed are actions in the field of international labor which shall be greater in scope, more careful in planning, and bolder in conception than those heretofore undertaken. I noticed in Paris last spring (1949) what seemed to me a telling symptom of the lack, in American official opinion, of full awareness of the problem. Along the walls of the corridors of the Embassy annex, where many of the ECA offices are located, there were displayed charts and tables designed to show the progress of the Marshall Plan in France. Comparative figures on exports and imports and on various aspects of the production output of different industries were in prominent evidence. I did not see a single chart (there may have been some, but they did not strike the eye) which referred to matters of specific concern to workers: nothing about labor's wages or social conditions or real standard of living. The attitude manifest in this absence has not a little to do with the success of the communists in persuading French workers to believe their version of the meaning of the Marshall Plan.

I wish to illustrate by concrete examples the kind of labor operation which can and should be undertaken:

1. The communists used the cover of the wartime Resistance to take over control of the French Federation of Labor (C.G.T.). During 1947, there developed in the Federation a loose movement of opposition to the communists, which took the name Force Ouvrière. In October and November, 1947, the communists staged a series of strikes which they tried to enlarge into a general strike. (This was the occasion of the fall of the Ramadier government, and the formation of the first of the present Third Force type of government.) These strikes were so obviously sterile, arbitrary, and "political" from a labor point of view that many workers rebelled against the communist leadership. Under pressure of this resentment, the Force Ouvrière broke away from the general Federation, and declared itself an independent organization.

The leadership of the now independent organization was feeble and confused. Its nominal head, the aged and outworn Léon Jouhaux, had shown the maximum of reluctance to split with the communists. Nevertheless, the Force Ouvrière expressed an anti-communist tendency which went deep into the entire French working class, and which had been stirred to action by the strike situation.

However, the Force Ouvrière began independent existence with no assets except this state of mind and feeling. The communists retained all of the material resources, the buildings and equipment and money, of the Federation. The leaders of the Force Ouvrière had nothing: no office; no typewriters or paper; no telephones (a utility infinitely painful to acquire in France); no stationery; no money to buy stamps, print membership cards, or send telegrams; no means for sending organizers into the provinces. What was required was immediate action to crystallize the opposition sentiment while it was still stirred up, and to establish the framework of a going concern, before the workers should relapse, as they were bound to do, into relative apathy. The means for such action were plain, simple things like typewriters and stamps and cars, and comparatively small amounts of money to buy gasoline and railroad tickets, to hire halls and to print pamphlets and dues books. There is good reason to believe that with these means, in that situation, a majority of the workers belonging to the old Federation could have been brought over to the Force Ouvrière: that is, could have been broken organizationally from the control of the communists.

There were Americans at that moment in France who understood what was happening, and what was needed. They made specific proposals for action; but action was not taken. The workers subsided. The Force Ouvrière lost its élan, and carried with it only a minority—and not the most important minority—of the workers. The communists have maintained their dominant position in French labor.

Conjunctures like that of November, 1947, affecting an entire national working class, do not occur every month, but they are not abnormal. Minor situations, similar in pattern, constantly arise—or can be made to arise.

2. In Italy, in correlation with the elections of the spring of 1948, an exactly similar situation arose, with exactly the same potentiality, the same failure to give quick and concrete support, and the same inconclusive result of a minor splitoff from the dominant communist-controlled labor federation.

3. In northern France, following 1945, there were some two hundred thousand German ex-prisoners of war working, primarily in the coal mines and textile mills. They were a carefully selected group of first-class men (many of them have since, or are to be, given French citizenship), in the key industries of the area, located near the significant strategic line of the Channel Coast. In 1947, there were circulating among them five German-language journals, all five communist controlled. An American, then in France, who knew these things, and their meaning, was in contact with a number of these German workers. He and they prepared a plan for an anti-communist German-language paper. Their estimate was that with only $50,000 as an advance, and a little help in getting supplies and modest machinery, they could launch a paper which would be self-supporting within three months. Neither officially nor from private sources could they raise that miserable sum (50 thousand against the annual 5,000,000 thousand of the Marshall Plan and the 40,000,000 thousand of the annual United States Budget) or get that help.

4. In most of the countries of Continental Europe, part of labor is organized into Catholic trade unions. Though the official policy of these Catholic federations is a strict syndicalism (that is, non-political "pure trade-unionism"), it is of course true in fact that they are strongly anti-communist. Like most trade unions in Continental Europe—except those controlled by the communists, who can draw on the resources of the Soviet Union and the world communist movement—these Catholic organizations are impoverished materially. They too need and deserve support, and do not get it. Indeed, they do not have even that intangible but powerful support that

could come from friendly and frequent personal relations with Americans.

5. When, in 1945, the Red Army drove into Germany, it was governed by a strategic aim very different from that which guided the armies of the Western Allies. The communist objective was (and remains) not merely the defeat of the Reichswehr and "the removal of the threat of future German aggression," but the absorption of Germany into the Soviet Empire. Their tactical implementation of this objective prominently includes, as in all such cases, the drive to win ascendency in and, finally, control over the German labor movement.

Hitler had purged all but a few communists out of the German labor movement, so that in 1945 they had to make a fresh start. Their plans had long been matured, and they were ready to act. They had carefully trained a whole corps of men, Germans for the most part, with a few others who spoke German perfectly, for the operation. These men were dispatched throughout the factories and working class districts of Germany—Western as well as Eastern Germany. In the East, where the communists had a completely free hand, new trade union organizations were at once set up, staffed by loyal party members, or by collaborators who could be counted on to yield to the promise of favors or the threat of terror. The small things, so large in effect, were not forgotten. The communist agents were healthy, and many of them young. They were provided with food enough for hard work, money, means of transportation, the materials for agitation: with, in short, the necessary tools for their trade.

The Western Allies had also thought about "the trade union problem," but they had not thought deeply enough. They were satisfied when they had brought together, often out of exile or concentration camps, a few men—by the nature of the case, mostly old, physically feeble, and out of touch with the present—and had given these men an organizational name, an unheated office, and a blessing on their efforts to recreate the German trade unions.

Though the results have not been as wholly negative as, under the circumstances, might have been feared, they have been far from as positive as the situation demands. There has not been built in western Germany a new organized labor movement both powerful and thoroughly anti-communist; and there has been almost no penetration, as there could have been, into the labor movement of the Soviet Zone.

What is required—and there is hardly anything else in Germany so imperiously required—is a German labor movement which shall constitute a massive social weapon operating continuously against the communist pressure. For this, much more is needed than labor attachés dining with mayors, and feeble old men with honorable records and impressive new titles but no energy, no close links with the rank and file, and no material resources. The communists, blocked temporarily at the top in the Western Zones, work assiduously at the bottom—in the individual factories and the local "Works Councils," as they are called, which may in time replace the higher union organizations as the form of proletarian power.

The problem has not been, and is not, insoluble. It is necessary to get to know individual German workers of ability, and individual activists in the labor movement, at the lowest as well as the highest levels. To those with whom discussion and cooperation are possible, adequate material support should be offered. Considerable numbers of German trade unionists should be given a chance to make lengthy trips to the United States, and while in the United States to participate in the great American labor movement. (A start toward this has been made during the past year.) Selected young men and women, from the most successful American trade unions, should go to Germany, not to make a speech or two and "survey conditions," but to settle down in German industrial cities for several continuous years, and to join intimately, from the inside, the task of rebuilding and orienting the German labor movement.* All of

---

* No comment seems adequate to express the absurdity of the occupation policy, in Japan as well as in Germany, which grants the communists freedom and legality.

the billions of dollars, and all of the immense effort and energy that are being poured into "the German problem" will have been much worse than wasted, after all, if Germany in the showdown swings to the eastern side of the balance.

6. The social weight of the labor movement is relatively less in less industrialized nations. However, even in the less industrialized nations, the potential strength of the labor movement is more than it would seem to be from bare population statistics. What industrial workers there are, concentrated in the larger cities, which are always also strategic centers of communication and transport, have much greater leverage, when they are organized, than the peasants dispersed over the undeveloped countryside. "Labor operations" are therefore called for in every nation, in Asia and Africa and Latin American as well as in industrial Europe, Japan, and North America.

Why, in China, for example, has the United States not become acquainted with the activists of the organized Chinese labor movement? No matter what the policy toward Chiang Kai-shek, there was no reason to turn over Chinese labor to the communists by passive default. In India, too, there are trade unions as well as Nehru and the communists.

During the '30's, the communists constructed, with only partial success, a general federation of Latin-American trade unions. For this campaign, they used as their spearhead the Mexican leader, Lombardo Toledano. In this particular trade union activity, the United States had a more than incidental positive part. Toledano became the darling of at least one group of United States officials (he was much admired and favored by Henry Wallace and his friends); he was fêted in the United States, and the meetings which he staged in Latin America were often spiced by the appearance of prominent United States citizens.

In recent years, an anti-communist Latin American federation (the Inter-American Confederation of Workers) has been formed to rival Toledano's communist-controlled outfit. So far there seems to have been much less United States cooperation with this new federation than there was in the old days with Toledano's.

When United States industry and government negotiate new agreements with Cuba on sugar, with Guatemala on bananas, with Brazil on coffee, with Venezuela on oil, with Bolivia on tin, with Chile on copper, it should be possible to recall that workers are also concerned, and that they might be brought into the negotiations in some further way than as subject of denunciations for wanting wages that threaten to raise prices enough to cut into importers' profits.

In relation to the present struggle for the world, the truth about labor's stake is the direct contrary of the communist mystique. Under communism, labor is worse off in all respects, material, political, and moral, than under any variety of anti-communism—capitalist, democratic-socialist, "mixed economy," or even fascist. With such a truth as objective starting point, there is surely no reason to feel defeatist about the contest with communism for the loyalty of the labor movement. The truth, however, does not automatically take care of itself. Apart from the long-term social problem of bringing about material improvements in the workers' conditions of life, it is specifically necessary to direct policy toward the aim of winning or keeping labor from communist control.

It is necessary that those men who carry out American policy, at all levels, should know labor—know its problems and its people; and, in fact, that personnel drawn from the labor movement should themselves be prominently included among those who carry out American policy. Labor has a full interest in all important actions, political, social, or military, and therefore must be accorded full rights, from the beginning, in these actions. Propaganda must be designed with labor audiences in mind—including in at least some cases the workers of the Soviet Union.

I have already mentioned, in connection with Germany, the importance of an exchange of labor personnel. Representatives of the

American labor movement—not only big-time officials, but young, active persons just getting started in the labor movement—should travel and live abroad; and members of foreign labor organizations should be invited and welcomed in the United States, and should be given an opportunity to see the American labor movement in action, and to join in its actions.

Diplomatic pressures on other governments can often be designed to serve the aim of winning labor organizations from communist control: by insistence that the other governments do not act in such a way as to throw workers into communist hands; and by helping to handle the delicate problems which arise from communist-led political and strategic strikes.

Most directly and simply of all, material aid is needed by the anti-communist labor organizations which exist or which can be made to exist. It is pathetic to ponder what battles have been lost on the labor fronts of the world struggle of our day for want of a second-hand typewriter, a truck and gasoline, a few hundred pounds of paper, or a usable printing press. If we can spend a million dollars for a fancy simultaneous translation system at a mirrored conference of well-tailored plenipotentiaries, where nothing is or can be decided any longer, we should be able to spare a few cents, and ideas, to provide our real friends—who will continue to be friends, if necessary, after the Red Army comes as well as before—with the simple means of proving their friendship in action.

CHAPTER XIII

The Cultivation of Political Friends

A BIG DIFFERENCE between traditional diplomacy and a political procedure adjusted to the present state of permanent war is in the people one sees. In this respect, the present period has similarities to other periods of social revolution, general or local: to Rome of the 1st century B.C., Europe at the time of the French Revolution, and even to the period of the American Revolution.

Traditional diplomacy is *official*. Though secret agents and private intriguers are never absent from international political life, in normal times (in, let us say, the century preceding the French Revolution or that preceding the First World War) the main international business of each nation is carried on by official representatives of that nation who meet, talk to, dine and correspond with, the official representatives of other nations. The officials chiefly see, in addition to their opposite officials, members of the established élite: noblemen in a still aristocratic society; financiers and industrialists in a capitalist society, and so on.

The United States, in spite of the internal fluidity of American society, has for several generations been probably more strict than most other powers in holding within the official limits. The pattern is easily enough displayed by the answer to a simple question: with whom do the diplomats and other governmental representatives have luncheon, drinks, and dinner? with whom do they spend weekends? Even our popular journalists express the customary limits. John Gunther, for example, is the most widely read of our writers on "foreign affairs." In the eyes of himself and his readers, his reports on foreign nations are authenticated by the innumerable interviews and personal talks he has had with Ministers, Premiers, Generals, Cardinals, Mayors, and Presidents, most of whom he seems to call by their first names.

This orientation toward the official makes good sense when it is a question of standard political problems and stable social structures. In a period when the government of France or Germany or Russia, say, is firm; when the government is genuinely representative of the nation in at least the practically crucial sense that it can commit the nation, with its resources and people, to the line of action which the government decides on; and when the relative rank of social classes within the nation is not being rapidly altered—in such circumstances there is no point in being anything other than official, except for personal amusement. For the purposes of international relations, the nation then *is* its officialdom (government representatives plus members of the ruling and established non-governmental élite). Agreements or treaties or conflicts, peace or alliance or war, depend on the relation that is negotiated through or with that officialdom.

In times like ours, however, which are not normal times, official relations are likely to be a very inadequate summary of real relations. It is a waste of political effort to spend many hours with dukes and bankers, if dukes and bankers don't count for much any more; and in not a few countries they now count for very little. An agreement with the officials of a government is not a very solid contract, if that government is not actually in a position to commit the people of its country and their resources.

In the world struggle against communism, the United States needs firm friends. What does it mean, in this struggle, that a friend should be firm? The meaning is simple, and grave: that he will go, if necessary, to the end; that his friendship will continue into any stage of war or revolution; that his friendship will remain in the face of death; that he will shoot, if it comes to shooting, in the same direction.

The present governments and officials of many non-communist

nations are not firm in this final meaning. I do not suggest, of course, that the officials are cowardly in a personal sense. As with most groups of men, doubtless some are cowards and some brave. Their lack of firmness is a social and a political characteristic. The governments are not firm, in some cases, because they are not truly governments, not sovereign in their own houses. The officials are not firm because their political ideas, traditions, and structures do not force them, or even permit them, to stand up unyielding to the communist attack. Because of the political vise which held them, neither Beneš in Czechoslovakia nor Nagy in Hungary nor Mikolajczyk in Poland could avoid becoming an accomplice of the communists: each was drawn irresistibly into a communist-dominated "coalition government" which was in reality only a link in the chain of communist conquest. In the same way, Léon Blum in France or Pietro Nenni in Italy or Henry Wallace in the United States could not resist the attraction of the communist united front. These men whom I have named are not, in the world today, atypical specimens.

Because so many governments and officials today are not firm, relations with them must be supplemented by closer relations with those who are unofficial, but firm, or firmer. I am not, certainly, proposing that the United States should stop taking seriously its official relations with other governments, and should give up all attempts to make agreements, contracts, treaties, and alliances. I am arguing that today these formal relations are not enough, and that the formal accomplishments which follow from them—even so spectacular an accomplishment as the Atlantic Pact—may prove very leaky shelters against the Soviet storm. To reach out, within other nations, beyond the official layers, is apt to be offensive to the local officialdom. But it can be done; and the officials themselves can become firmer when they feel the pressure of firmness upon them. Moreover, the present governments and the present officials are not eternal. They change, in time, even in the normal course of affairs. In the crisis of war or revolution they can disappear with amazing speed. It is necessary to seek the friendship not only of the man who today is Minister of Foreign Affairs, but of the man who will replace him tomorrow. The latter friendship may well be the more decisive.

What I have already written on the labor movement, and what I shall write in succeeding chapters on exiles, liberation movements, and the Resistance, bear directly on this task of cultivating political friends. We must seek out those who are or could become firm friends, seek them wherever they are to be found, even in places rather sordid and dreary (there are some of them who do not patronize the Ritz or the Excelsior, and who have no country houses). We should come to know them, to discuss and plan with them—and to learn from them, for they have, some of them, a good deal to teach. In some cases we can provide them, carefully and quietly, with what they often greatly need, and which, at least, we can supply: money, ease of travel, radio facilities, a magazine or newspaper ... and arms.

2

It is a little awkward to illustrate concretely this tactic of the cultivation of firm friends. The application of the tactic demands, in the case of each nation, a rather intimate knowledge of the internal situation. The appropriate operations are delicate, and can be tarnished by public discussion. Nevertheless, I do not wish to rest in the comfortable armchair of abstraction. I shall attempt to suggest a few examples.

1. I have already referred to the Costa Rican crisis of early 1948. There, before the civil war, the official government was in a united front with the communists, and was trying to negate the results of an election which had repudiated it. Figueres represented both the strongest anti-communist force in the country and also the will of the people as democratically recorded. Surely this was a friend to be aided. Since the usurping government had the official machinery in its hands, he needed aid—in understanding, money, and arms. He and his friends made their need known, to the State Department

and to the United Nations. At the acceptable time, the aid was not forthcoming.*

2. In France, the very name "Third Force," which is applied to the coalitions which have since November, 1947, constituted the government, is a sufficient symptom of official France's lack of present firmness. Not only are the government and the parties which make it up infirm. So also, and worse, are the principal backers of this government and these parties: bankers and ineffectual bourgeois who find the government's weakness the most favorable medium for their own narrowly motivated manipulations.

Apart from the communists, the Gaullist movement is the most serious force in France. From 1940 on, official America has disliked, avoided, distrusted, or repudiated De Gaulle. I do not wish to deny De Gaulle's publicized "difficulty"; nor do I wish to argue here the general question whether De Gaulle and his Rally of the French People "ought to be" running France. I do wish to insist on certain verifiable facts. De Gaulle himself, certainly, is firm: what other leading Frenchman was absolutely firm in June, 1940? (His firmness then, his absolute rejection of Vichy and his absolute pledge that the war would not end until victory, was, indeed, a notorious instance of what Churchill and Washington then regarded as his "difficulty.") His movement has drawn in a certain amount of riffraff, as all mass movements do. But the R.P.F. includes also a larger number of Frenchmen who can be relied upon to resist communism *to the end*—through, if necessary, another war, another defeat, and another occupation—than can be found in any other French formation. An official French army, built under the aegis of the Atlantic Pact by a French government which does not dare to remove Joliot-Curie from his chairmanship of the Atomic Commission, or to jail self-proclaimed traitors, may well collapse even much more quickly than the army of 1940. The core of the Gaullists—for the most part already trained in the fierce school of the revolution

---

* I have been told that, as a consequence, he was forced to accept help from sources that have subsequently caused him, and us, embarrassment.

or the Resistance—will not collapse, and will not yield. Are these not reasons enough—what reasons could be greater?—for seeking a somewhat closer liaison with De Gaulle and his colleagues?

In France (as in other countries) there are also other groups than De Gaulle's—some of them most antagonistic to De Gaulle—which contain men who will be firm, but who see very little of official, or unofficial, Americans. For example, there are not a few anarchist-minded workers, like those in Paris who live on the sacred ground of the Commune beyond the Canal Saint-Martin, and who have now, in their disgust, withdrawn silently from trade-union and political squabbling. Many are to be found also among the supervisory and managerial personnel of French industry, who in France are organized, in part, in syndicates of what are called "cadres."

3. In Italy, the two serious forces are at present the Communist party and the Catholic Church. Throughout Continental Europe (including, of course, Eastern Europe) and Latin America, the Catholic Church is probably the strongest present anti-communist force. Stalin himself knows well the incompleteness of his scornful question, "How many divisions has the Pope?" The present war is not a war merely of divisions; and in the non-military phases of the war, the Church has formidable resources: a faith with which to oppose in the hearts of men the secular religion of communism; a disciplined organization which penetrates society from its upper reaches deep into the masses; two thousand years of historical experience, and the lessons digested from those years.

The plainest common sense therefore dictates to non-Catholics— nations as well as individuals—what can be called a "united front with the Vatican." In the world struggle against communism, this united front is firmly grounded in objective interest. No matter what may have been (or may still be) the illusions of some members of the Church Hierarchy, the fact is that the Church cannot survive under the communist totalitarian monopoly of social power. To this fact, Balkan events during 1949 have been bearing most eloquent witness. The Church is thus compelled to share the central objective of the world struggle. The Church and the anti-communist secular power have each, moreover, much to gain from the other by united action. The Church, from the time of Constantine at least, has understood the uses of the secular arm; and the Church can contribute, in one or another way, remarkable means for intelligence, persuasion, planning, organization.

Close practical cooperation with the Catholic Church is distasteful to some Americans. These are, I think, being misled either by a failure to rate problems in their proper order, or by prejudices which the communist propaganda machine is at some pains to keep fanned (the communists in the United States, besides their underground propaganda on this issue, have vigorously supported such openly anti-Catholic publications as *The Protestant*). The supposed argument that the Catholic Church is just another "international totalitarian movement" is, quite apart from its abstracted truth or falsity, simply irrelevant to the present historical context. Whether or not Catholicism ever was, or ever might be, successfully totalitarian, the world is not *now* under any threat of Catholic totalitarianism. The totalitarian threat of this historical period is directed from an address considerably to the north and east of Rome.

A united front of action—not the communist variety, which is a device for swallowing partners, but a loyal united front—does not mean that the parties to it abandon their distinctive ideas or their integrity. A united front is not "unity"; it is a merely practical collaboration for specific and shared purposes. For Washington to hold back from the fullest possible measure of such collaboration with the Vatican is a victory, and a considerable victory, only for Stalin.

4. Though Mohammedanism is not, in our era, a coherent organized structure comparable to the Catholic Church, and though the most part of its faithful are materially backward, it too is actually, and even more potentially, a powerful anti-communist force. From shortly after the Russian Revolution, the communist high command has sought to penetrate Islam. Agents and agitators have been trained in large numbers at special schools, and mass propa-

ganda campaigns have been carried out. The success has been much
below expectation or hope. The Mohammedan faith has proved a
difficult barrier to the communist ideology and communist methods
of action. In fact, there is some reason to believe that this has been
the principal barrier which has slowed the communist advance
across the land bridge to Africa.

The strategic significance of the Mohammedan areas is striking.
Not only do they comprise the greater part of the Near East, but
also much of the northern coastland of Africa, Pakistan, and sections
of China and Indonesia. More than this, Islam extends deep within
the Soviet Union itself, and even there the communists have not
been able to destroy or assimilate the Mohammedan faith and culture. A special attention to Islamic relations is therefore not only
necessary from the defensive point of view of holding further communist advance. It offers also major offensive possibilities. A Mohammedan Resistance movement inside the Soviet Union is by no
means a fantastic project.

5. I have already stated, in an earlier chapter, that the present
structure of the political parties in western Germany is artificial.
It does not provide an adequate or natural expression of the political
sentiments of the population. The present major parties are ad hoc
creations of the occupation authorities, drawn out of the dead file
of the Weimar Republic. This means that the present parties are a
historical anachronism. Their arbitrary re-creation simply wrote off
nazism, the Second World War, the rise of communism, the split-
ting of Germany, and the western migration of 11 million refugees,
as if these had never happened.

Though it is possible that the party structures will prove flexible
enough to adapt themselves to a new political content, there are
already many symptoms of distortion. New splinter parties are constantly bursting out of the old containers; in many cities, local
"circles," nominally within the parties, have developed in such a
way as to overshadow the formal party organizations; the refugees

have tended, whatever their party label, to become a distinctive grouping.

Because of this situation, adequate political liaison with Germany cannot be sustained by confining relations to the top national levels of the present parties. These parties, moreover, and their national leaders are not, or not yet, to be numbered among the firmer of friends. However, there do exist in western Germany, in not a few localities, individuals and groups whose political orientation toward the world struggle is far more promising than that of any of the political parties. In some cases these individuals and groups have important local influence, and are even in control of local organizations of the major parties (the Christian Democrats or the Social Democrats). I have talked to some of these men, and their story is disheartening. Their needs are great (though not too difficult to fulfill), but the need they feel most profoundly is merely to have some friendly and cooperative contact with Americans (or British or French), to have some discussion of plans and perspectives, and a small measure of mutual confidence.

6. In the Far East, American policy seems often to be implemented in such a way as to ensure the antagonizing of every potential friend within every camp. It must be confessed that Americans tend to see the Far East through a heavy cloud of liberal sentimentality. "The awakening of the Asiatic masses," about which so many books and articles have been written, is in reality the awakening of a thin layer of Western-educated intellectuals, who are able to arouse and use, on some occasions, some sections of the masses. They, and our own intellectuals, talk about Java and Ceylon and Burma and Sumatra—and it is necessary to add India and China—in terms of 19th century Western-type parliamentary governments, as if political forms floated around in a historical vacuum, and could come to rest on any material base through the magical repetition of formulas. A land in which 95 per cent of the people are impoverished, illiterate, disease-ridden, in which there are hardly any communications or transport or industry or doctors or engineers

or scientists, and no traditions of self-government, is not going to change overnight into a new England or France or United States. The best intentions can easily produce social chaos. Social order is a problem more difficult and more prolonged.

In most of those lands, what order has existed during the past several generations has rested on the guns and the bureaucracies of the Western imperial powers. With these withdrawn, the available internal forces are not adequate to establish their own new order and to begin a progressive social development. The totalitarian order of the communist imperialism, stiffened and sustained from without, offers itself—and imposes itself—as a solution which cannot fail to have tremendous attractive power. In spite of the anarchist myth, the worst condition for most men is to live under no-government. Under no-government, all is absolutely insecure; and it takes only a short taste of anarchic freedom for the majority to be ready to accept any government—that is, any order—at all, even despotic government, rather than nothing. The Western nations are often enough accused, and often rightly, of failing to be "liberal" enough in the Far East, of failing to make "concessions." They are equally guilty of failing, at appropriate times, to make suitable use of regulated power.

The objective facts are: (1) that the social development of the Far Eastern peoples is impossible without the aid of the resources and skills of the Western nations, in particular of the United States and Europe; (2) that the communist power threatens to destroy the Western nations; (3) that if successful in this, communism would thus indirectly make impossible the development of the Far East; (4) that communism also acts directly against the Far Eastern peoples, in pursuit of its goal of Western destruction, by its course of Far Eastern conquest. These facts are an objective foundation for cooperation between the Far Eastern peoples and the Western nations against the communist empire. The terms of cooperation are implicit in the facts. The Far East requires economic and technical assistance, on a massive scale, and military protection against communist conquest. The Western nations require political assurances (against communism or a communist orientation), military collaboration in the world struggle, and strategic protection.

Within all of the countries of the Far East (and they are not nations in the Western sense, it should be remembered), there are many persons among the (comparatively restricted) groups which influence affairs who understand these conditions. Suitable formulas must, of course, be found for the collaboration. The example of the Philippines proves that this is not impossible; and events in India, if chaos can be avoided there, seem to be moving toward a similar solution. It must be emphasized that any solution is a problem of power as well as of good will—the communists do not advance in the Far East through a policy of constant concessions in the liberal mode. The Dutch East Indies are not yet by any means lost to the communists. They will not be saved by a return to the untrammeled imperialism of two generations ago. Equally, they will not be saved by a total withdrawal of the Western nations, and an abandonment of those islands to a local ersatz-nationalist movement which does not have the resources, the guns, the tradition, or the personnel to establish and maintain sovereignty.

The disaster in China has gone too far for formulas, however adroit. Nevertheless, even if the communist armies reach the southern and the western borders, China is not altogether lost. There remain, and will remain, firm friends and potential friends in China. China is too vast and too loose for the communists to control tightly, and these friends will be able to live and to act, perhaps on a considerable scale. The communists, moreover, will manufacture new friends of the West, as the meaning of their rule comes into the open. Even if the State Department's White Paper is correct in arguing that Chiang Kai-shek could not under any circumstances have maintained a national government over all China, Chiang is still, as I write, in spite of his abandonment by Washington, fighting communists. His record of the past fifteen years does not particularly suffer by comparison with the records of the other leaders of that period. If at the moment it is impossible for the United States to mount the effort which would be required to throw the communists back out of China, the moment is not eternal. Granted the will, the resources are available to keep alive and nourish in China an anti-communist hope, a Resistance which, blocking meanwhile the consolidation of the communists' Far Eastern position, will be able to join in the offensive that can come when the wheel enters another cycle.

CHAPTER XIV

Refugees, Exiles, Liberation

WITHIN THE NON-COMMUNIST areas of the world, there are at present great numbers of refugees, exiles, and "displaced persons" from all the various nations of the communist empire. The two largest groups of these refugees, numbering in all more than ten million human beings, are German: the Sudeten Germans, displaced from Czechoslovakia, and the Silesian and other Germans from the parts of eastern Germany which were ceded to Poland. The status of these two groups is different from that of the rest, since their displacement was the direct result simply of the German defeat. They constitute a special problem, with which I am not here concerned. The other refugees and exiles come from every one of the nations now included within the Soviet Empire: Estonia, Lithuania, Latvia, Finnish Karelia, Poland, Czechoslovakia, Hungary, Rumania, Bulgaria, Albania, Manchuria, northern Korea, communist China, and also from the Ukraine, Great Russia, and the other original Soviet "republics."

Some of these refugees are old-timers: Czarists and liberals escaped from the very first stages of the Russian Revolution; Mensheviks, Social-Revolutionaries, anarchists, and others who got out as the Bolsheviks liquidated the opposition parties; and a constant trickle of individuals who year by year broke with the regime. The bulk of the refugees, however, is the product of recent years. Many of them are persons who, at the conclusion of hostilities in 1945, found themselves west of the Soviet line, where they had been prisoners of war, impressed laborers or soldiers of the Nazis, or in some cases voluntary Nazi collaborators. They refused to return to the lands of communist dictatorship, and maintained their refusal in spite of threats and blandishments and force, in spite of the pressure exercized through first UNRRA and then the International Refugee Organization, in spite of the shameful collusion of the Western allied authorities. Since 1945, these have been joined by many tens of thousands who have made their painful exit from the communist police paradise.

Among these exiles there is every type of human being. Some of them are scoundrels, guilty of collaboration in the more infamous of Nazi deeds, or of common crimes outlawed by all societies. These, however, are a small minority. Most of the exiles will not return to their homes, or have escaped from them, because they passively or actively reject the communist tyranny. There are among them scholars, statesmen, artists, engineers, scientists, as well as workers and peasants. There are a great many soldiers, from privates to generals. Besides individual soldiers from all the nationalities, there is, in fact, a good part of a great army of soldiers: the heroic army of Poles which General Anders formed on Soviet soil, out of his fellow prisoners whom Stalin released after Hitler struck, and led through the Middle East into the harsh fighting of the Italian campaigns.

These human beings are, in origin, exiles or refugees, not emigrants. That is, they did not abandon their homes in order, out of some positive want or need or ambition, to find homes in some other part of the world. They had, as they understood it, to seek a temporary refuge because their homes—which remained in their hearts still their homes—were usurped by strangers, by an enemy. In the course of time, many of them are being transformed from exiles into emigrants. Losing the hope of return, they try to settle permanently in new lands. Some have been so transformed; but many have not, and, while they live, will not be.

This vast group of exiles from the communist empire is a major and symptomatic historical phenomenon of the mid-20th century. Its mere existence, more even than the existence during the '30's of the much smaller and much less broadly representative group of exiles from nazism, is a profound comment on the nature of the regime from which these human beings have fled, a comment alike upon its inhumanity and upon its potential weakness.

These persons displaced from the communist empire have been a trial and tribulation to the victorious powers. Motives both humane and expedient have urged that they should be given food and shelter. However, if we may judge by policy and action, the overriding wish has been to slough off the responsibility, to get rid of them. To this end, the Kremlin had an easy answer: send them back. The communist high command is not easily reconciled to the loss of a single one of its slaves; there is plenty of room in the labor camps for all; and the communists know what a potential danger these exiles are if they remain in the free world. The Western powers, during the years immediately following 1945, did their best to comply with the Kremlin's wishes. The displaced persons were deluged with propaganda designed to persuade them to return. When persuasion failed, they were not seldom herded by bayonets into the eastbound trains. Still they remained, in hundreds of thousands. The lying propaganda and promises struck ears turned politically deaf. The soldiers—of England and France and America—who came to drag them to the trains found them with throats cut. Month by month new thousands came west to join them.

The eastbound trains slowed finally, and stopped. The Western powers undertook to "liquidate the refugee problem." The exiles began to scatter, or be scattered, throughout the world. Of those who were Jews, many made their way to Palestine. Many of the Poles of Anders' army settled in England, others in Australia, Canada, France. Many of the Balts were in Sweden. Argentina and other Latin American nations drew increasing thousands. Slowly and grudgingly the doors of the United States were pried open. In 1949 several hundred thousand still remained in western Germany, and there were many thousands, also, in France.

There is no doubt: the exiles have been an expensive problem, a painful headache. Only slowly has it come to be realized that, in the world situation which we now confront, they are also a promise and a possibility. Their act of going into exile, and their actions in exile, prove that these exiles, or most of them, are persons who take freedom seriously. Men do not lightly decide to taste, for long years, the bitter salt of strangers' bread. Their very existence, in such numbers, is both a promise of the breakup of the communist empire and at the same time a weapon for the accomplishment of that breakup. As exiles, their line of force is not out, but in, back to the homes which they have left but not abandoned. They are thus, or can be, the outward projection of, and link with, the Liberation movements inside their homelands. Their fulfillment as exiles can only be a return to freedom.

2

In the plan for the defeat of the communist power, operations with and through the refugee-Liberation movements should be assigned a high priority. They are a lever which can pry apart whole segments of the communist empire. The aim should be to activate these movements to the maximum, and to coordinate their strategy in order to concentrate its effect.

Many of the exiles are, of course, dissolving into the environments where they find themselves, and are thus becoming, one might say, no longer exiles. This is inevitable, under the given circumstances, and not unfortunate. It is only the more dynamic who can, and will, enter into active operations.

A considerable number of exile groups and individuals have been persistently active without external impetus or aid. In Stockholm, London, Paris, Washington, New York, and various cities and camps in western Germany, organizations have been functioning. Part of their work is concerned with the practical matter of helping their fellow refugees to live, to get food and shelter and visas and jobs. They aid in the escape of fellow countrymen whose lives are in danger. They are publishing information and propaganda bulletins, magazines, and books which are in many instances both valuable and effective. Some of the groups have been able to maintain liaison with the homelands, and have thereby kept up an intelligence and propaganda exchange.

Most of these groups have had to operate under the most discouraging of material conditions. They have almost no money, whether for the implementation of their political plans or for the support of their active members. The members are often without valid passports and labor permits. They are under direct danger from the MVD, and indirect adverse pressure, often, from the police and authorities of the country of temporary residence. Many of the bravest and most intelligent of them suffer also, perhaps most of all, from the terrible isolation of the exile: an isolation both from his own people, and from the strangers around him who do not wish to be bothered with the troublesome being who has come to lodge like a germ in their city, and who can best, it seems, be exorcised by indifference and avoidance. A first main step in the expansion of refugee-Liberation activities is simply to get to know the exiles, who and where they are, and what they are doing.

"Politics in exile" is usually dreary and stultifying. The exiles are removed from the primary scene of action, and from that daily contact with their own people which controls the resentments and vivifies the abstractions of political minds. With no sufficient practical outlet for their energies, and in an environment often of hardship and always of bitterness, they tend to split into minute factions, to puff small differences into unbridgeable "theoretical conflicts," and to sharpen their organizational talents on café intrigues.

In the case of the exile representatives of the peoples of the Soviet Empire, there are peculiar added troubles. On Eastern Europe lies the weight of a long history of divergent claims and aspirations. Poles and Ukrainians yield nothing to each other in the belief that the mantle of East European leadership fits most gracefully on their own respective shoulders; and Czechs find them both not fully issued from barbarism. Poles and Germans, Poles and Czechs, Czechs and Hungarians, Hungarians and Rumanians, Rumanians and Bulgarians, all are convinced of the justice of contradictory claims to provinces and cities. Refugee Great Russians, who are opponents of communism, are nevertheless not seldom in agreement with both the Czars and Stalin that Russia has a mission to rule over Ukrainians and even Bulgars, and a clear title to warm-water ports on the Mediterranean, the Baltic, and the Pacific. The present medley is made still more discordant by the addition to the exile ranks of a growing number of dissident communists, and the appearance within the communist empire of the successful dissident, Tito.

It is naïve to suppose that Resistance movements (for that is what is in question in the attempt to coordinate and activate the exile groups, and through them the internal Liberation forces) are fulfilled by the bare goal of "freedom." Julian Amery correctly observes: * "Resistance Movements, like the States to which they are embryonic successors, wage war for political ends. Now those ends are not, despite all propaganda, 'Victory' or 'Liberation' [it would be more accurate, I believe, to say, "are not *merely* 'Victory' or 'Liberation'"], but the recovery or the gaining of political power."

The difficulties are so formidable that some analysts have concluded that work with and through the present exile groups would prove futile. Even if this work contributed to the overthrow of the communist power, and if that overthrow were accomplished, the result would not be an improvement. All Eastern Europe, including European Russia, would be thrown into a bewildering series of nationalistic, racial, and civil wars. This conclusion, if justified, really means that we ought to give up the struggle against communism—that is, accept communist world domination. If the communist ill that we bear is preferable to the risk of future troubles that we know not yet of, then let us bear it.

However, the conclusion does not seem to me to hold. It is certainly probable that at the collapse of the communist power in a large part or the whole of its present empire, there will be plenty

* "Of Resistance," in *The Nineteenth Century and After*, March, 1949.

of trouble. Even if that trouble is the maximum that can be feared, it is still a lesser evil than the present situation, and far less than the situation which will come about if the communist power is not smashed. From an American and a world point of view, communism is not a major threat and enemy merely because it is communism. If the communist empire were confined to the limits of Afghanistan or Liberia, no one would have to worry about it. Communism is a major threat, a threat which must be removed, because it is both communism and also a great world power, holding under a unified sway a vast section of the earth's area, population, and resources, and attempting to use this section as the base from which to conquer the rest of the earth. To break up this unified and aggressive control is an enormous gain, no matter what internecine disturbances might follow. It goes without saying that our aim should be, so far as possible, to destroy the communist control with a minimum of social loss and chaos. Correct work with and through the exiles, the Resistance, and the Liberation may well be the principal means of succeeding in that aim. The anti-communist Resistance, linking the exile groups and the internal opponents, is, precisely, the potential successor to the communist power.

There are others, less pessimistic than those who would drop the whole operation, who argue from the difficulties, and from the divergences both within each national group and among the various nationalities, that America should insist, as a condition preliminary to collaboration with the exiles, on a full programmatic agreement among all the exile factions. This conclusion also seems to me unrealistic and unnecessary. Full programmatic agreement probably cannot be attained as a preliminary. If attained in form, it would probably be violated in practice. Significant agreement will be, if it is possible, the product, not the condition, of action.

It is action, action of some moment and consequence, that is the supreme medicine for the sterility and the freneticism of exile politics. If action does not cure all the disputes—some of them are historically justified and therefore cannot be cured but only decided

—it at least eliminates those disputes which are personal, subjective, trivial, the product of spleen and idleness. Our prejudice should be in favor of those exiles who are firm, and who are ready to do something, to act. With such we should be ready to work, despite the laggards and the unresolved ideological puzzles.

After all, the present situation imposes its own imperatives, once we decide to act in relation to it. The exiles, and their internal friends, are against the communists; they are for the overthrow of communist rule, and the liberation both of their own homelands and of all the peoples now subject to the communist tyranny. That is not a small measure of agreement on which to base a united front of action, and to develop a reasonably coordinated, reasonably unified strategy. Many of the ablest of the exiles are aware that they cannot pulverize the present communist empire into a crazy stew of small jealous nations. The best of the representatives of the East European states (including the Ukrainians) accept and explore the perspective of an East European Federation within the larger perspective of a Federated Europe. They, indeed, and not the West European leaders, may well be the ones through whom Europe receives the unification without which it cannot survive.

3

I should like to list, as examples, some of the urgent tasks which can be carried out in collaboration with the exiles, and with the internal Resistance movements, actual and potential, which the exiles represent.

1. It is fairly well understood how much the exiles have to offer in the field of Intelligence. From the point of view of the struggle against communism, they are a rich mine which is already being tapped, but which could produce at a much higher rate from a more systematic and continuous exploitation. Moreover, the vein of paying ore is daily expanding as new refugees cross the borders, or, already outside, renounce allegiance. The metaphor is incomplete,

however. The exiles should be regarded not as passive material to be used by Intelligence, but as active participants in the work of Intelligence.

In part, the problem is to discover what the exiles already know, the information which they have brought with them, but the relevance and importance of which they may not themselves be able to evaluate. Among them are men of all kinds and degrees, from all levels and sectors of society. What can be found out from them is a great deal: about industries and roads, inventions and plans, social attitudes and armament, new construction and military training, purges and rewards. In the case of those who know most, routine questioning is insufficient. Careful study, reflection, cross-checking, research, interpretation are required. A proposal for a large center in which exiles themselves could undertake such enquiries has been publicly announced. It is to be hoped that this proposal is being, or will be, put into effect.

What the trained scholars, scientists, and soldiers among the exiles can do in the field of Intelligence is not confined to supplying passive facts. They are admirably fitted to join in the continuing analysis of developments within the areas from which they come, or within the Soviet Empire as a whole. Their knowledge and ability are needed, moreover, not merely for the gathering of information, but in the formulation of plans.

Finally, there are many among them who are or could be in active liaison with their homelands, and who, having escaped as defeated oppositionists, would be willing and able to re-enter as advance couriers of the Liberation.

2. How much the exiles might do in the field of propaganda, in both its preparation and its transmission, would seem to be self-evident. It is better, in most cases certainly, that Poles should speak to Poles, Russians to Russians, Hungarians to Hungarians, and especially that the communication should be between those who have shared the same experiences. I have talked to many refugees who have been puzzled as well as disheartened that there have not

been assigned to them or their colleagues regular radio periods during which they might talk to their countrymen. It will be a tragic waste if the Bulgarians are permitted to forget, as all things unrenewed are forgotten, the firmness of George Dimitrov; or the Poles, the heroism of Anders. In written propaganda also, in creating it and in distributing it, the exiles can accomplish much, if they are given confidence and means.

3. Among the exiles, there are scholars, scientists, and teachers. There are also many young persons, in their late teens or their twenties, who would today, if their lives had not been so violently interrupted, be in college or graduate school. With these two groups in mind, a project has been put forward in explicit detail by a number of refugees now centered in Paris, for the foundation of an East European Institute, or University.* Their conception (which is capable of practical alteration without injury to the principal aims) is of a center located either in Western Europe or in North Africa. The primary direction and the chief material support would come from the United States. A faculty would be formed from the East European scholars (including Russian scholars), American teachers, and possibly also some British and Continental teachers. The student body would be selected from the young exiles, and would also include Americans and West Europeans.

This project is less modest in its potential, and more urgent, than it might at first seem. Even from a purely educational, academic point of view, an East European Institute is sufficiently justified. The teachers, scholars, and students are there; they want and need a University; without sustenance, their knowledge and intellectual abilities will wither and be lost, no less than their bodies. At the same time, the communists are destroying knowledge and education throughout Eastern Europe, and substituting for them the falsified myths of communist ideology and propaganda. The destruction is

---

* Similar proposals have been made by other individuals and groups. A "Baltic University" was in fact started in Germany, but, lacking support and proper guidance, it has not succeeded.

quite literal: books are burned and chopped up; histories are re-written; independent teachers and students and scientists are purged, and sent to slave-labor camps. The actual knowledge and the most advanced cultural tradition of Eastern Europe will be simply lost if the field is abandoned to the communists. To save them, it is necessary to assemble living carriers of that culture—scholars, teach-ers, writers, together with the material records of the knowledge—books, papers, manuscripts; to enable the scholars to work at that for which they are qualified, which they cannot do in dispersion or when forced to make a living by cleaning latrines or sorting gar-bage; and to bring the scholars into relation with the youth who will continue the tradition.

The young among the exiles are, indeed, a more considerable problem than has yet been widely recognized. Their uprooted pres-ent existence, their lack of challenging tasks, the failure of the adult world to provide them with a clear perspective, are producing their natural effects. Two types of response are already spreading widely: a passivity, cynical or indifferent, toward all political, social, and even moral values; and a fierce nihilism not unlike the nihilism of the lost German youth after the First World War, which then ex-pressed, not nazism, but the social despair out of which nazism could breed. For the exile youth, not only for those who attended it but for the others in whose eyes it would establish a sense of direction, the projected Institute would be a substantial counter-influence to these tragic, and dangerous, moods.

There is much more, however, to the idea of an East European Institute. Its beginning, even on the smallest scale, would have an enormous propaganda effect, direct and indirect. Presumably the Institute would publish magazines, treatises, even books; and these would not be less effective as propaganda for being qualified as scholarship. Quite apart from any specific publications by or about the Institute, word of its existence would spread immediately throughout the exile groups, and throughout East Europe also. It would be, for the youth, especially, and for the most intelligent, most ambitious of the youth, a symbol and a sign that the world had not abandoned the peoples of Eastern Europe to the communists. The Institute would be a visible covenant of Liberation. I have talked to many refugees who believe that the indirect propaganda effect on Eastern Europe of such an Institute would much exceed that of a ten times multiplied Voice of America.

The Institute would be a solid link between the United States and Eastern Europe, of a kind that does not now exist and has never existed. America and Eastern Europe know very little about each other, and in the mixed faculty and student-body as well as in the Institute's research and publications, that ignorance could start to be overcome. Personal acquaintance, and a common life together, would add to the solidity of the relation. These are not small matters. What happens today and tomorrow among the peoples of Eastern Europe has consequences both intimate and weighty for America. This will continue to be the case long after the communist power has ended.

Finally, the Institute would be recruiting some of "the cadres of Liberation." If our general plan and our political perspective are serious, then we are heading toward a time when the communist power will have withdrawn or been overthrown. As it collapses or retires, someone must take over the leadership and organization of society. The communists' method, as we have seen, is to try to perpetuate their rule by destroying all alternatives to it, by eliminating all non-communist personnel who could exercise political, administrative, or technical direction of society. What will be needed when Eastern Europe is freed—under whatever circumstances—will be not merely a political faction able to take over the power, the sovereignty, but also trained administrators and technicians. Through the projected Institute, a nucleus would be created around which, even though it might be small, the new, or renewed, social order might in part be formed.

4. I have noted that men who are "exiles" in origin are transformed into "emigrants" (and finally into men of another country)

when, giving up the idea of return, they seek or accept new homes and new lives in a new land. Many of the exiles of this period are going through this transformation. For many, for the majority in fact, this is doubtless the best human solution. Many others, however, remain and will remain exiles: that is, whatever practical steps they have to take in order to keep alive and fed, their hearts will still be pointed toward return; they will not be reconciled to new homes in new lands. It is desirable that this should be so. The irreconcilable attitude is a symptom that the span of communist rule is temporary, and is an omen as it will prove a partial cause of that rule's overthrow.

The irreconcilable exiles (even those from the Ukraine or other sections of the original Soviet territory) regard their homelands as *enemy-occupied country,* and themselves as at war with the communist empire. Because of this attitude, because some of them are professional soldiers, and because jobs are hard to get, many of these irreconcilables do not fit well into a routine, peace-assuming existence. There seems to be no good reason why they should not be given something to do: assembled into organized groups, and assigned various tasks. The exact manner of organization, whether under military or civilian auspices, is less important than the fact. The suitable tasks range from conservation and reconstruction projects (in Europe and throughout the world) through constabulary and semi-military assignments to the outright military. The appropriate organization of the exiles would, that is to say, have elements of a Civilian Conservation Corps, a police force, and a Foreign Legion.

For some obscure but potent cause, a suggestion of this sort shocks many Americans. I have, however, heard few grounded arguments against it. There are important jobs, highly productive and beneficial, that could be done today by such an organization, if it existed. At the same time, the organization of the exiles would be a really serious preparation for the Liberations. Even if the Liberations take place altogether peacefully, or by purely internal shifts in which the exiles have no part, there will still be the need, as I have already pointed out in discussing the "cadres of Liberation" that would be formed at an East European University, for trained social forces to replace the communists. If the fighting is general, as it may be, there will be an incomparable advantage in having, from the beginning, Ukrainian, Polish, Czech, Chinese, and the other units on the anti-communist side.

If the United States made the decision, there would at once be, from among the exiles, enough recruits to man the organization at almost any quantitative level that might be wished.

5. The destiny of the exile movements from the countries of the communist empire is to return to homelands freed from the communist dictatorship. The exile movements are therefore in reality an extension of internal Resistance movements, even though at a given moment the internal movements may be silent, and the external extensions alone articulate and active. The exile groups are a channel, and doubtless the principal and essential channel, to the internal Resistance, both as it operates, half-alive, today, and as it will operate as it gains skill and power and confidence tomorrow. I shall reserve for the next chapter a further discussion of work with the internal Resistance.

CHAPTER XV

The Scope of Resistance Warfare

IN THE FIVE preceding chapters, I have confined my discussion, for the most part, within the limits which I imposed in Chapter IX. I have tried to direct attention to types of informal, unorthodox operations which fall within the field of "political-subversive warfare," or what may be called in the most general sense, "Resistance warfare." I want now to call renewed attention to the fact that this field is not clearly separated from that of the more conventional, traditional operations: diplomatic, military, economic, and psychological. What is at issue is a general plan for attaining the central objective: the destruction of the communist power. In this plan, Resistance operations are obviously only one section or phase.

If the general plan is to be intelligently applied, then its various phases must be coordinated with each other; at the very least, they must not conflict with each other. For example, let us suppose that it is judged possible to overthrow the Cominform government of Albania, and thereby to break Albania off from the communist empire. In such a project, Resistance methods would presumably have the principal role. It would naturally be stupid to accompany their employment with economic and diplomatic measures the effect of which would be to strengthen the Cominform government. Or suppose that it was decided to invoke the penalty clauses of the peace treaty with Bulgaria, and to compel Bulgaria to make an accounting. In that case, adequate military provision would have to be made, not only to cover the demand on Bulgaria, but against the general risk which, however slight, would be incurred. Or again: if it were decided to support, by missions and supplies, anti-communist armies or detachments which could be kept in existence in China, then not only would correlated military and economic measures have to be taken, but a correlated information and propaganda program ought to make the Chinese action intelligible to the European and American publics.

The function of Resistance operations, as of all other types of operation, is to implement the general plan—that is, to lead toward the attainment of the objective. In their preliminary stages, even without the support of other types of operation, Resistance methods fulfill this function in a double way. Negatively, they weaken, disorient, and undermine the enemy. Positively, they encourage, organize, clarify, and strengthen our own and allied forces, and win over new forces. In the broad sense that I am giving the term, "Resistance" does not mean merely opposition movements behind the enemy lines. As a matter of fact, there are no lines in the present war, since the forces of the enemy are deployed and active within every area of the world. The Resistance operations can and should be taking place in the United States itself, in Europe and Latin America and Africa and India and southeast Asia and the East Indies, as well as behind the Iron Curtain.

The aim of Resistance operations does not stop short, however, at merely "weakening" the enemy. Resistance is not necessarily limited to the secondary function of an "auxiliary arm." Resistance operation can properly, at least under favorable circumstances, seek a *decision*: that is, the overthrow of the enemy. That this extension of aim is not illusory has been proved by recent history. Tito took power in Yugoslavia, and Hoxha in Albania, by methods which remain fundamentally within the framework of Resistance. The communists have taken power in the greater part of China, also, through Resistance operations. Moreover, from the point of view of the United States, the Greek civil war has been a Resistance operation, and has, within the limits imposed, come close (as I write) to a fairly decisive, if negative, result (a result, however, which can only be temporary so long as the communist power is deep in the Balkans.

It is true, on the other hand, that as the scale and decisiveness of operations magnify, Resistance measures tend to merge into other measures, lines are obscured, and available forces of many kinds from many or all fields are brought to bear in the degree that seems required.

2

Julian Amery, in the article from which I have already quoted, uses the term "Resistance" more narrowly and perhaps more appropriately than I have been doing. "Resistance is the name which we give to operations directed against an enemy, behind his lines, by discontented elements among the enemy or enemy-occupied populations. (The term 'enemy' is used here in its broadest sense. It applies equally to belligerents, opponents in a cold war, malevolent neutrals, or indeed to any state against which it is decided to conduct Resistance operations.*) . . . Resistance . . . differs from Revolution (or Counter-Revolution), only insofar as its operations are supported by an external Power or conform to the general military and political strategy of that Power. By definition, therefore, a Resistance movement draws its strength and inspiration from two sources; from the local forces of which it is composed, and from the outside Power which supports it. Its nature is thus determined by the proportion in which these two elements, the local and the external, are mixed. This proportion varies from case to case."

Up to this point I have omitted mention of many of the most familiar methods used by Resistance movements operating within the enemy lines proper. Among these, Amery lists: "revolt, guerrilla,† sabotage, terrorism, civil disobedience, strikes, 'go-slow' tech-

---

* Amery here suggests the reason that makes me think it legitimate to use the term "Resistance" to refer in a blanket way to all of the "informal" operations of the present war. To one or another extent, every country in the world today is "enemy-occupied."

† By all indications, the military services of the United States are not devoting

niques, non-cooperation, the spreading of hostile or diversionist propaganda and the harboring of enemy agents or escaped prisoners."

Though any public discussion of it must for a variety of reasons be restrained and rather vague, it is necessary to raise the question: how many of these and similar methods are appropriate and possible in the present stage of the war against the communist power? In other words: What scope are we to assign to the anti-communist Resistance?

Let me first observe that all of the proposals which I have made in the five preceding chapters are both appropriate and possible. There is no insuperable material or technical obstacle to carrying them out, and they are called for by the nature of the present situation. Some of them are, of course, already in effect. In their case, the proposal is only to expand them, and to direct them more consciously to the central objective. To begin the others requires only the relevant decisions.

It is believed by many, among whom are men neither timid nor inexperienced, that it is impossible to conduct Resistance operations within communist-controlled territory. They argue that the apparatus of repression is too strong, that the embrace of the police terror is too tight. I have recently read reports of speeches to this effect made by General Anders, and by General Bor-Komorowski, the leader of the great Warsaw uprising against the Nazis, so shamefully betrayed by the Red Army. Presumably having their own Poland primarily in mind, they argued, according to the reports (which were not complete), that any attempts at internal actions—sabotage, strikes, disobedience, terror, agitation, and so on—would only provoke reprisals and countermeasures which would, in the net, aid the communists. Their reported view is that such actions must wait for either open war or internal chaos (spontaneously

---

anything like the amount of attention that seems warranted by the situation to the technical problems of guerrilla warfare, and the training of guerrilla personnel.

arising?) or a virtual war situation created by the presence of Western armies at or near the borders.

It seems to me, however, that one cannot generalize about the possibilities of internal Resistance operations. Our attitude must be open and experimental, and in a sense opportunistic. The truth is that the situation within the Soviet Empire differs from country to country, and even from local area to local area. The degree of police control is different, as well as the extent and consciousness of opposition. Social and geographical factors are also relevant to the possibilities: what is possible in mountains and forests differs from what is possible on the plains; what is possible in the countryside differs from what is possible in the cities.

Something is always possible. It is continuously possible at least to communicate with some persons in every section of the communist empire, from the disorganized parts of China to Russia itself: by radio, and, with more but not hopeless trouble, by written or printed message. It is usually and in most places possible to have some direct liaison, and at least a skeleton organization. And of course it is possible to exert, from the outside, economic pressures and boycotts which can have direct and significant internal effects. Moreover, the awareness, internally, that the outside world has not accepted the communist domination, that the outside world holds the perspective of Liberation, an awareness which cannot be blocked once the perspective is established in propaganda and action, will have an effect profoundly stimulating to the spirit of opposition as well as demoralizing to the spirit of the communists and their supporters. This awareness will give meaning to opposition, meaning which has been until now in doubt.

Even if such seemingly nebulous results were the maximum, they are not to be lightly dismissed. The nature of communism is such that it requires an absolute, a totalitarian hold on society, on minds and spirits as well as on bodies and things. For this reason, even the smallest germ of opposition, or independence, has a surprisingly extensive repercussion throughout the communist organism.

Much more than this is undeniably possible. Let me be concrete in demonstration.

When the Ukraine was occupied by the Reichswehr, and after the local population had learned the insane viciousness of Nazi rule, much fighting was carried on against the Germans by partisan and guerrilla bands. When the Red Army, and the MVD, returned, many of these bands did not dissolve, but remained in existence in order to struggle against the communists. They formed themselves into the Ukrainian Insurgent Army, and functioned as an anti-communist Resistance. In spite of gigantic efforts by the communists to wipe it out, the Ukrainian Insurgent Army continues to exist, and is unquestionably the symptom of a far wider implicit Ukrainian Resistance. The reality of the Insurgent Army occasionally thrusts itself into the international news. During the past year, for example, several of its members have been forced to escape into non-communist territory. A number of them, who had been captured in Czechoslovakia, were given a public trial at which they successfully insisted on their right to wear their uniforms, and based their defense on the contention that they were members of an army at war.

In at least Poland, Hungary, and Czechoslovakia, the Roman Catholic community constitutes a powerful Resistance element, linked moreover with the outside world by the policy and actions of the Vatican. The Catholic Resistance is effectively preventing the complete totalitarianization of these nations. Small and great public demonstrations of the Resistance are in effect taking place under the forms of the Church: a religious procession, the celebration of a Saint's Day, attendance at Mass and other religious rituals, not to speak of the harboring of priests and others wanted by the secret police, are not only spiritual expressions—and for many perhaps not even primarily that—but also Resistance actions.

In Poland, and elsewhere, the introduction of Stakhanovite (intense speedup) methods in the factories has been followed by sharp increases in absenteeism and illness. These are in reality the forms of strike and slowdown that are used by the workers in a situation which, for the present, rules out forms more open.

Even in the tiny Baltic states, after the deportation to Siberia of hundreds of thousands, the communists have still not succeeded in wiping out the Resistants who find refuge in the woods or the stables of peasants.

The Soviet and satellite press carries hundreds of articles about inefficiency, breakdown, deterioration, and sabotage in industry and agriculture. We know from past experience that much of this talk is humbug, the chief purpose of which is to excuse the errors of the bureaucracy by finding scapegoats for difficulties. Nevertheless, a certain amount of the economic trouble is undoubtedly caused by Resistance sabotage. There are subtler ways of sabotaging the economic process than by throwing sand or monkey-wrenches.

In the Soviet sector of Berlin, and to some extent throughout the Soviet zone of Germany, the continuing spirit of Resistance has been quite openly manifested. In spite of the elaborate rigging of elections, large opposition votes are returned. Fugitives are protected, persons wanted by the MVD are helped to escape. Communist directives get entangled and held up in local administrations. Economic and financial decrees are widely and often quite blatantly violated. Western newspapers and magazines are read, and radio programs listened to. Communist spies and informers (their names often made known by the American radio station) find their doors marked, and themselves the objects of mysterious telephone calls, curious letters, and the cold stares of their neighbors.

In judging the presence and strength of Resistance, we must not tie our vision to precedents. The expression of the Resistance spirit must adapt itself to the actual conditions, including the political conditions. In Bucharest or Leningrad, the silence of a crowd might have the same significance as a mass riot in Detroit. A slight lowering of the production rate in the Donbas or at Magnetogorsk may be the social equivalent of a spectacular strike in Pittsburgh.

Such incidents as those to which I have been referring are publicly known. There are many others, more extensive and more directly challenging to the regime, about which news filters out only slowly and partially, or is altogether suppressed by the defensive censorship. It is certain that there could be many more, still more challenging, if we made the appropriate decisions, and undertook the appropriate actions.

3

We have not yet nearly sounded the limits of Resistance possibilities. Let me continue to be concrete.

It is a fact that Tito broke with the Kremlin, and (at the date when I am writing) has successfully maintained his defiance for a year and a half. Even if he is liquidated in the near future, he has nevertheless proved that the Kremlin can be challenged; and he has given, to those who wish to learn them, some very instructive lessons on the methods and terms of challenge. For the people of Yugoslavia, it is not much of an improvement to be ruled by Tito as an independent fuehrer rather than by Tito as satrap; morally, there is little choice between Tito and Stalin. From the point of view of world politics, however, the change is substantial.

We shall wish that in the end the people of Yugoslavia will find a sovereign more endearing than either Tito or Stalin. But if we grant the desirability of Tito's eventual overthrow, we must keep in mind that it makes a momentous difference who does the overthrowing. If the Kremlin succeeds in overthrowing Tito and in re-establishing its authority in Yugoslavia, that would be a disaster for the anti-communist struggle which would, in my opinion, exceed in political effect the disaster in China. It follows, therefore, that, while we have no motive for aiding Tito positively, we must nevertheless prevent the Kremlin from reconquering Yugoslavia. If we are serious, we must be ready, to this end, to employ those means which prove necessary.

If an open showdown comes over Yugoslavia, then those means would have to include military means. If so, then the action would carry the risk of general war. It does not follow, and it would not be the case, that this risk would be appreciable. There has been fighting, and fierce fighting, over the same fundamental issues, in Greece, and general war has not followed. There has been fighting in southeast Asia and the East Indies, and major campaigns by great armies in China, but a general open war has not been thereby stimulated.

On Tito's southwestern flank is situated Albania. Albania controls the Straits of Otranto, the communication between the Adriatic and the Mediterranean, a principal historic entry to Central Europe. Albania borders northwestern Greece, and has served as a communist base for the Greek Civil War. In Albania, there are now under construction Soviet air and submarine bases. By Tito's defection from the Cominform, Albania was strategically isolated; under its present Cominform government, Albania's position is strategically untenable.

Internally, the position of Albania's government is also untenable. Its roots in the population are slender and shallow. The primitive, semi-feudal economy of Albania's mountainous sections is not adapted to communist social structure. The mountaineers are not permeable by communist ideology. Only the special conditions at the end of the Second World War, the incredible stupidity of Western policy, and continuing support from Moscow have enabled Hoxha's regime to establish itself and, most uneasily, to be maintained. Both inside Albania, and in exile outside, there are opponents who are courageous, determined, and well known to their countrymen.

Far from being utopian, vigorous action to overthrow the Hoxha regime and break Albania away from the Cominform would be almost certain to succeed, at a cost in blood and material aid much below what has already gone into Greece. The results to be reasonably expected would be of almost incalculable value. The Greek problem would be virtually solved; the Kremlin's base on the Adriatic, at the rear of the Balkans and the entrance to the Mediterranean, would be eliminated; a disintegrating impulse would spread throughout the communist organism.

In China, even if the vulgar "business" point of view succeeds in bringing about acceptance and diplomatic recognition of communist rule, and a subsequent buildup of the communists by trade for the sake of short-term profits, it will still not be possible for the communists, or for anyone else, to establish in quicktime over that inchoate, undeveloped land anything like centralized totalitarian rule. Cracks and seams will remain loose and open. Resistance will remain alive, in individuals and whole social strata, and will be able to sustain organized forms, from secret cells on up to opposition armies. If the United States cannot now spare the massive aid that would result in the ousting of the communists and the reconquering of Chinese freedom, or if an operation on that scale is judged (as it is by some) to be strategically unnecessary, there is at the same time no barrier to a more limited cooperation with the Chinese Resistance. Even limited cooperation would enable the Chinese Resistance to prevent the communists from exploiting their victory, and would so tie up the Chinese communists within China itself that they would not be able to help their comrades in India, Japan, and the Southeast.

The least secure territory of the communist empire is, at present, eastern Germany. Eastern Germany is also the section in easiest and fullest communication with the West. Through any of several possible combinations of action, resolutely pursued, it is not at all unlikely that the communists would have to retreat from eastern Germany. Part of such action would be of a traditional diplomatic or economic kind. Part would have to be of the unorthodox Resistance order. Moreover, if eastern Germany is won tomorrow, then, the day after, Poland and Czechoslovakia can become the points of maximum disintegration.

North of Greece and east of Yugoslavia lies Bulgaria. As a defeated enemy power, Bulgaria is legally bound to a Peace Treaty of which the Western powers, as well as the Soviet Union, are parties, enforcers, and guarantors. The communist government of

Bulgaria has brazenly violated the provisions of this treaty. It has violated international law and peace by its actions in relation to the Greek civil war; it is a mechanism of the Kremlin in the Soviet assault on Tito; it is a center of communist manipulation of the "Macedonian question." There is no reason in the nature of things why the Bulgarian communist government should not be called fully to account for violations of the Treaty and disturbances to the peace. But to call the Bulgarian communists fully to account cannot be done by diplomatic notes and protests.

The necessary action would, again, entail the risk of general war. Let it be repeated: any action or no action, in the period ahead, entails the risk of general war. Because the action is firm, it does not follow that the risk is greater. The contrary follows, and is proved by the entire history of American relations with the communists, not only during the years since 1945 but since the beginning. The demonstrated law is: the firmer the action, the less the risk; the firmer the action, the better the results. Yielding, compromise, conciliation, always and invariably result in increased communist boldness, increased demands, further aggressions. Faced with firmness, with genuine and sustained firmness, they retreat. Even the half-firm, limited, and defensive measures of recent years have brought about their retreat. Was this not the case in Iran, in 1947, when Britain and the United States stood firm diplomatically, and Britain began mobilizing in Iraq, across the gulf? Sloppy and incomplete as was the conception of the Greek operation, its firmness, within the limits imposed, is paying off. The Berlin airlift, an action of truly Quixotic firmness, broke the blockade, and, since it kept firmly running, never ran into the anti-aircraft shells and "maneuvers" that were weekly threatened. What have we ever lost by firmness toward the communists? and, let the shadow of Yalta remind us, what have we ever won by yielding?

4

We cannot calculate in advance just what can be achieved if we take the initiative, adopt a conscious and coordinated plan directed toward the central objective, and add to traditional methods the diverse measures of political-subversive warfare, of the Resistance. At the minimum, we can be sure of positive results. We can be certain that at least in some measure we can, if we so will, weaken the enemy and strengthen the forces opposed to him.

At the maximum, we can, without general open war, achieve the central objective: the overthrow of the communist power, or at any rate its reduction to a degree of impotence that no longer threatens world security. This maximum, however unlikely it might seem to the conventional or the skeptical, is at least a real possibility. It is therefore almost infinitely worth trying for, since the only genuine alternatives are either an acceptance of communist world triumph, or a final commitment, without the trial, to a general open war.

There is no reason to rule out in advance a maximum success. The communist power is neither almighty nor eternal. I have analyzed, in Chapter VIII, a set of weaknesses which render it exceedingly vulnerable. These weaknesses exist or have developed, one might say, naturally, without aggravation from the outside. Some of them, if the communists are allowed time and quiet, can be overcome; but all of them can be exploited and deepened until the vulnerability becomes mortal.

There is an additional and profound potential weakness, which I have briefly touched on, inherent in what might be called the dynamics of communism. A totalitarian enterprise is by its nature highly unstable. Once well under way, it cannot stand still, it cannot even move equably. It *must* retain the initiative. It *must* keep the political and social situation in a perpetual turmoil: starting gigantic plans, and beginning new gigantic plans before the first are finished (which they never indeed are) or well begun; purging and counterpurging; turning diplomatic heat on with threats of war, and off with promises of peace; seeking always to upset, unbalance, confuse its opponents; starting united fronts and breaking them; winning victories in this field and triumphs in that. Its leadership *cannot* make mistakes, *must* be infallible. There is a totalitarian *rhythm* which must be sustained. And since totalitarianism is always at a fever pitch, always on a war footing, always keyed taut, it lacks, relatively, the reserves that are at the disposal of a system which is looser, less tempestuous.

This same dynamic law of the expansion of the totalitarian enterprise has its fatal inverse. If the initiative is lost, if the leadership not only errs but *fails* in actions too notorious to be hidden or ideologized away, if the fierce rhythm is broken, if the opponents are not unbalanced but cool and determined, then the totalitarian current can reverse, and with the same impetus sweep smashingly back through the whole monstrous structure. Just as the totalitarian victories are cumulative in their force, each preparing and easing the next, so are the failures—whether Hitler's in the past or the Kremlin's in the future. A positive and unmistakable anti-communist victory—not a merely negative, defensive victory as in Greece or Berlin—could start a process of disintegration that would astound the most sanguine.

How long have we to reach the objective? An answer in exact dates cannot be given. We must conclude, unfortunately: not long, not many years. The condition of the answer is simply the following: the communist power must be reduced to relative impotence before it succeeds in accumulating a sufficient quantity of the weapons of mass destruction, and of the means for delivering those weapons.* A plan of action such as I have here discussed is not an end in itself, nor can it be left suspended in a temporal void. The plan is a means to an end, an objective; it seeks a *decision;* and the decision must be realized in *time*. The plan, therefore—not merely the plan of political-subversive operations, but the whole plan, pro-

* For a full discussion of this point, cf. *The Struggle for the World.*

jected in every relevant field—must point toward a time of decision, a time not known exactly in advance, but which can be approximated by an estimate subject to correction by new evidence. If the decision is reached by the methods which can be, and I think will be, meanwhile used, then the problem which gives birth to the plan is solved. If the problem still remains, unsolved, when the time limit approaches, then the decision must still come, by other means.

Part Four

ORGANIZATION

CHAPTER XVI

The Direction of Political-Subversive Warfare

THROUGHOUT PART THREE, I have, by intention, omitted any reference to a question which necessarily arises whenever a plan is presented not for mere abstract discussion but for action. Who is going to conduct such operations as I have been discussing? Who, in the sense not of particular individuals, but of agencies or organizations?

It is my own conviction that Americans too often give this "organizational problem" a priority which it does not deserve. Americans are prone to believe that if they can find an apt name and draw up an imposing organizational chart, then matters will more or less take care of themselves. The blueprinted outfit will somehow, after it comes into neat existence, discover and fulfill its mission by an intuitive trial and error. This approach is the purest bureaucratism. The appropriate order is the reverse: first we must understand clearly *what is to be done*. Then we seek instrumentalities for doing it. These we may find by adapting to the new use organizations which already exist, or we may feel that a new, specifically designed agency is preferable. The name doesn't make much difference, and exact organizational charts can wait upon the teachings of experience.

The communists do not have any special organizational difficulty in relation to subversive and Resistance operations. The communist enterprise in its entirety is a subversive and Resistance agency in continuous action. Therefore the highest body of the communist enterprise (which is, *de facto,* the Politburo of the Russian party) is automatically and naturally in direct charge of these informal activities, which are rated as the primary international work of the enterprise. For the communists, it is the conventional operations which sometimes create organizational difficulties. For example, it has proved rather hard for them to devise a suitable administrative relation between the Politburo and the conventional army. They have had to try and reject a variety of expedients.

The non-totalitarian nations of the West, however, have not in the past been much concerned with propaganda, subversion, or Resistance. The operations in these fields do not fit comfortably into the normal structure either of their governments or of private institutions.

During the Second World War, all of the chief Western powers were nevertheless forced to undertake these operations on a considerable scale. In part, their conduct was placed in the hands of existing agencies, civilian and military, where they seemed to have some plausible connection with what these agencies had been doing. For certain of the tasks, including the more unorthodox, it proved necessary to improvise special agencies like the American Office of Strategic Services or the British "D" Organization and "SOE." *

These special agencies were, operationally, subject to the military high command (or, in certain cases, to the appropriate theater commander): that is, they functioned as subordinate units of the armed services. This arrangement seemed reasonable. The national effort was directed toward a unified objective which was military—the winning of the war. The military high command, subject to the ultimate control of the highest political leadership (which, however, was also working toward the unified objective of winning the war),

---

* As I understand it, there was no single British organization directly comparable to the American Office of Strategic Services.

was in charge of the effort, and responsible for the practical attainment of the objective. The unorthodox operations had obvious effects, both positive and negative, on military strategy, and therefore seemed plainly to belong to the province of those who were charged with the military strategy.

It is hard to see how any other reasoning could have been used. Nevertheless, the relation between the military chiefs and the special agencies was an uneasy one. It is of some importance to try to understand why this was so. In the first place, the military leaders were for the most part not experienced or trained, in either theory or practice, in the field of the unorthodox operations. They therefore tended to be suspicious or deprecating, or to expect the wrong kind of results. They did not trust the new methods; they could not anticipate what might come from them, in how long a time; and in general they just did not know enough about them to direct and exploit their possibilities. In the second place, it became clear at the start that the armed forces did not have the personnel to man these agencies. To soldiers from every military branch, many civilians—not a few of types antipathetic to the traditional military mind—had to be joined.

In fact, many of the soldiers (in the OSS, for example) were in reality only civilians arbitrarily given a military status in order to make the agencies seem more warlike.

These two factors alone were a source of abundant practical trouble. A third, though less noticeable on the surface, was more fundamental. In the social hierarchy, the political function is, so far as the two can be separated, dominant over the military. This is true even when a country is under a military dictatorship, since *the goal* is political, and the military dictatorship only a possible means for reaching the goal. (The only exception would be a tribe or nation the sole occupation of which was to make war.) The relation between the two is summed up in the familiar doctrine of "the subordination of the military to the civilian power," a doctrine accepted as firmly by Clausewitz as by democratic theoreticians. More exactly, however, the doctrine should be phrased: "the subordination of the military *function* to the civilian (i.e., political) *function*." It is conceivable, and it not infrequently happens, that a military captain becomes the chief of state. That does not violate the doctrine in this second form, since his function as chief of state is political, and separable in analysis from his military function.

If a nation reaches, or is forced into, the political decision that its interests require the armed defeat of another nation, then the military power undertakes to carry out that decision. This is how American and British military doctrine has always understood the function of the military, in spite of the political sidelines of individual military leaders. The military command can rightly advise on the military feasibility of the political decision; it can rightly claim precedence in determining the purely military means that are to be used for enforcing it; but the military strategy as a whole is subordinate to the political aim. In practice, when the military command interferes in the realm of political aims, then serious trouble starts.

In the past, these relations and limits, and the traditional doctrine, seemed fairly obvious. The difficulty with the unorthodox, subversive, Resistance operations, however, is that in them the military and the political are inextricably mingled—a fact which was symbolically expressed by the mingling of civilians and soldiers in the special agencies. There is no longer a clear line. What is done in the unorthodox fields has a simultaneous effect both on military strategy and on political aims. The fusion was constantly illustrated during the Second World War. Shall Tito or Mihailovitch be supported in Yugoslavia? Is that a military or a political question? Or Hoxha or Abas Kupi or Kryeziu in Albania? If we are to support the French Resistance, then which Resistance, or which faction of the Resistance—De Gaulle's, Giraud's, the socialists', the communists'? Which Resistants in Italy should our agents befriend, our planes supply, our Intelligence trust? And so on.

What happened, as a consequence, was that the special agencies could not be confined to their spots on the organizational charts. Not merely for the original political directive, but on frequent occasions, and sometimes in relation to issues which were quite trivial from a practical standpoint, the regular chain of command had to be broken through, and direct appeal made not to the military high command, but to the political leadership, and often the highest political leadership. This was very disruptive to "orderly procedure."

I do not think that there is any way to solve these confusions wholly. They are given in the nature of the problem. Both experience and analysis seem to suggest that, even in what is officially recognized as wartime, the direction of the unorthodox operations does not properly fall under the military command.* The political is prior to the military. If the unorthodox operations are a fusion of both, then their political phase should be given priority over their military phase. This conclusion holds with less question in a time like the present, which is not legally and formally recognized as war. In the present period, conventional military operations are for the most part preparatory, indirect, or secondary, whereas the unorthodox operations are, or rather should be, active, ample, and primary. It would be almost a reversal of the real relations, in the present situation, to put the direction of the unorthodox operations in direct subordination to the conventional military command.

At the same time, however, since the unorthodox operations are *also* military, and since they both use and profoundly affect conventional military means and resources, their conduct cannot be altogether independent of the military command. There must be the most intimate and continuous liaison between the two, and this must be provided for in any adequate organizational solution.

---

* In the United States, there is a special factor reinforcing this conclusion: the inter-service rivalries which make it almost impossible to have an objective head of the "unorthodox branch" drawn from the regular armed forces. A military officer, since he is only a single being, must be from the Army, the Navy, or the Air Force, and from only one of these. Almost inevitably, since he is a subordinate of some other office of the same service, and himself part of that service, the agency would tend to become an Army (or Navy or Air Force) "show."

It might seem, from the preceding considerations, that the direction of the "unorthodox branch" falls most naturally within the province of the State Department (to concretize the discussion in terms of the structure of the United States government—the same principles would hold for other democratic governments). To assign it to the State Department would, in fact, be a possible organizational solution. During recent years, the State Department has taken on a number of the kinds of operation which are here in question: propaganda notably, and even, on a smaller scale, some of the more irregular measures. It is the highest political department of the government, and it is charged in general with foreign affairs.

There are, however, at least two objections to the State Department's assuming the direction. In the first place, the State Department has too many other things to do. Its officials have already great difficulty in coordinating effectively, and guiding actively, its multitudinous affairs. A new major division would either get lost in the shuffle, or would interfere with the handling of established tasks. Moreover, the kind of thinking, the kind of "mental set" required for these newer measures is different from that appropriate to most of the other State Department activities. It is hard for the same administrators to shift at will from one to the other. In the second place, the unorthodox operations, though in one aspect they are undoubtedly related to the function of the State Department, in others (the military and the domestic, for example) are outside of its normal boundaries.

However, just as in the case of the military command, there must unquestionably be the closest liaison between the State Department and the unorthodox branch: the policies and actions of each continuously affect and are affected by the actions of the other.

There is a third very close link between the unorthodox branch and Intelligence. Plainly, political-subversive, Resistance operations require the best possible Intelligence. The link in this case was shown by the history of the Office of Strategic Services. The OSS was first planned, I believe, as simply a special type of Intelligence group, and its Intelligence activities were always a major portion of its work. From this point of view, it might seem that the unorthodox branch should be set up as part of the Central Intelligence Agency. This also, I think, is a possible solution for the organizational problem. The objection, once again, is that Intelligence is only *one* aspect of political-subversive warfare, and, since the controlling aim is action, not knowledge, it is essentially a secondary aspect. For the same agency to undertake both would run the risk of their mutual interference. A full and objective Intelligence coverage might be biased by the particular actions which were being carried on, or planned. Actions might be hindered by an occupational tendency of Intelligence toward passivity. Nevertheless, in this case also, the liaison between the Central Intelligence Agency and the unorthodox branch must be the most intimate possible.

I have discussed here the relations between the unorthodox branch and the three established governmental institutions to which, by virtue of its tasks, it is most nearly tied. It is true that its tasks relate it to nearly every other sphere as well. However, the tie in the other cases is not so intimate, and with them there are indirect ways, already established, in which coordination can be obtained. The State Department, for example, is already designed to coordinate foreign economic with foreign diplomatic policy.

There is one further preliminary point, arising out of a peculiarity of the United States' governmental structure, which should be noted before attempting to draw a positive conclusion.

The American executive power is structurally separate from the legislative power. Both together (plus the judiciary, which is not here relevant) constitute the nation's organized leadership, the embodiment of its sovereignty. The national stake in political-subversive, Resistance operations is as crucial as in formal war. Moreover, many of these operations can only be carried out through a lack of publicity unprecedented in American tradition, with funds "unvouchered"—not publicly accounted for, and a personnel also largely removed from public scrutiny. For these reasons, and what they imply, it would seem that the Congress ought to have some special mode of liaison with the direction of the agency which carries on these operations.

2

The organizational problem of the unorthodox branch is too complex to permit anyone to feel certain that he has found an ideal solution. With the preceding analysis in mind, what seems to me probably best is more or less along the following lines:

There should be an agency established at the very highest governmental level: that is, the head of the agency should be directly under the President. He, and he alone, should be the chief of the agency, responsible to the President only. However, he should work continuously with a board or commission on which would sit direct representatives of the State Department, the Joint Chiefs of Staff, and the Central Intelligence Agency, and a representative or official of the Congress. This board would be the mechanism both for running the agency and for obtaining the necessary closeness of liaison. The director himself should have civilian status, even though he might be drawn from the armed services.

The function of the agency should not be primarily operational, but rather to plan, initiate, guide, subsidize, and coordinate operations undertaken, wherever possible, by other institutions already existing, or brought into existence by the agency for some special purpose. Of course, some operations would have to be undertaken by the agency itself. Most of the time, some other instrumentality would be more effective: and in any case there is none but a bureaucratic point in creating new institutions to do what can be just as well done by old. Many of the operations could be best carried out, for example, by the armed services, the State Department, various of the financial or economic institutions of the government, the Departments of Commerce or Labor, or still other governmental divisions.

It is, however, both expedient and, from a democratic point of view, most desirable that very many of the operations should be the task not of any governmental institution but of private groups or individuals. Many of those fields of activity which I have surveyed in Part Three are best cultivated by private citizens: by trade unions, educational, scientific, and charitable foundations, publishers, universities, business corporations (especially those with extensive foreign interests), voluntary associations of citizens formed for specific purposes, committees (and even governments) of exiles and refugees, students, tourists, and businessmen who travel or reside abroad. It is apparent, for example, that associations with foreign trade unions are usually handled more profitably by American trade unionists than by American governmental representatives. One of the great foundations might effectively interest itself in the project for an East European University, and in similar projects. American publishers can devise ways to increase the flow of newspapers, books, and magazines throughout the world. With a little guidance and help, American students in Paris, Rome, London, Munich, Heidelberg, Sweden, Holland, Geneva would find it not uninteresting to get to know more of their surroundings than classrooms, museums, and cafés: the labor and political movements, and the people active in them, are a most stimulating object of research and excitement. A newspaper published in Milan or Frankfort or Tokyo or Rio de Janeiro does not have to be "published by the U.S. Government" in order to express a point of view of advantage to the American side of the struggle for the world. Already, of course, private groups are active in not a few of these fields.

There are certain deficiencies in those activities of private groups which bear (whether or not the groups understand so) on the political-subversive war. One set comes from ignorance. The private groups are often misled by false or inadequate information into sponsoring causes or persons with whom they have nothing in common. In other cases, private individuals do not know what needs to be done, but would be quite willing to act if particular problems were merely brought to their attention. From a more general point of view, the completely unguided activities of private groups tend often to a misuse of effort, through unnecessary conflicts, bad timing, overlapping, etc. Finally, the private groups, in order to carry out some of the most important activities, lack the required funds and resources, and have no way to get them except through direct or indirect subsidy. It is for such reasons as these that, even in relation to the private groups, a guiding and coordinating agency, with adequate resources at its disposal, is required.

I have said that a highest level agency, set up as I have here outlined, seems to me the best organizational solution of the problem of the direction of the informal war. If the best, it is not the only solution; there may be one still better that I have not thought of. Moreover, even without any orderly solution, the informal war nevertheless continues, and, whether admitted or not, continues to be fought by our side as well as theirs. No one has to wait for a formal declaration or official action in order to take part in this war. There is much that any individual, or any group, private or governmental, can accomplish, whenever the responsibility is accepted and the decision made. It is absurd to wait for official orders to seek survival: and it is survival that is at stake.

3

The struggle against communism is not an exclusive domain of the United States. By virtue of the present relationship of world forces, the United States must supply the major resources for the struggle, and only the United States can lead the struggle. The struggle is itself, however, the concern equally of all nations and peoples, including a greater part of the peoples today subject to the communist power. In whatever actions the United States takes in the struggle, therefore, it must strive for the maximum of collaboration with the maximum number not only of its own nationals but of the nationals of all other countries.

It is desirable that, where possible, the collaboration should be

official as well as private. To collaborate, outside of any official sanction, with individuals of another nation is a delicate and difficult
business. Besides other objections to it, it is wasteful of time and
energy, and it excludes many persons who will not act in these matters without at least the implied approval of their acknowledged
government. The number of men in the world well equipped by
temperament and experience for the struggle against communism
is not so large that any can willingly be spared.

If, for example, a major action were decided upon for the Balkans
(support of a revolt in Albania, let us say, or protection of Yugoslavia against Cominform attack, or a showdown on the Bulgarian
Peace Treaty), it would be almost indispensable to secure full British understanding and cooperation. Britain has more men trained
in Balkan affairs than the United States possesses. She has also a
considerable tradition of irregular warfare. For the Near East, the
Far East, Africa, and India, the case is the same, or nearly so. It
follows that, just as we expect complete British solidarity in a general open war, if it occurs, so we ought to try to have solidarity with
Britain in the informal war of the present period.

With Britain this seems possible. No matter what disputes between Britain and the United States arise—and some of them are
not trivial—the destiny of the two nations is fused. Britain may try
to temporize with the Soviet Union, she may even, in momentary
nostalgia for the old balance-of-power technique by which she once
dominated the world, dream occasionally of playing the Soviet
Union off against the United States. In the final analysis, she cannot line up with communism, and she will not surrender to it: she
is not ready for suicide.

Britain, then, can be relied upon in almost any undertaking, even
the most confidential; and to the success of some she can contribute
a disproportionate share.* But, unfortunately, for the work of such
an agency as I am advocating, for the conduct of political-subversive,

---

* It is my own view, motivated in *The Struggle for the World,* that the United
States, Britain, and the Dominions should be united.

Resistance warfare, there are not many nations toward whom, at present official levels, we can feel the same full confidence. We can hardly coordinate plans and operations with an official agency of a government that permits communists to penetrate all of its agencies, or a government that has no real authority or permanence. The awkwardness is not confined to the problem of informal war. It is already plaguing the United States in connection with military plans for the nations of the Atlantic Pact, as it has in connection with Latin America.

The paradox is painful. The United States must have allies—and it needs allies, not mercenaries. And yet it cannot be sure who is, or can be, an ally, or of what degree. There is no formula for an answer. In politics, as in individual life, the foundation principle seems to be: the first responsibility is one's own; accepting that, one does what one can.

CHAPTER XVII

The Suicidal Mania of American Business

THE UNITED STATES has been, as all the world knows, the promised land of "business." It has been the "businessman's" country. Until, perhaps, recently, the "businessmen" have for more than a century been its leading citizens—its "ruling class," Europeans would say. From a sociological point of view, the American concept of "the businessman" is complex, and not a little obscure. It covers a variety of individuals whose functions and status are by no means identical: outright owners of personal or family enterprises; corporation directors with substantial but minority holdings in the corporations they direct; directors, managers, executives who have little or no ownership interest; certain "professional men," like lawyers, advertising men, engineers; bankers and financiers as well as industrialists; small enterprisers as well as large, real estate operators as well as road contractors. Still, we all know, or imagine we know, who the "businessmen" are. We can all recognize a businessman when we see him, and, when we go to a town, we know pretty well where to find him. The "business community" appears in public, and is on record: there it is, in the files of the Chamber of Commerce, attending the Rotary luncheon, sending its delegates to the convention of the National Association of Manufacturers, subscribing to the Community Chest.

The dominance of business in this country's development is something visible, palpable. In a land so enormously spread out, sprawling, so geologically varied, so mixed in religion, climate, ethnic roots, physical types, it is business that ties together the remarkable whole into some kind of cultural unity. In every scene and context, the externalized realities of business are there, presented. It is not so, or in such degree, in any other nation. So much of France, for example, as it is known to the senses, is Braque-colored stone walls and village houses, Norman and Gothic spires and windows, vines pruned in just the French way, a certain tilt of berets, trees lining canals and narrow roads, unspeakably dingy provincial streets, chestnut blossoms and blossoming fruit trees unlike any others, a style or set of styles that is somehow manifest in everything made—houses and churches, furniture and printed books, paintings and clothes, a certain kind of shutter for shop windows, special chairs and tables and glasses for sidewalk cafés. So, when we think or feel of England—in spite of the Midlands, in spite of Liverpool—do we not somehow combine in immediate imagination green-set spires, like those of Winchester or Salisbury, with the Thames Embankment and the great public buildings of London, hedgerows with Tudor stucco and timber on rural shop fronts, the wonderful country houses with the Roman architecture of Chester or Bath, the incomparable gardens with, of course, the suburban villas? Italy differs at once from France in the way the vines are trained, the look and stones of the churches, the location of villages, the placing of big houses—castles, fortresses, rather. Almost any nation with a real unity appears to us in terms of art, architecture, housing, landscape arrangement, dress, music, gesture, town planning, characteristic colors and shapes, and ways of tending shrubs and flowers or fields; or, if we look through the mind instead of the senses, in terms of religion, philosophy, literature, morality.

If we try to grasp the United States as somehow a whole, not by reading and thinking about it in an apartment or library of the eastern seaboard fringe, but by going to look and feel, the principal key to the reality seems to be of a different kind. There is no pervading national style in the arts or buildings; the people of different sections, and within sections, do not look alike, or even talk alike; there is no shared folk foundation in custom, style, or thought, no common music, no particular way to arrange pictures or gardens.

But everywhere is the externalization of business—not just of the local business of this or that area, but of a single, a national intertwined business system. Far across the Great Plains, it is not a cathedral spire that is seen against the sky, but a towering grain elevator. As the traveler draws near, he will see the label dedicating it to Pillsbury or General Mills as often as he will find a church in France dedicated to the Virgin. At the small shop in lonely places he will find no wood carved or lace made on centuries' sanctioned patterns; but he will refresh himself from the Coca-Cola freezer, buy Wrigley's Spearmint gum, and get for his car (the same in kind as cars he will see however many thousand miles he goes) his Texaco or Esso gasoline that will pour from a pump brought there and to twenty thousand other wayside stops from the same plant in Indiana. As he crosses the plateau of Montana, he will see against the evening sun not a moated chateau, but the poles and wires which he knows mean American Telephone and Telegraph or Western Union; and he will be advancing alongside the endless steel tracks —from Gary or Pittsburgh—that will never be far away. His wayside shrines will be the billboards, beckoning him to Chesterfield, Luckies, Chevrolet, Rinso, their colors mixed by International Printing Ink, their paper from Crown Zellerbach or Kimberley, the boards of their structure from Weyerhauser, the nails from U.S. Steel.

In the remotest wilderness, the bulldozers of Allis Chalmers will have blazed a lumber trail up the mountainside, the heavy trucks of General Motors will be grinding under their piled load which the quick whine of the portable continuous saws has carved into exact lengths. In desert, city, and seaside, the ice boxes of Westinghouse and Philco will be there, the light bulbs of General Electric, the radio receivers of Zenith and RCA. Across the prairies of the Dakotas in the autumn he will not see compact villages clustered within their walls, but in the air around him will rise the dust from the threshers by International Harvester, heaping their golden piles; and across the Delta of the Mississippi he will hear the clash of

Deere & Company's cotton pickers. As he begins the long approach to Great Falls, it will not be another Chartres that lifts before him into the air, but the great smokestack of Anaconda; and as he swings down the coast of southern California or the Gulf, no monastery like St. Michel will spring from the sea before him, but the derricks of Standard Oil or Phillips. As he penetrates a wasteland, he will not come upon the ruins of a Roman theater or a Norman castle; but out of the sage will spring the curious form of a booster station for the pipeline, forged by Bethlehem or Republic, through which gas from Texas flows fifteen hundred miles to warm northern homes or drive northern turbines. Around the water-hole conjured out of the desert by the steel windmill from Toledo, he will exchange stares with the white-faced Herefords who have been summoned into existence by the far-off call of Armour, Swift, or Wilson from Chicago. Overhead the bright plane, sheathed by the Aluminum Company of America, powered by Pratt & Whitney, braked by Borg-Warner, super-charged by General Electric, tired by Goodrich, held to course by the Sperry Corporation, follows the airways which, marked by radio beam and searchlight, now tie together the air of the nation as the ground was earlier tied by the rails. Wherever he goes, he will see and hear and touch the material extensions of the mills and assembly plants and lathes and presses of Pittsburgh, Detroit, Chicago, Schenectady, Bridgeport, Youngstown, Birmingham, Beaumont. In whatever town he enters, there in the windows he will find spread before him the brand names that are his litany: Del Monte, Frigidaire, Parker, Remington, Duz, Birdseye, Wearever, Silvertone, Ford, Hotpoint, Bandaid, Arrow, Nylon, Singer, Kodak, Calverts, Sunkist.

I have no sympathy and little patience with those inverse Philistines—my fellow intellectuals, often, or the junior sons of the creatively wealthy—who sneer so easily at business and businessmen. Business and businessmen have opened and built this continental nation, on the perspective and scale of Alexander Hamilton's unprecedented vision, and they are to be therefore honored. If they acted, as a rule, for the love of money rather than of their fellow men, there are motives more injurious than the search for profit; and they did not need slave camps to people their frontiers. If this country is "basely materialistic" in its "philosophy," then let it be noted that such materialism is the cause of less suffering and more joy than most idealisms which history records.

One afternoon of the heat wave in August, 1949, we were driving southwest from Detroit, past the Willow Run plant, just as the shift had ended. Out of the wide entrance of the plant yards, the cars of the workers—workers, not bosses—came rushing by the hundreds, and swinging into the highway. Were they more miserable because a great machine, under their control, was taking them where they wanted to go, and because they were not trudging dustily on foot or swarming into dirty trams toward miserable rooms without light or baths? Twenty-five miles further on, we turned off into a State Park of trees and small hills. We saw ahead, again, many hundreds of cars, many of them the same that had come from the plant a little earlier, but now stopped. Beyond them were dozens of acres of wooded grounds, with tables, benches, stone fireplaces, and heavy iron charcoal grills placed on iron posts (mass produced, no doubt, by Midland Steel Foundries). It was beginning to darken, and the reddened charcoal in the grills gleamed among the trees like lampposts. At the tables, hundreds of families—of workers and clerks and stenographers—were finishing their steaks and hamburgers and hot dogs, and Cokes and beers. Beyond them was a large lake; and there hundreds more were swimming, laughing, diving, shouting, and in the deeper water sweeping or drifting along in canoes, rowboats, and outboards (mass produced by Evinrude). There seemed to be values present there in abundance—of friendship and love—that were something more than "material"; and yet without the material, without those cars and that iron, that processed wood and well-preserved meat and skillfully bottled drink, neither the values nor the people rejoicing in them would have been there.

2

The American businessman is a genius in his kind. He is on the average remarkable, and from his ranks have come authentic individual geniuses in remarkable number. He has proved himself the master of the techniques of production. In the auxiliaries of production, in financing and distribution and sales, he is scarcely less astounding.

Within his own field, he is alert, inventive, keen, perceptive, quick to change and adapt. Confronted with a new process, a new machine, a new method, he drives quickly through cant to realities. And, in his field, he has a magnitude of vision which puts to shame the businessmen of other nations. Who else drives railroads two thousand miles into nowhere; thinks of pipelines in thousands instead of dozens of miles; puts up a thousand houses at once, as Levitt does, or creates whole towns in a year, as at the atomic projects; links every citizen, or nearly every one, with every telephone in the world; within a decade encases the female legs of half the world with a new chemical?

All this is true. But the American businessman, alas, suffers also, and most grievously, from the hypertrophy of occupational function. Within his arena so accomplished a performer, he often proves an oaf when he ventures, or is forced, outside. His alertness, vision, quickness, invention are somehow transformed into their opposites. In art, philosophy, and in political or social affairs of any but the crudest sort, he is likely to be drearily prejudiced, emptily pompous, narrowly unperceptive, hopelessly backward-looking, naïvely credulous. At his banquets, his conventions, his clubs, and in his family circle, he tirelessly repeats the most banal of ritualistic abstractions, without relevance, content, or style. It is as if his entire creative spirit were channeled into his special field, and for all else there remained only a paltry set of conditioned verbal reflexes. Ah, how infinitely wearisome a thing it is to listen to the after-dinner speech of "a leading businessman"!

Because this country has been so predominantly a land of business, and because businessmen are still so powerful a segment of the national community, we cannot lightly dismiss this extra-curricular ineptness of the typical businessman. Unfortunately, he is not a tamed domestic who can be chained within his corporate boundaries. His stupidities, as well as his genius, have their momentous effect on the national destinies. In relation to the struggle against world communism, there is grave question what effect that will turn out to be. I am inclined to believe that the attitude and actions of the businessmen are the factor in the struggle about which we must have the gravest doubts of all.

3

In relation to the struggle against communism, the American businessman is too ignorant, too greedy, too reactionary and, in a certain sense, too cowardly. I am not, of course, qualifying individual businessmen by these adjectives; I am referring rather to social or "class" characteristics of the businessman as a type. As individuals, businessmen are no more frequently ignorant or cowardly than individuals from any other social group. They are perhaps somewhat more often greedy and reactionary, but that is no doubt an unavoidable response to their social function. I want to specify my meaning with some care.

American businessmen seek, and often obtain, really enormous personal incomes for themselves, and colossal profits for the corporations which they own or manage. During these past few years, corporate profits in the hundreds of millions have not been extraordinary, and in one case (General Motors) a single year's profit has gone beyond half a billion dollars. In the published lists of the salaries of corporation executives, we read the names of hundreds of men who are being paid from one hundred to more than five hundred thousand dollars by a single company. These figures tell only a part, and sometimes a relatively small part, of the story. Each of these men, and their wives and children, have other sources of income—from other companies, from bonds and stocks and mortgages, from expense accounts (which have expanded into a major racket) and trust funds—that boost the total figure as much as several hundred per cent.

I am aware that the income tax takes a big slice of the personal incomes. That fact, however, seems to give less, rather than more, excuse for adding more hundreds of thousands in the upper brackets where only 15 per cent or so is left. Besides, there are ways—expense accounts, capital gains, farms worked at a loss, pensions, tax-exempt securities, streamlined gifts—for softening the edge of the income tax. I am aware also that most of the arguments of the labor leaders and their "labor economists" about corporate profits are the grossest demagogy (as if, in an economy like ours, wage-increases could "come out of profits" rather than be added to the cost base, as if in any case the spread of profits over the wages of all the workers would make in the long run any appreciable difference, other than to ensure an increased number of bankruptcies . . .). I also know that profits in the hundreds of millions can always be shown to be "very small" by altering the base to be used in calculating them: "total turnover" instead of invested capital; reproduction cost instead of original cost; profit per unit instead of total profit—the "business economists" are just as ingenious as the labor economists.

All these pseudo-economic rationalizations are beside today's point. That point is that these monstrous incomes and profits have an antagonizing and demoralizing effect upon the workers, and the rest of the poorly or normally paid members of society, in this country and throughout the world. These income statistics are emotional explosives handed gratuitously to the communist propaganda machine.

Even where they do not lead to conscious communist tendencies, they promote that "alienation of the proletariat" which Marx rightly believed to be so essential a condition for the victory of communism. They also, in themselves and by their psychological effect of justifying the most extreme trade union demands, stimulate inflationary processes and economic disharmony. Objectively considered, their direct economic impact is comparatively slight. Nevertheless, in the present condition of the world, their psychological, political, and social impact is enormous. In a world where there is not only so much poverty and misery, but where more men than ever before are conscious of that misery, they call forth a moral rejection of the system that permits a few to be so blatantly and self-indulgently greedy.

I do not myself believe that American workers, and the American masses generally, are equalitarian in their social thinking. So far as I have been able to tell, they feel not only that some men inevitably do get greater material rewards than others, but that things ought to be so; and they are more often pleased than jealous when some-one "gets up in the world." They show this attitude by the size of the salaries—and expense accounts—which they vote their own union leaders, or which they do not object seriously to when the leaders take them without a vote. But they, and most men in the world, think that the line ought to be drawn somewhere, and somewhere considerably short of the spot where the heads of the great American corporations are drawing it.

Let me turn to another business attitude, where we find a combination of greed, ignorance, and a kind of economic cowardice. The United States imposes a "protective" tariff on most imports at the same time that the rest of the world is groaning from a lack of dollars. All suggestions for radical reduction of the tariff are immediately fought by the lobbies of the industrialists, who want to block even a minor foreign competition in the home market. Even the mild and still high-tariff Hull "reciprocal trade treaty" program was initiated and continues only against the opposition of much of the business community. Nevertheless, the businessmen insist on their right to sell their own products anywhere in the world, and they complain at any measures of discrimination. They show their greed by wanting to exploit the home market to a maximum without any interference that might (though it would not necessarily) cut into volume and prices, while simultaneously wanting a hog's share in foreign markets at whatever detriment to the economies of other nations. They show their timidity—these same businessmen who lament so piously the "growth of statism"—by relying on the tariff-shield of the state to shelter their home monopoly. They show their ignorance in their failure to realize that the two parts of their program—to sell but not to buy—are contradictory. (That the world's principal creditor nation should operate its foreign trade on a virtual free-trade basis should be among the most elementary of economic lessons.) And they prove their lack of any vision of the fact that the present stage of industrial civilization demands a perspective of the development of the world economy as a whole.

More directly ominous is the mounting, though still partly hidden, pressure from the businessmen for "trade with the enemy." They are irked by the State Department's restrictions on exports to the communist empire. What does world policy matter when there are a few easy dollars to be made? As the signs of partial economic recession appeared in 1949, the longing for those dollars grew in intensity. Shabby schemes for evading the restrictions, by indirect sales through Holland, Belgium, and other intermediary nations, were worked out with the usual ingenuity. As the communists swept south in China, the businessmen in the China trade bowed to the ground before them, and asked only for the privilege of supplying them with what they need to consolidate their conquest: but Mao Tze-tung is proving a rude host, even to suppliant businessmen.

In this instance, the greed (provoked, it is true, by economic compulsions) is manifest enough, but the ignorance is even more devastating. Though the British aid to German rearmament and the American sales of iron and oil to Japan are the freshest and most painful of examples, history, experience, and common sense are fatuously disregarded. It would not, of course, be sensible to stop all trade with the communist empire. A small flow facilitates a certain desirable contact, permits some importation of needed supplies, and exercises a certain political leverage. But to trade on a big and unrestricted scale is to prepare suicide—or, rather, to build the guillotine for one's own executioner. The inability of the communists to solve their economic problem is probably their greatest weakness, and our greatest protection. Are we, then, going to solve it for them?

Businessmen are ignorant, abysmally ignorant, about what communism is, what communists are. Of course the businessmen are, almost all of them, in their own minds the staunchest of "anti-communists." But because they do not understand communism (and because they are greedy and short-sighted), they act frequently in ways that help communism. They really cannot believe that the communists mean what they say—just as they could not bring themselves to believe Hitler. They do not believe that the communists are serious when they declare that they are going to conquer the world. They cannot comprehend the certainty that, if the communists conquer, they themselves—these same businessmen flanked in their splendid offices by their corps of secretaries, relaxed in the expensive furnishings of their suburban houses—will be shot like cattle, or driven to die more slowly and terribly in some Arctic or tropical wasteland. Mass rape may be possible, and recorded, in Berlin-Zehlendorf, but it is not even conceivable in Greenwich. Can the president of General Motors or U.S. Steel or the Chase National Bank, with whom an ordinary fellow citizen cannot even make an appointment, be yanked from his chair by a common ruffian who has not even been announced? It is too absurd. The businessmen, for all their rhetoric, can think of the communists only as rivals or competitors of the same fundamental type as themselves. And every businessman knows that all businessmen have, in the last analysis, their price, that, no matter how hard the bargaining, it is always possible to make a deal if you want it badly enough.

Very many businessmen do not know the difference between a communist and an anarchist, democratic socialist, or mere eccentric dissident. They pick up a pompous phrase like "socialism is the halfway house to communism," and imagine that by repeating it they are being profoundly philosophical. I have had Minnesota businessmen tell me that Senator Humphrey—who drove the communists out of the Democratic-Farmer-Labor party in Minnesota—is a communist. Not a few Michigan businesmen look on the Reuther brothers as communist. I have even heard John L. Lewis called "a communist at heart." The social-democratic labor governments of Britain, Australia, and Finland, all three of which in 1949 smashed major communist internal offensives (the London Dock strike, the Australian coal strike, the Finnish lumber and attempted general strike), are all "sort of communist" in many Rotary and Chamber of Commerce circles. Many businessmen have asked me about my colleague, Sidney Hook, one of the world's leading anti-communists, and also a democratic socialist and "radical": "He is a communist, isn't he?"

In the struggle against internal communism, these negative qualities of the American businessmen are discouragingly apparent. Some of the businessmen, plain and simple reactionaries, are absolutely anti-union. They would like literally to smash the trade unions. Since their likes become known, they too help to "alienate the proletariat" and to heap up grist for the communist propaganda mill. How modern mass industry could operate without trade unions they have never stopped to speculate. Others, from ignorance or greed or both, act toward unions in such a way as to aid communist-led unions against anti-communist unions. I shall illustrate this particular stupidity by two specific examples.

In 1947, the anti-communist leader of the United Automobile Workers, Walter Reuther, was in the midst of a bitter and gallant internal union fight against the faction led by the communists. His success in that fight had as one condition his ability to win a reasonably advantageous contract with General Motors. Though the majority of General Motors employees are members of the UAW, a considerable number (in the non-automotive divisions) are members of the United Electrical Workers (United Electrical, Radio and

Machine-Workers Union), which is under communist control. In the midst of negotiations with Reuther, the General Motors management suddenly made a settlement with the United Electrical Workers, on terms which Reuther had publicly rejected. The General Motors management no doubt thought this a very smart trick whereby to cut the ground from under Reuther's feet. They were unaware that they were the dupes, not the instigators of the trick. The trap was in reality sprung by the communists: they—as so often sacrificing to party policy the interests of labor solidarity—offered the seductive settlement in order to weaken Reuther's position in relation to the company, and to force him, as they hoped, into public defeat which would undermine his position in his own union. Reuther, fortunately, was a better and a braver general than either the management or the communists. He got a good settlement with the company, and smashed the communists in the autumn convention. For the latter result—a major victory in the present war for the world—no thanks are to be given to the executives and directors of General Motors, those fulsome defenders of "the American way."

On the Pacific Coast, the sailors and allied workers are organized in a group of unions led by the Sailors' Union of the Pacific, the leader of which is the militant and extremely anti-communist Harry Lundberg. The union of the Longshoremen, warehouse workers and others, is under the control of the communists, represented most publicly by Harry Bridges. In the late summer of 1948, Bridges tied up all the principal Pacific ports. The shipowners fumed and blustered. Up and down the Coast, they declared that this time it was not a matter of wages and hours and working conditions; it was now a matter of principle, American principle, to throw the "foreign, communist agent," Bridges, out of the labor movement. Never, never would they negotiate with Bridges! The time had come for a showdown. And so for a while it seemed. For more than three months, the ships were idle, the harbors empty. But lo and behold, suddenly at the beginning of winter, there were the photographs again of Bridges and the shipowners smiling at each other, and the happy announcement of a fine contract satisfactory to both parties, and ready to go into operation tomorrow. There was a little catch in the announcement. Harry Lundberg's sailors had, during the strike, also presented their demands to the shipowners. But somehow these demands had been lost sight of in the shipowners' get-together with the foreign communist agent. The ships were to sail tomorrow, but no contract had been signed with the Sailors' Union of the Pacific. They did not sail. Fortunately for America, Lundberg, like Reuther, understands both communists and shipowners, and fears neither. His sailors blocked the sellout, and manned the ships only when their contract, too, was signed and delivered. I wonder whether the shipowners have reflected on how the greed, the ignorance, and cowardice they displayed in this 1948 Pacific Coast deal with Bridges paid off in 1949, in Hawaii?

The American businessmen are ignorant, dangerously ignorant. Some among their great publishing houses have distributed millions of copies of propagandized books by communists and their fellow-travelers. In the case of China particularly, these books are weighty among the causes of the disaster that has taken place. With all the devotion in the world to free speech, could they not at least leave it to the communists to publish their own, instead of using the resources and ability of business to smear the country with this mental poison? In their million-copied magazines, they print articles skillfully advancing the communist line. While the *New Leader,* the finest anti-communist paper in the country, and a journal of real distinction, tilts permanently on the verge of bankruptcy, and keeps barely going only because of the goodwill of its first-rate but unpaid contributors and the enlightened backing of David Dubinsky, the businessmen write their checks to newspapers and magazines run by communist united fronts or hospitable to communist-line authors. How many communists and fellow travelers, how many communist causes, have drunk deep of the many-millioned streams which Marshall Field has poured into journalistic gutters! Funds from the great foundations are dispensed to communist-line writers, artists, teachers. The endowments of great universities, supervised by businessmen trustees, maintain in the comfort to which they are accustomed notorious apologists for communist causes. How many pamphlets, books, speeches, and reports pleasing to the Kremlin have appeared under the benign sanction of the Foreign Policy Association or the Institute of Pacific Relations, both recipients of such generous support from the suicidal statesmen of the business community! Whittaker Chambers is fired from his job ("allowed to resign," in the formal phrase) by the lord of streamlined business journalism; and Alger Hiss (whether he is legally guilty or not does not affect the contrast) is coddled by the businessmen trustees of the Carnegie Endowment. How strange that Hollywood and Broadway, which so readily and easily ground out pro-Soviet movies and plays during the war and immediate postwar period, seem so inhibited in their output of anti-communist productions—though they have never had a subject with half the potential drama of the communist struggle to destroy and conquer the world!

4

The communists have studied the American businessman with meticulous care. They have learned how to seduce him, while he remains unaware, through his greed and ignorance and lack of vision; and they have learned how easily, because of his political and moral timidity, he can be intellectually terrorized. During 1949 they opened a beautifully planned new front in their campaign for the demoralization of the American business community.

It began with the Jessup-Malik conversations at the United Nations, the lifting of the Berlin blockade, and much talk about "East-West trade." Then came a masterful thrust on the propaganda flank. From a source anonymous and obscure in its channels but unmistakable in origin, an article appeared in the magazine, *United Nations World*, supported by a long list of our best citizens. This article was at once headlined as major news by the principal newspapers. With all the rhetoric of "inside stuff" and "most confidential," it "revealed" that Andrei Gromyko, during his stay in the United States, had held a series of private conversations with several dozen of the leading American businessmen. From these conversations, Gromyko, so the article declared, underwent a change of heart and outlook. He became convinced that the businessmen were not such terrible imperialists as the communists had theretofore imagined, that they had not decided on a war to smash the Soviet state, and that they were anxious to get together with the Soviet Union on a constructive basis. Gromyko returned to the Soviet Union, so the story continued, an altered man with an altered mission. He told Stalin about his experiences in the United States, and about these conversations. Stalin, at first skeptical, finally saw the light under Gromyko's insistent guidance. With a sigh of relief, Stalin realized that here was his chance to liquidate the cold war (which, apparently, he never wanted in the first place, but was driven to by his fear of American imperialism), and to enter a period of world cooperation and reconstruction. Toward this happy consummation, Stalin then set his course.*

Shall we laugh or weep at the naïveté with which this sugared dose was swallowed? It is really humiliating to reflect on how easily the Kremlin propaganda directors can pull the stops of American public opinion and the American press. Today a fortissimo of war and revolution, tomorrow the throbbing Vox Humana of "the peaceful collaboration of capitalism and socialism," the deep pedals of fear and anxiety alternating with the treble chirps of the longed-for dove: and for total effect in the responsive audience, a chronic schizophrenic imbalance that paralyzes action, as the schizoid individual is paralyzed when his finger, following a string, reaches a point where the string splits into two branches.

I do not know who the author of this article (and its sequel) is,

* Two months later, a follow-up along the same lines was published in *United Nations World*.

why he wrote it, or where he got (or was fed) his material. It is quite likely that Gromyko talked with leading American business-men, and that he proved an affable conversationalist. But the pic-ture of the junior errand-boy, Gromyko, acting on his own, getting bright new ideas, and then persuading Stalin to change *his* mind about the nature and intentions of American "finance-capitalist imperialism" is comically absurd. To the dewiest sophomore in com-munism—the businessmen are for the most part pre-freshmen—the Kremlin's play should be obvious. Gromyko, so far as there is any-thing to the story, acted, as he always acts, under the instructions, precisely, of the Politburo and its chief, Stalin. (If he had not so acted, there would no longer be any Gromyko.) He visited his businessmen not at all to "sound them out" but to manipulate their greed and ignorance and timidity. Stalin, well pleased apparently by the response, did not "change his mind" in the least—as if, at this point in his career, he is going to go to school to Gromyko for first lessons in Marxism—but advanced the play a stage further, and secured for the game a world audience. He is simply holding up a big, juicy sugarplum before the eyes of the sweet-toothed political children of the business community: now you see it, now you don't. And what a chuckle for him and Gromyko as they watch the mouths water!

Just here is the danger, perhaps the greatest danger, for the entire world struggle against communism. The businessmen are shrewd in their own eyes, and fancy themselves shrewd bargainers. They believe that a deal can always be made, and they want a deal. What Stalin is doing is to encourage them to keep that belief and that hope. Communists, however, do not make deals; they make traps: an oath to an infidel does not bind. By such tricks as these articles (and whatever confidential discussions have accompanied them), the communists are tempting the businessmen to look upon the American "policy of containment" as a bargaining maneuver lead-ing to a general deal, a "settlement," instead of as a bridge to the offensive. Come unto me, Stalin is calling, and you will have abundance of profits, and peace of political mind. In public he does not add: give me the time, the materials, and the lack of interference which I need, and you won't have to worry any longer about a "general settlement."

5

According to Marxism, these characteristics of businessmen upon which I have been commenting are, as they put it, "not accidental." The greed, ignorance, timidity, and lack of vision—in short, the ineffectuality—are, in the Marxian analysis, "inevitable expressions of the decadence of capitalism." The actions of the business class, the "capitalists," are determined not by individual choice but by economic necessities.

Maybe so. Perhaps Marxism is right about the capitalists, or about most of them. If so, and if the businessmen are the predominant influence in deciding American policy, then the outlook is not promising.

Marxism, however, like all closed monistic doctrines, is oversimplified. Whatever American businessmen have been and done in the past, it is possible for them to learn, and some of them have been learning. The American reality does not, in any case, conform to the crude Marxian scheme. The "businessmen" of the United States do not constitute a solid, socially coherent "capitalist class" or "bourgeoisie." As I pointed out at the begining of this chapter, those whom we call "businessmen" include a considerable variety of classes and sub-classes. The economic compulsions which operate on a "capitalist" in the strict sense of the term (a legal owner of means of production which are labored on by others) are not the same as those which affect non-owning managers or engineers. Even if human actions were altogether determined economically, and if capitalists were, in the present period of history, prevented by economic interest from carrying out an adequate policy in the struggle against communism (neither of which suppositions is true), even then it would not follow that economic interest would affect in the same way the other, non-capitalist sections of the "business community." The differing social functions of the various sections permit, indeed promote, a differentiation in ideas and perspectives. There is no reason, yet, to despair of the "businessman" as such.

Still further: Even if business as a whole, all the businessmen, are disqualified, it does not follow that the struggle against communism cannot be correctly conducted. From the second quarter of the 19th century—from the Civil War almost without challenge—until a decade or two ago, the businessmen (in the broader, vaguer sense) were in fact the dominant or ruling class of the United States. During the past generation, however, there has not only taken place a social differentiation within the business community. New groups from the population (some of them socially related to the managerial groups developed within business) have been rising to positions of influence and power. These prominently include: the leaders of the organized labor movement (or "labor managers"); the governmental administrators (operating the gigantic governmental machine which has become by far the chief single element in the national life); various professionals; and the soldiers, or rather the leaders of the soldiers. The interests of these new, or newly powerful, groups, are not tied to old forms or old ideas. The new groups are in a position to be, and are proving to be, more flexible, more daring, more ready to try the new and abandon the old, than the businessmen have shown themselves.

During the past two decades, almost all of the major changes in the United States have been put through by these new groups, and against the initial opposition of the business community. It was they, for example, who launched the Tennessee Valley Authority, the great dams elsewhere for irrigation, power, and flood control, the other vast measures for conservation, the Reconstruction Finance Corporation, the Export-Import Bank, the International Bank for Reconstruction and Development, the Marshall Plan, the strengthening of Pan-American relations, the Atlantic Pact, and all the various structural reforms such as the Securities and Exchange

Commission, the Federal Deposit Insurance Corporation, and so on. It was they who declared that 50,000 airplanes could be produced in a year, and they, to be frank, who carried us into the Second World War some time before it was formally declared. I do not wish to imply that I think that all of these and of the other major changes of this period have been "good." But most of them have been almost inescapable adaptations to the quickly changing world in which we are living. Moreover, these changes could not have been carried through, in most cases, without the cooperation, however reluctant, of the business community. Roosevelt could call for 50,00 planes, but it was the businessmen who built them. Marshall could announce his Plan, but the bankers and industrialists have had to implement it. It is, however, noteworthy that businessmen have almost never been the first to advocate any of these changes and actions, but have met them with sullen or bitter complaint. In the end, they have usually gone along, and have often, after the fact, not only accepted what has happened but found it to be of benefit to themselves.*

It is true that the greater flexibility of the new groups contains a danger of its own. Though the actions of the businessmen have often been of indirect aid to the communists—through omission or commission, the businessmen have seldom been seduced subjectively by communism. With only rare exceptions, the businessmen have proved to be ideologically immune to communism, as if the American business tradition had set up antibodies in their thought streams. This immunity has by no means extended to the new groups, perhaps just because they are not the product of any settled tradition. Many of the governmental administrators, professionals,

---

* Wendell Willkie made his public reputation as the representative of Commonwealth & Southern in battling TVA. I wonder how many stockholders of Commonwealth & Southern have reflected on the fact that their properties, almost insolvent at that time, are now paying dividends, and are immeasurably better off as a direct result of the area development brought about by TVA? Not many, apparently, to judge by the same dreary business opposition to the project for Missouri Valley and Columbia River Authorities.

and labor managers have been infected in varying degrees of intensity with the Bolshevik virus. The symptoms have ranged through innocent "fronting" to persistent fellow-traveling to full (though often secret) party membership to espionage service for the MVD and the Soviet Military Intelligence.

It would be wrong to minimize the danger from this susceptibility, the damage that these infected individuals have already worked, or the still greater damage that will perhaps be done in the still more perilous days that are yet to come. This particular danger, however, is not altogether a disadvantage. For almost all persons, communism is one of those phenomena like artistic creation or earthquakes or love, which must be experienced, lived through, in order to be fully understood. The congenital immunity of the normal businessman to communism is probably no more than an expression of his inability to understand communism. The members of the newer social groups are not, it is true, gifted with any innate understanding —communists are made, not born. But they are able to acquire an understanding by the very process of undergoing, and passing through, the communist or near-communist experience. The anti-communism of an individual who has successfully cured himself of communism is usually of a different order from the anti-communism of one who has not only not experienced communism but has never even felt its immense attraction to the disheveled modern soul. The latter is based very often on prejudice and ignorance; the former springs from knowledge and inner torment. Moreover, the immunity to communism acquired by having harbored and then thrown off the virus is far more absolute than the congenital immunity. It is my own belief that those who have been communists, or who have at least wanted to be, are the best soldiers in the fight against communism; and that they will, and must, have a prominent and even leading part in the conduct of that fight.

John L. Lewis is a better anti-communist today because of his period of collaboration with the communists at the beginning of the C.I.O. Walter Reuther of the Automobile Workers and Philip

Murray (both once in willing united fronts with the communists), Michael Quill of the Transport Workers and Joseph Curran of the National Maritime Union and so many other labor leaders who were once themselves party members or close sympathizers, are better, and immensely more effective, anti-communists than Charles E. Wilson of General Motors or Thomas J. Watson of International Business Machines. When compared to the standard commercial writer (the businessman of letters), Arthur Koestler's books do not suffer in excellence or in anti-communist influence from the fact that he was for many years a party member. Professors George Counts and Sidney Hook, both formerly very close to communism, get more as well as more enlightened results in the present struggle against it than their unsullied pompous colleagues who bleat so emptily about "American ideals." And among governmental administrators (both those now in and at present out of office: in this case names are best omitted), the group that has been through communism or was once touched by it is not the least reliable.

To become a communist today, of course, is a very different thing from becoming a communist in the '30's or through the years of the Second World War. Then Hitler was felt by most men of good will to be the main enemy. Communism seemed a potential and, during the war, even an actual ally. A combination of ignorance, blindness, and utopian idealism could hide what communism was in fact doing, what the Soviet Union was like in truth, and what the great Purge Trials meant. Today, not merely is communism much more completely and publicly exposed (though the exposure can never be altogether complete), but, in the case of the United States above all, the world struggle with communism is already joined. Therefore, today, it requires a greater ignorance and blindness, a more utterly confused and sentimental idealism, or treachery, to become a communist. (I refer here to the "intellectualized" classes. Workers in desperate conditions, members of minority groups, etc., can become communists even today for quite different, and more legitimate—though mistaken—reasons.) This means that a new generation is being deprived of the educational luxury of the direct communist experience; that luxury, at any rate, has become too expensive to be voluntarily permitted. But even without the direct experience, the members of these newly influential social groups, or some of them, show themselves better able than the businessmen to understand and combat communism.

This is conspicuously true of some members of the armed services. During these years since 1945, many officers, themselves never touched by communism, have been advancing remarkably in their understanding of communism. I think that the reason for this is that the soldiers *know* that both the future of the country and their own lives are at stake, whereas civilians, though it is true also for them, do not have this knowledge so directly and continually in mind. Furthermore, the soldiers, in their thoughts about communism, have to deal with the most concrete and inescapable problems of victory and defeat. This concreteness of the presented problems is also a stimulus to the labor leaders to seek the truth instead of phrases, as it is increasingly to the governmental administrators— even to lower levels of the ponderous bureaucracy which is an object of such distaste to business.

If businessmen in general continue to be as shortsighted and incompetent in the struggle against communism as they have been in the past, if they are incapable of leading that struggle, there are, then, other forces available to conduct it and to carry it through. These other forces, newly powerful in our society, with new men and new interests, together with newly developing sections of the business class itself, are in any case gradually pushing the old-line businessmen aside.* The businessmen of the United States, whatever their special views, are loyal. They are not like the capitalists of Russia, who, in 1905, were indifferent to the outcome of the Japanese war when not actively in favor of Japanese victory; or like the many French capitalists in 1939 who were ready to accept the organization

---

* I have described this process, which is going on throughout the world, in *The Managerial Revolution* (New York: The John Day Company, 1941).

of Europe by Hitler. The businessmen are still very influential in United States affairs. They can, by their stupidity and negation, block the timely adoption of an adequate policy, and thereby make the struggle more costly and more difficult. But they will not actively sabotage it. In the end they will go along, when they see more clearly what is the case: that this struggle cannot be absorbed in any deal, no matter how adroit; that, sooner or later, it must be decided.

CHAPTER XVIII

The Inevitability of Communist Defeat

IF WE WEIGH IN a static balance the results achieved between 1946 and 1949, in the struggle for the world, we shall record a net gain for the communists. The Chinese addition much exceeds the half-loss of Yugoslavia, and the many other items pretty well cancel each other out. A static balance, however, is not a proper instrument for historical measurement. History is temporal, dynamic; it is the direction, the trend that counts. Two men who are at the level of the 60th floor of the Empire State Building are not in identical condition if one is rising in an elevator, and the other has just jumped off the parapet. In a pneumonia patient, the meaning of a body temperature of 104° depends upon whether the patient is getting well, or dying.

Dynamically considered, the years 1946–49 show a net *trend* against the communists. If the communists are not yet losing— and they are not—their rate of advance has at least been slowed. For all temporal phenomena, it is this that is the most significant index. When the rate of advance, the "growth curve," begins to flatten, we can reasonably wonder whether it is not approaching its maximum, and the start of its decline.

The principal cause of this reversal of trend has been the change in the attitude and policy of the United States. I once more insistently repeat that the present policy of the United States is inadequate; but I again also repeat that the direction of change of United States policy since 1946 is correct: correct, that is to say, in relation to the world power equilibrium. Both halves of this estimate are essential to its truth; either alone is a falsification.

Though the change in United States policy is the principal factor, an analogous change has also, in varying degrees, taken place elsewhere. The anti-communist Resistance has begun hardening on a world scale, as when the body begins forming an indurated wall against an advancing abscess, or a loose spring, so easily pushed at first, begins to assert its latent tension.

This process has taken place more quickly, and gone further, than I anticipated when, in 1946, I wrote *The Struggle for the World*. It is true that the reversal of trend is by no means firmly established. It is true that the curve of development is not smooth, but rather the resultant of vacillations, of irregular peaks and valleys. Nevertheless, the present pattern of the graph is unmistakable.

Let us then ask: will the present trend continue? In other words: will the objective be attained—if not the wider objective of a democratic world order, at least the narrower and specific objective of the defeat of world communism, with which this book is primarily concerned? The answer to this question, hazardous enough with respect to the facts, is also psychologically intricate. The answer we give may itself alter the facts.

If we say, "No, the objective will not, or probably will not, be attained," then we may induce attitudes of discouragement or despair which in turn will adversely affect the struggle for the objective. Shortly before the communist Czechoslovakian coup of February, 1948, I received a letter from a Czech with whom I had been occasionally corresponding. In first writing me, he had described himself as "not important," an ordinary worker in an office. In this last letter (no reply could be risked), he told me that he had managed to get a copy of *The Struggle for the World,* the publication and sale of which had of course been prohibited in Czechoslovakia. After discussing it for several pages, he ended, in his approximation of English, to this communicable effect: We know what will soon happen here. But you, and the others, must make always clear to us that the victory of democracy is inevitable. I know that it is, because I can see *their* failure, but they have fooled many people with their talk of historical necessity. You must make us believe that the victory of democracy is inevitable. We can hold out, if we believe that. If we do not, I am not so sure.

If, however, we make this reply to our question, and assert that the objective will, or will very probably or inevitably, be attained, we then run the opposite risk of quieting a sense of urgency, and arousing feelings of complacency. In talking over the contents of this book with friends of mine, I have found that a number of them objected, on such grounds, to its title and to some of its conclusions. They have argued: It is a time to cry havoc, not to pat on the back. The imbecile statesmen and stupid publicists who congratulate themselves on their astuteness, and tell us that "the cold war is being won" and "the tensions are lessening," are playing into the hands of the communists, lulling the public to sleep. After the disaster in China and the Soviet atomic explosion, after the communists' 1949 demonstration of their control of two-thirds of the world's harbors, it is one's duty to sound the alarm, to rouse what of the public can be reached to the prospect of total defeat, enslavement, and death.

The two arguments neutralize each other. I shall therefore try to consider the question, briefly, on its merits.

2

A candid survey will, I think, show that our side—that is, the democratic side,* the side led by the United States and including all other nations, peoples, and persons who are sure to stand with the United States—is at present superior to the communist side in all relevant major factors except two. These two are strategic posi-

---

* There is no demagogy in calling this "the democratic side." Democracy is a matter of degree, not an absolute. In spite of the fact that "our side" includes reactionaries and dictators, and in spite of the fact that it may be compelled to restrict freedoms further during the course of the struggle, it is and will remain incomparably *more* democratic, *more* free, than the communist side.

tion, and political leadership. In everything else that bears on the decision, not only in economic plant and technology, but in science, invention, culture, adaptability, health, usable (not merely theoretical) reserves both of material resources and of human energies, we are at present better, and in most instances immensely better.

The Soviet base is constructed on the best strategic position that exists on the surface of the earth. It is not advisable to dismiss this advantage. Nevertheless, we may properly qualify its importance. Strategic position is, after all, a static, not a dynamic, factor. New techniques of long-distance warfare, and of subversive warfare, have reduced its relative weight. And strategic position is never in itself decisive: there is no position that cannot be taken, if sufficient intelligence, determination, and power are brought to bear against it. The possession of the superior strategic position sometimes proves a disadvantage in the long run. It can prompt carelessness, and promote that guarantor of ultimate defeat, a defensive point of view.*

The entire question, therefore, turns on politics, on the quality of the political leadership. Assuming the continuing superiority of communist politics, we may ask: can political strength overcome all the other relative weaknesses? On the evidence of history, we must answer that, if the disparity is great enough, it can. This is proved by the history of almost all tribes, races, peoples, or nations which started (as all groups must) from little and went on to greatness. At the beginning, by the nature of the case, each was inferior to its older rivals in almost everything except leadership. (I should add that political leadership is not necessarily identical with the presence of great individual political leaders. Certain attitudes of the group can produce, or rather find and select, an effective leadership, or compel an existing leadership to become effective; whereas different group attitudes may favor, or almost guarantee, mediocre leadership.) However, if the disparity in political leadership is less than very great, then the other factors will outweigh it, and the side

* Cf. the discussion in Chapter VIII of the defensive Soviet military doctrine.

with the poorer politics can win.* Even now, the inferiority of democratic to communist political leadership is not so considerable as to make democratic victory impossible. A comparatively minor improvement in our politics would heavily swing the balance. This is why I wrote, in *The Struggle for the World,* that, "with a determined leadership in, and by, the United States . . . the policy of democratic world order would prove successful."

The problem, then, can be reduced to the question: will our politics improve?—I refer to our international politics; our ward-heeling politics are too good already.

Political ability is a synthesis of knowledge (partly native talent, or intuitive knowledge), intelligence, and will. Presumably the amount of intelligence and native talent distributed among us is on the average equal to that distributed among the enemy. At least, this average equality would follow from Mendelian principles, which are still permissible for a bourgeois analyst, though they lead to the concentration camp in the Soviet Union. Our knowledge, about matters relevant to the present political struggle, is increasing, and will certainly continue to increase. The crux, then, is in the will.

Does the United States *choose* to win? Can it make the necessary *decision?* Is it going to have, at the required tension, the *will* to survive? The answer to this triply phrased single question is the determinant of the future. There are those, not only among the Marxists but among ourselves, who reply that the United States has already reached a stage of cultural decadence in which the needed will has vanished. This conclusion is implicit in the theories of "the mature economy" and "the closing of the frontier"; it is supported, so it is argued, by such symptoms as "materialism," "aesthetic barrenness," "cosmopolitanism," social separatism, cynical indifference to patriotism, and so on.

To try to answer, for myself, this question was among the motives

---

* I am inclined to think, for example, that the German leadership, both military and civilian, in the First World War, was superior to that of the Allies. In most other major factors the Allies had the clear advantage.

that led me to take, in 1948–49, a slow, twenty-thousand-mile trip through the United States. Once out of the often brilliant but in-grown intellectual circles of the northeastern seaboard, which draw their spiritual fuel from Europe and the Soviet Union rather than from America, and whose members have for the most part never seen a factory in Detroit, an oil well in Texas, the vegetables in the Imperial Valley, a grain field in the Big Bend, range land in Wyoming, fruit along Hood River, ore ships crowding the Sault, copper mines in Utah, the generators at Grand Coulée, steel mills at Gary, logging in Oregon, chemical works at Beaumont, not these or the people who man them; once looking at America and not reading about it, the direct impression becomes gradually too clear for interpretative doubt. Some of the symptoms magnified by the theorists of decadence are undoubtedly there. They are seen in con-text to be signs, not of melancholia and cynical old age, but of dis-turbed and disturbing adolescence. The United States is not, not by centuries, ready to quit. The United States is, in Mackinder's meaning, *a going concern;* and a young concern. It may be that Western civilization as a whole is old and decadent—relatively old, that is to say, on the vast time scale of the histories of civilizations. An impressive case has been made out by Spengler and Toynbee. If so, the United States is the youngest child of Western civilization, its Joseph, who has not only his own manhood ahead, but the chance through his strength to revivify his parent. The death even of civil-izations as a whole is not decreed by any unchallengeable court. Civilizations die, in truth, only by suicide.

The uneasiness of the United States is not that of the awareness of death, but, rather, the tormenting pause before the leap into maturity. The will to exist and to advance is powerfully there, though for the moment in partial suspension. Because it is there, the suspension will be, sooner or later, resolved. The political question will be answered; the objective, attained: at greater cost, perhaps, and greater delay and suffering than need be; but attained.

I have, a number of times in the past, discussed the problem of "inevitability." For anyone at all trained in methodology it is an easy assignment to show that no statement about future events can be asserted as "inevitable." What we say about the future (or about events past and present as well, for that matter) can never be certain from a scientific and descriptive point of view; it is always more or less "probable," on the evidence. From this point of view, we may conclude that the defeat of world communism is, on the evidence, probable. Just when, under what circumstances, and with what measure of benign or disastrous indirect results brought about through that defeat, is not clear from the evidence. But an objective assessment of the evidence does not seem to leave much doubt that the ultimate defeat is itself very probable.

This descriptive interpretation of the word "inevitable" is, however, trivial, a mere exercise in linguistics. The significant meaning of "inevitable" is not as a description of facts (to which it has, in reality, no application), but as an expression of will. When a captain, before a battle, proclaims to his soldiers, "Our victory is inevitable," he is not so naïve as to mean that the victory is, as a matter of scientific fact, objectively certain. If that were his meaning, he would not bother to address them. What he is doing through the word "inevitable" is to unify and express the *resolution* not to yield, to fight to the end.

The defeat of communism, probable on the facts, is also *inevitable,* because there are enough determined men in the world—and their number daily grows—who have so resolved. The knowledge and intelligence, which enter into the synthesis of politics, are still needed in order to make that defeat as fruitful as possible a victory, as sparing as possible of blood and treasure. But the issue is no longer in doubt. Doubt is vanquished by the act of will which makes the decision. The future becomes servant, not master.